WRITE
smart
WRITE
happy

CHERYL ST. JOHN

WRITER'S DIGEST
BOOKS

WritersDigest.com
Cincinnati, Ohio

For more resources for writers, visit www.writersdigest.com.

22 21 20 19 18   5 4 3 2 1

Distributed in Canada by Fraser Direct
100 Armstrong Avenue
Georgetown, Ontario, Canada L7G 5S4
Tel: (905) 877-4411

Distributed in the U.K. and Europe by F+W Media International
Pynes Hill Court, Pynes Hill, Rydon Lane
Exeter, EX2 5AZ, United Kingdom
Tel: (+44) 1392-797680, Fax: (+44) 1626-323319
E-mail: postmaster@davidandcharles.co.uk

Library of Congress Cataloging-in-Publication Data

ISBN-13: 978-1-4403-5179-2

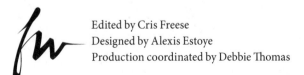

Edited by Cris Freese
Designed by Alexis Estoye
Production coordinated by Debbie Thomas

DEDICATION/ ACKNOWLEDGMENTS

This book is dedicated to Robyn Roberts, who always offers proofreading help and is excellent at spotting mistakes. On my music team, she keeps me on track by planning ahead and efficiently working behind the scenes. I definitely get by with a little—or a lot of—help from my friend who is always there in a pinch. Thank you, Robyn.

I'd like to acknowledge the generous members of my Romance Writers of America Chapter, Romance Writers of the Heartland, as well as my long-time friends, the Harlequin Historical authors, a.k.a. The Hussies, for their patience with my questions and their honest and helpful responses as I was deciding which issues needed to be addressed in this book. Their insights into the vulnerabilities we all face were valuable contributions.

My thanks go to Blythe Gifford, Peggy L. Henderson, MK McClintock, Rain Trueax, Hebby Roman, Danni Roan, Kirsten Osbourne, MA Jewell, Diane Gaston, Lenora Worth for their input. Ruth Logan Herne, Sherri Shackelford, *lizzie starr, Holly Jacobs, Charlene Sands, MK Meredith, Carla Kelly, Carolyne Aarsen, Caroline Fyffe, Kit Morgan, Erica Vetsch, Julie Miller, Debra Ullrick, Stephanie Ludwick, and Pam Crooks have my gratitude for their time and contributions.

ABOUT *the* AUTHOR

Cheryl St. John has always loved discovering the exciting and diverse worlds between the covers of books. As a child she wrote stories and drew covers, then stapled them into books. She cut all the tiny book images from the book club advertisements in the Sunday newspaper and glued them to bits of cardboard so Barbie® had a full library.

Cheryl is the author of more than fifty fiction novels, both historical and contemporary. Her stories have earned numerous awards and are published in over a dozen languages. Many of her books made the *USA Today* and *New York Times* lists. One thing all reviewers and readers agree on regarding Cheryl's work is the degree of emotion and believability. In describing her stories of second chances and redemption, readers and reviewers use words like, "emotional punch, hometown feel, core values, believable characters and real-life situations." Amazon and Goodreads reviews show her popularity with readers.

Her straightforward and encouraging advice makes Cheryl a popular speaker and her workshops a standout at conferences. With a 4.9 star rating on amazon, her best-selling non-fiction book, *Writing With Emotion, Tension & Conflict* published by Writers Digest Books, is available in print and digital.

TABLE *of* CONTENTS

PART 4
emulate success while being yourself

PART 5
conquering fear

PART 6
time management

PART 7
celebrate success

introduction

Writing is a vulnerable occupation; it is personal and intimate. It requires commitment, honesty, curiosity, courage, resilience, sacrifice, and—above all—miles and miles and miles of heart.

I'm often asked for the best piece of advice for aspiring authors. I know the answer, but it's something that takes constant work and attention to achieve. This advice applies to writers at every stage of their career: *Believe in yourself.* There will be times when no one else believes in you, times when you hear negative comments, see another writer achieve more, and receive a rejection letter or pages of revisions. At those times you will need to believe in your ability, in the strength of your dream, in the hard-won wisdom that *you* are the only *you*, and only you could write your unique stories.

Circumstances are often out of our control. For example, I have no power over a critical Amazon review. What I can control is how I react to those words, how I let them affect my mental attitude and feelings, how I let them affect my writing day. While brainstorming how to begin this book, I surveyed several groups of writers with one question: *What about writing makes you feel vulnerable?* I received well-thought-out and honest replies, some deeply personal. The responses were amazingly similar, confirming much of what I already knew.

Many writers feel as though they are imposters. They feel as if they are faking it until someone discovers they're not any good and then their career falls apart like a house of cards. It's common for a writer to get "The Call," make that first sale, and then think right away there was some mistake and that the publisher will call back to say it was a mistake.

Some writers worry that once friends read their book, their opinions of them will change negatively. Many are concerned that they'll be judged for their writing and perceived as "not good enough." Writers are often anxious about how friends and family will perceive their desire to write, or if their spouses will wonder where the material comes from—especially if there's a level of heat or romance in the book. If I write about a taboo topic or a relationship, will people who know me think I've based it on experience?

Several authors question their lack of reviews. They see books with hundreds of glowing reviews and can't figure out how theirs have only a few or none. Lack of feedback might lead to a "Why bother?" attitude.

Writers working in the corporate world by day feel as though they have an alter ego they can't reveal in their professional world, for fear of judgment or ridicule. Writing reveals an intimate side that could easily be misconstrued as weakness.

Being compared or comparing oneself to other authors who have millions of readers and followers is common. "Why don't you write a book like Jodi Picoult/James Patterson/Maeve Binchy/Jonathan Kellerman?" Even after explaining genre and voice, the conversation ends with, "Well if you wrote like one of them, you'd be a bestseller."

Comparison makes writers feel defensive. It's unfair to compare apples to oranges and find one inferior.

It's human nature to compare ourselves to others and feel we don't measure up. There are always better writers: writers getting more reviews, earning higher advances and greater royalties; those with throngs of fans and thousands of social media followers; writers courted and promoted by their publishers. It's the same in the corporate world, in Hollywood, in journalism, in real estate, and in most professions. There's always someone younger, more attractive; someone who dresses better, makes friends more easily, attracts followers; someone with a better education, who possesses more marketing savvy, produces more work, and on and on.

And many of these concerns are grounded in reality, not simply un-supported concerns. Like many authors, I've been asked when I'm going to write a "real" book. Trying to understand the questioner's perspective, let's suppose they like to read John Grisham. John Grisham is great. I can't criticize anyone for enjoying his stories. But I'm not a lawyer specializing in criminal defense or personal injury litigation; I don't have the same experience and knowledge he has. Does that make the experiences I do have and write about less real? No. It's all fiction. If every book were a legal thriller, how boring would the reading world become?

When I consider in this situation, I always fall back on one of my heroes in this business, Stephen King, who said, "If you wrote something for which someone sent you a check, if you cashed the check and it didn't bounce, and if you then paid the light bill with the money, I consider you talented."

I've paid a lot of light bills and car and mortgage payments with my earnings over the years. I've paid a whole lot of taxes. I think that qualifies as writing *real* books. Of course, I don't respond that way when the thoughtless question pops up at a social gathering. I have my standby quips, and the one for "When are you going to write a real book?" is "When they stop paying me so well to write these fake ones."

It's important to remember we're not the only writers who have feelings of inadequacy. That's why I maintain that writing requires commitment, honesty, curiosity, courage, resilience, sacrifice, and—above all—miles and miles and miles of heart. It takes courage to read your writing in front of another person, hand over a chapter for feedback, and send writing out into the publishing world for consideration for publication, reviews, criticism, and possibly rejection. And it takes resilience to keep writing after that criticism and rejection. Heart is required—passion, if you will—to continue year after year in the face of adversity, a saturated marketplace, and, sometimes, downright scorn.

As writers, we have to remember that our work has meaning and importance. This never struck me as strongly as it did early in my career: Following the release of my fourth book, *Saint or Sinner*, my perspective began to change. In this historical novel, my female protagonist suffered physical and emotional abuse at the hand of her father. She had escaped him and attempted to live the life she always wanted to live. But he finds her. Back then, I used to drive to the small neighborhood post office once a week and collect my reader mail. On one particular day, I received a letter that I've held onto ever since. (Who am I kidding? I've kept all of them.)

In her letter, the reader shared her personal story—how she had been abused by her stepfather and lives with permanent nerve damage in her arm because of it. I can remember sitting at my desk in my office with tears running down my cheeks, experiencing a feeling of complete hypocrisy. There I sat in my comfortable air-conditioned office, with everything I needed at my fingertips, a cup of coffee and a cozy chair, reading my mail. Out in the real world, people were experiencing horrible things, while I was safe and sound, making things up.

That feeling lasted only a few minutes. Because in the rest of her letter, this dear young woman told me my story made her feel good; it gave her hope that one day she would find someone who loved her like Joshua loved Addie. I cried even more at that. But after that day, I knew my writing was not meaningless.

That's why I write. I write for those who believe in love, justice, and happily-ever-afters. People want to see good triumph over evil and the bad guy get his comeuppance; they want to see the little guy have his day in the sun. I write to give people hope.

In this knowledge, I find my confidence to go forward. There are no guarantees. We can't force publishers to buy our books. We can't force readers to buy, like, or review them. The most we can do is write the best possible book—and then let it go. We're vulnerable, but we're not alone.

Sharing our experiences and fears creates connections. Knowledge dispels shame and embarrassment. In the article "The Creativity Trinity: Truth, Empathy, Hope" on Writer Unboxed, MM Finck says, "War stories are gifts to people in the trenches. What's happening to us has happened to others. And they survived. Their survival gives us hope. Their advice arms us for the fight."

Advice from the trenches is what I offer you with this book. I think most writers fear that their words won't read as well on paper as they sound in their heads, and that's the battle I'm overcoming as I write this book. I want to help you rid yourself of the obstacles that hold you back and help you give your writing the energy that confidence infuses.

The following quote has been attributed to everyone from Tony Robbins and Mark Twain to Albert Einstein and Anthony DiNozzo on *NCIS*, so I can't be certain who to credit, but the truth of these words couldn't be more pertinent.

If you do what you've always done, you'll get what you've always got.

Our choices drive our actions. Our actions drive our results. And behind our choices and actions are our deeply held beliefs about ourselves and our abilities. Believe in yourself.

PART 1

Goals

career planning

Focused, hard work is the real key to success. Keep your eyes on the goal, and just keep taking the next step towards completing it. If you aren't sure which way to do something, do it both ways and see which works better.

—JOHN CARMACK

HOW BADLY DO YOU WANT THIS?

As a writer, you must have something in mind—a story or a career—or you wouldn't have picked up this particular book to read. I know excellent writers who never get past the first five chapters when writing their books. I know gifted writers who published a couple of books that didn't get much traction, so they became discouraged and quit.

There's something each of us must ask ourselves and answer honestly: *How badly do I want to reach my goal? How badly do I want to see my name on the cover of a book? How badly do I want to see my book on the shelf at Barnes & Noble or online at Amazon.com? How badly do I want to quit my job and support my family on a writing income? Am I willing to make the sacrifices necessary to make my dream come true?* Because, in the end, it all boils down to commitment and sacrifice.

You might look at another writer and see how effortlessly she seems to complete books, publishing them one after another. But I can guarantee you that behind the scenes, the process is not effortless. That writer has sacrificed to make time to write. She's created a plan and followed through.

It sounds deceptively easy when I put it like that. It's a simple strategy, but it's not easy to carry out.

Nothing about writing is easy. Nothing about writing is a given or a guarantee. No one has a crystal ball that will tell you whether or not you'll succeed in this business. But I can promise you one thing: Success as a published author is often predictable. After being in the same writing organization for thirty years, I can pretty much spot those who will succeed as soon as I talk to them and learn their work ethic, watch how they react to teaching, the market, and constructive criticism—whether or not they even want feedback speaks volumes.

Want to know how I can spot them? I ask these questions: *How hungry are they? How badly do they want this? What are they willing to do—what are they willing to sacrifice—to make it happen?*

Occasional overnight successes do occur, but truthfully, most overnight successes have been years in the making. Success is almost always the result of sweat, sacrifice, and tears. There are no secret handshakes, fast passes, or instant successes. Success is absolutely achievable. But to reach your dream, you are going to have to evaluate what and how you've been doing things up until now, and decide if you want to improve. I can't promise to help you sell your books. But I can encourage you to write better ones and to write with less frustration. In these chapters, I'll do my best to help you remove the exasperating hurdles that you'll face in the process.

When I used to teach a much briefer version of this book as a class, I'd pass out slips of paper for the participants to write down behaviors they wanted to change. At the end of the class, we'd throw these slips into the trash, symbolic of ridding ourselves of the stumbling blocks that hold us back as writers. As you read through these chapters, you can make notes on scraps of paper or sticky notes and do the same. The important thing is to evaluate your behavior at each step of the way: *Have I done this in the past? Is this an activity or thought that's preventing me from moving forward?* Own up to bad habits now and choose to change them for the better. You have a whole bright future ahead of you in which to make better choices.

Do Things Differently to See Better Results

Sometimes writers unintentionally harm their own interests with their poor habits. They often need a good friend to tell them to shape up. The chapters in this book are designed to help you look at your habits, both good and harmful. You'll be asked to take an honest inventory of your writing life and make decisions about moving forward with greater productivity and a healthier attitude.

I won't mislead you: Some time ago, I dragged my feet on proposing this project—even though it was something I wanted to do—because I knew how challenging it would be. I've given a class online and in person for years that is similar in content, but writing it all down and developing concepts is an entirely different undertaking. I asked my good friend, "Am I shooting myself in the foot by not stretching myself and writing this book?" Without a moment's hesitation, she replied, "Yes." Sometimes, we all need friends to tell us the truth about ourselves.

Were you satisfied with your writing accomplishments last year? Can you see room for improvement? This year will turn out just like the last unless you take the steps to make choices and changes. About half the American population makes New Year's resolutions. According to www.statisticbrain.com, the top resolutions in 2016 were as follows:

1. Enjoy life to the fullest
2. Live a healthier lifestyle
3. Lose weight
4. Spend more time with family and friends
5. Save more, spend less

Past years' resolutions included quit smoking, quit drinking, be debt free, learn something new, help others, become organized.

University of Scranton research suggests that only 8 percent of people achieve their New Year's resolutions. Some might live with their goals in mind for a week, others a month. Many allow the resolution to slide away but then pick up the same resolution the following year.

Why is it the norm to fail? We make excuses out of fear or lack of motivation. *My job has been really busy this year. After a day at work, I don't have any energy left. I have only an hour before I have to pick up the kids.*

If you've been making excuses, ask yourself the following questions now:

- Why haven't I started this book?
- Why haven't I *finished* this book?
- Are excuses getting in the way of progress and accomplishment?

I took a quick poll in my writer's group to hear their thoughts. Here are the excuses my honest chapter mates make for not writing. Maybe you can identify with some of them:

- There's not enough time to get into the story.
- I have too many projects and can't focus on just one.
- The house needs to be cleaned.
- It's too noisy to concentrate.
- My husband keeps reading me the newspaper.
- My husband is retired, and we go places together.
- I'm spring cleaning.
- The dog needs to be walked.
- I'm too tired.
- I need to unclutter my desk.
- I have to read the books I'm judging for a contest.
- Nobody reads my stuff anyway, so why bother?
- I haven't finished my critiques from last week yet.
- The cat box needs to be cleaned.
- My website needs to be updated.
- It's too late. I'll start tomorrow.
- I need to research first.

Write Smart, Write Happy

- I'm stressed.
- I work full-time.
- My office isn't organized.
- I have writer's block.
- Everyone else's needs are more important.
- I'm just not there yet.

This is only a partial list. As writers, we come up with a lot of reasons why we can't focus on the task of writing. If you're honest with yourself, you'll recognize some of these excuses in your own habits.

Grab Your Notebook

Make a list of the excuses you've made for not writing right now. Look at each one and check the validity. Is it an excuse? Is there a fear behind it, or are you just being lazy?

Excuses are counterproductive in that they make you feel bad about yourself. Look at each excuse and shift your thinking to accept responsibility for these excuses. Ask yourself, "Is this a genuine reason or an excuse?"

Now come up with a positive perspective on how you will change your thinking. In this case, don't regret your behavior. Simply put it behind you. *I accept that these were excuses, but from now on I'm going to plan ahead, focus on my goals, remember the big picture of what I want to accomplish, and take measurable steps to reach my goals.*

If you resolve to do something that you've failed at repeatedly in the past, you're already programmed to think you'll fail again. A negative pattern will develop because you've never dealt with the negative habits you've built up and nurtured. Guilt and regret have no place in moving forward; we learn from the past, but we don't have to focus on it. We can use it as a platform to build new, positive behaviors.

Think about your writing career today and the tools you have available right now. Focus on where you want to be in your writing career tomorrow, next week, and next year. See yourself typing "The End," holding your book, admiring the cover, signing a copy. The next time you catch yourself with an excuse forming in your mind, deny that negativity and imagine a cover with your name on it. You might even create a mock-up cover to remind and motivate yourself.

Remember your priorities. Don't spread yourself so thin that you can't possibly keep up with everything. It can be difficult to stay focused when there are so many bright and shiny things we want to try our hand at in addition to our responsibilities outside of our writing careers and the necessity of some much-needed downtime. So how do we fit it all in?

We don't. Instead we make choices. We eliminate other activities to pursue our writing goals. And we stick to the plan.

I'm asking you to take an honest, in-depth look at your behaviors, thought processes, and the things holding you back. Self-examination may be difficult, but it's always necessary for improvement and growth. Negative patterns and poor attitudes will influence your ability to assert effort into a project. If you start out with an attitude of failure, you're going to fail. Here are the obvious, but not so simple facts:

If you're unhappy with your achievements, you must stop what you've been doing. New patterns must replace old patterns. New behaviors must cause change.

Think about it: Negative behaviors and attitudes are like weeds in the new garden you're planting. Weeds are hardy and can withstand just about anything—drought, overwatering, new plants, lack of sun. However, new plants are fragile and tender, and need the right conditions to thrive. The only way to get rid of a weed once and for all is to pluck out its entire root system. If the roots remain, the weed will come back—just like bad habits and negative thinking. Nurture the new plan, put a fence around it, water it, give it sunlight.

MAKE A CAREER PLAN

First, we must know where we want to go. Looking at a career as a destination is difficult because there are no guarantees in this business. Calling it a dream sounds lofty and irresponsible, however, so deciding what and where we want to be should be part of our plan. Not all writers set out with extensive career plans. And every writer defines a career—and a successful career—differently. Maybe you want to sell and publish books the traditional way consistently. Maybe your goal is to write and publish independently and give your books away to friends and family. There is no right or wrong plan. There's a plan that fulfills our dreams—whatever those may be—and that's the goal to reach toward.

"I want to be a writer" or "I want to be paid for writing" is too vague a plan. Literary agent Chip MacGregor helps his authors with career planning, and he gives a very simple explanation of what they need to do: "Figure out where you are, decide where you want to go, then determine a plan to get there."

Where are you currently? Have you just started writing? Have you been writing for years? Were you previously published? Is writing a second career? If you're holding down a full-time job, your plan must work around your available writing hours.

Consider your strengths first (we'll go over this in-depth in chapter 5). Consider your experience and what aspects of it will benefit your career. Perhaps you're familiar with writing on deadline. Maybe you're a social media guru or a marketing genius. It's possible your skill set includes knowledge and hands-on experience that will contribute to the type of books you write.

Define Success

Take time to figure out what you want. How do you define success? Everyone is different. Success to one person may simply be earning enough to quit his day job, while another wants to earn enough to send her kids to college. Perhaps success is the pride in seeing your name on a book cover. As you achieve goals, the next step to your vision of success might change. Only you know what you want to achieve. When my critique partner, Sherri Shackelford, started out, her image of success during her first year was to have her name on a book cover. The second year, she imagined success as a two-book contract.

When I started, I simply wanted to write and publish books—and I wanted to get paid for it. I wanted to know others enjoyed my stories the way I enjoyed books I read. My career goals have changed over the years, though, and my writing career became a desire to provide for my family. One of my critique partners, *lizzie starr, said she didn't have a goal other than publication when she started writing seriously. She didn't know the difference between dreams and goals. She didn't even know what a writing goal was. Many of us don't when we first get into writing. At present, her career goal is to pursue traditional publishing to become a hybrid author while continuing to learn and improve her craft. I've seen her action steps: She watches online for opportunities to pitch books and then adjusts submissions to the house, imprint, or editor. Diligence pays off.

Define your idea of success at this current stage of your career. And make a plan to reach it.

Sample Career Plan

WHERE I AM NOW: Full-time job; a few short stories published, a few classes under my belt; this book in my hands

DESTINATION: Multipublished; work less hours at job

ACTION STEPS: Find an accountability partner/critique group

- Join a writer's group, online or in person
- Find writers in my own genre on Facebook

Study the market

- Buy the current *Writer's Market*
- Subscribe to *Publishers Weekly*, review magazines or online groups
- Subscribe to publications in my genre

Get recommendations and study books on the writing craft

- Ask writers their favorite craft books
- Check out the *Writer's Digest* website
- Look for books on Amazon covering conflict, dialogue, plot, etc.

Take an online writing course every three months

- Learn about upcoming classes in writing groups
- Check out the Writer's Digest University website
- Check out the RWA University website

Do three things every day to educate myself or move forward

- Read a chapter of a book in (or even outside) my target genre, or in a craft book
- Read an online blog or article
- Listen to a book in the car
- Outline a chapter
- Complete a writing exercise

If you're planning a career, stay on track with Action Steps:

- Study grammar and sentence structure, and read various genres.
- Learn editing techniques.
- Attend one writers conference a year.
- Outline a book.
- Write a synopsis.
- Set writing goals for the year and stay on track.
- When book is completed, pay for copyediting, query agents, query publishers; or, pay for an edit and learn about independent publishing.
- Plan the next book.

A wise young man, Pastor Anthony Odhiambo, said, "Success is an inward condition; not an outward demonstration." There's nothing wrong with pushing harder and reaching for more and better, but if we don't find contentment in the steps along the way, we'll never find joy in our achievements. By thinking we're not doing enough, and then falling short, we create a stressful and counterproductive environment.

Grab Your Notebook

Before you begin to set goals and commit to projects, take some time to decide what kind of writer you are. Some writers can write a book every year. Others sit down and write a chapter a day. There's no wrong way or incorrect pace, but knowing how you work and planning your time productively will prevent a lot of headaches down the road. Proposing unreasonable page counts will only set yourself up for failure; we want to be productive and to stretch ourselves, but we don't want to discourage ourselves either.

Write down your career writing goals and prioritize them. Add actions to each one, deciding what you will need to do to make them happen.

Writing an excellent, marketable book is imperative. But we're not talking about craft; we're taking a look at your future in publishing.

If you're looking to publish for the first time, having a unique style, a solid brand, and the ability to write marketable books gives you an advantage. Your signature style will define the decisions you make and the books you write. Educate yourself on your desired genre and the market. Research editors and agents, and what they're currently seeking. Keep your career goals firmly in mind when you decide which books to write and which conferences to attend, as well as which editors you will approach.

TIPS FOR CONFERENCES

- Dress professionally, but comfortably.
- Sit with people you don't know and engage them in conversation. I have friends who met agents who didn't identify themselves until handing over a business card and requesting a submission.
- If you get into a workshop and a) the speaker is unprepared, b) the material doesn't apply to what you're writing, or c) the material is too basic and you're past that level, do not sit through the workshop to be polite. It's your time and money, and you don't want to waste it. Get up and find another workshop that is beneficial, or network in the hallway, reception room, or bar.
- On the backs of business cards you collect, note who gave it to you and where you met this person, and find her online later.

Whatever stage you're at in your writing career, create an online presence that solidifies you and your brand. Find a writing niche that you're passionate about and pursue it. A lot of agents and publishers will look for you on social media to see if you have a following.

Be an approachable writer who's easy to work with and open to suggestions and change. If an editor suspects or learns you are difficult to work with, or that you don't accept revisions well, he can opt to buy the next person's manuscript because that writer isn't a hassle. Once you have several books under your belt, you'll have proven yourself and will have more room to weigh in on revisions and changes. Being easy to work with will serve you well if your first book doesn't do as well. A publisher will take another chance on a dependable writer, and will be more likely to let the pain-in-the-neck writer go.

If you've been thinking you want to do more—whether it's in terms of accomplishments, writing, or publishing—but you're waiting for a season to pass or a current life situation to change, I'm here to tell you it will never happen. The stars will never magically align to give you more time, a better work space, or more money to attend conferences or buy that fancy laptop you want. You have to make the decision to get serious by taking the bull by the horns or satisfying yourself with a comfortable hobby. If you want this badly enough, set goals and make them happen.

As I write this chapter, I'm also helping my youngest daughter plan her wedding, a task that includes helping get her fiancé's house ready to sell and taking care of grandkids over winter break, snow, and sick days. In addition, I have been summoned for jury duty four days before this manuscript is due. Does that sound like the ideal time to write and revise a book? Of course not. There is no ideal time, because we are people with families, responsibilities, and (often) other jobs. We get sick, need surgery, take care of elderly parents, lose loved ones, open our homes to our grown children, attend graduations, host parties, celebrate holidays, have the furnace cleaned or replaced ... you get the idea.

As an author, one of the most irritating things I hear is, "I have a book to write, too. I just haven't had the time." Those words are like nails screeching on a chalkboard. As though a spare weekend or a vacation in a secluded cabin would enable this person to pop out a book. No one has the time. Hear me? *No one has the time.*

How can you achieve your goals?

- Be clear about what you want to achieve; visualize your destination.
- Start now; don't develop a habit of procrastination.
- Get your family, children, or significant other on board; share your dream.
- Read, read, read: fiction, history, writing craft, cereal boxes.
- Research publishers, markets, agents, trends.
- Work on your grammar, punctuation, and editing.

- Stay fresh by improving one or more skills each year: conflict, plotting, dialogue, description, setting, etc.
- Join a writing community or, better yet, more than one.
- Find an accountability partner or group.
- Create goals, record them, commit to them.
- Learn to pitch your ideas and books.
- Attend conferences, workshops, and retreats.
- Teach yourself to write to deadlines; set and stick to a schedule.
- Develop habits that help you reach daily/weekly goals.
- Track your progress: Make a habit of tracking words and pages.
- Create and maintain a professional image; treat other writers, editors, professionals, and readers with respect.
- Learn organizational and record-keeping skills; track submissions, sales, deadlines, income, expenses; keep lists and contacts.
- Keep yourself motivated for the long haul: give yourself breaks, visit interesting sites, take an art or language class, listen to music, sing, pray, do yoga.

Get Organized

You might want to develop an editorial calendar. Plenty of writers accomplish this with a hard copy calendar dedicated to their writing schedule. If you're more technical or desire to save space, use an Excel spreadsheet, a Google Sheet, Scrivener, or any one of a number of online tools, such as Trello, CoSchedule, or Evernote. You can use these tools as much or as little as you want to track your submissions and marketing, blogging, and social media efforts.

Keeping the managerial aspect of writing in its place and continuing to write efficiently is a balancing act. A professional writer must remain focused on the oftentimes overwhelming amount of work that is not actual writing. Many writers hire assistants to handle the tasks of tracking, accounting, publicity—and all of the paperwork it entails. Whatever you do, treat your writing time as the sacred commodity it is. We are writers, but to be professional writers, we must also be businesspeople.

Committed writers make the time. We wanted this badly enough to give up bowling leagues, television shows, home-cooked meals, clean houses, tidy desks, fresh-baked cookies for the Parent Teacher Organization, and Friday nights at the movies to make it happen. We scrimped and saved for books, conventions, online classes, postage and paper, and good computers. We taught our families to respect our writing time. We stayed up after the family went to bed and set out for work the next day on four hours of sleep.

I'm not saying this because I'm special. Not by a long shot. I'm one of thousands of writers who have sacrificed the same things. Plenty of writers will read this and enthusiastically nod in agreement. I'm telling you so you will understand that if you want to be a writer, *today* is the day to start.

WHAT IF YOU DON'T REACH YOUR YEARLY GOALS?

First, I don't use the word *failure*. You shouldn't either. We only fail when we neglect to set goals and work toward them. Falling short is not a failure. Think of it as an opportunity to rework the plan and recommit. When we set achievable, realistic goals, we have the power within us to accomplish them.

Let's say one of your goals was to organize your entire office, but you only made it halfway through. Did you fail? Should you waste time and energy on regret? No, you shouldn't. What you should do is admit the goal was unreasonable (considering the allotted time), forgive yourself, and move forward. If it's something you really want to do—and you believe it's within your capability to do it—set the goal again for the next year (or whatever time frame). I always keep organization and decluttering on my to-do list and goals.

If you had a goal of completing a book, but didn't finish the manuscript, you'll need to ask yourself what you could have done differently.

- Did you plan according to your abilities?
- Did you make writing time a priority?
- Did you ask for help when you ran into difficulties?

- Did you give 100 percent?
- Did you hold yourself accountable to another person?

If the answer to any of those is *no*, you should look again at your goals and rethink your action steps as well as your level of commitment.

- Did you waste time on things that didn't move you forward?
- Do you feel like you let yourself down?
- Did you overestimate the time and energy the task would take?

If the answer to one or more of these is *yes*, you should ask yourself again, *How badly do I want this?*

Career planning should not be a one-time thing. We have annual checkups with doctors and dentists; our children receive quarterly report cards. Writers should at least review their career plans on an annual basis. It's not difficult. It's not something to dread or put off. Review the past year and reflect on how your plan is working and where you might want to make changes. A career plan is a road map that will aid you in reaching your destination.

Now picture yourself where you want to be and get on the road.

2

yearly goal setting

Goals are pure fantasy unless you have a specific plan to achieve
them.

—STEPHEN COVEY

I never make New Year's resolutions. Instead, at the end of every
December, I set *goals* for the year ahead. A resolution is a passive
statement about what you want to change or wish to change. A goal
is an active plan with a specific date of achievement in mind, steps for
progress, and motivation—or a reason you want to accomplish the plan.

I'm a firm believer in goal setting. My critique group shares our
yearly goals each January. In July, we go over accomplishments made toward our goals and make adjustments in our plans for achieving them.
If you're reading this book in March or September, it's never too late in
the year to create a plan for the upcoming months. It's not important
when you start. It's important *that* you start. Period.

Here are the two most important action steps to remember when
setting goals:

1. Have a plan.
2. Have someone to hold you accountable to the plan.

Writing down your plan and sharing it with an accountability partner
makes you more likely to accomplish your goals. If you're serious about

the changes you want to make, sharing your goals keeps you accountable. Not telling anyone is the cowardly way out. It means you can fail and no one will know. If you don't have a critique group, find a writing partner who is willing to be on the buddy system with you. Share your goal plan and expect your partner to hold you accountable to it. Likewise, hold *them* accountable in a caring and gentle manner. In my group, we have our goals written in our planners. In past years, we've also posted them on a board for everyone else to see.

A good way to stay accountable is to report back to each other every week or month. Some partners meet in person over coffee or lunch. Others stay in touch via e-mail or Skype. When reporting, each writer should explain the steps he took toward reaching his goals. It's important to be committed to your partner's goals as well as your own, paying close attention and offering encouragement.

If you check Amazon for goal or achievement journals, you will find a selection of tools you can consider using to help you stay on track. One of the best—because it accommodates goal steps in an easy-to-record method—is *6 Month Goals and Accountability Planner for Authors*, by *lizzie starr. My writers chapter uses this book, and it works for both simple and more complicated planning.

There are people who meet every attainable goal year after year. What quality do those people share that helps make that happen?

Theodore Roosevelt said, The one quality that sets one apart from another—the key which lifts one to every aspiration while others are caught up in the mire of mediocrity—is not talent, formal education nor intellectual brightness, it is self-discipline. With self-discipline, all things are possible. Without it, even the simplest goal can seem like the impossible dream."

Self-discipline is the key to doing all the things we aspire to. And for many it's also one of the most difficult qualities to achieve. With self-discipline, we have the ability to work at a goal, bit by bit, making progress until we finish what we set out to do.

Repeatedly reaching small goals, and then bigger ones, encourages us to move to our next task and the one after that. Reaching goals gives us confidence. Once you've achieved something you've been working toward, your brain processes it as a win. It basically tells itself, *I did it. I can do it again.* Confidence must be nurtured, and knowing how to set goals aids us in doing that.

Pep talks are fine and support groups are good, but motivation to reach our goals has to come from within. When we're working toward a goal that comes from the desires of our hearts, we are naturally inspired and compelled to do our best. Direction and satisfaction come from working toward those things we believe in. Completing a book is one of the most gratifying experiences a writer can have.

In January 2007, I began a yearly goal sheet:

- January–February: write proposals for three historical novels and three contemporary novels
- Write one hundred words for one hundred days
- Submit the proposals
- Writing improvement: work on techniques, like segues and time lines
- Learn my brand and incorporate it into website, promotion, etc.
- Use my planner and consistently plan out page counts for deadlines

Several of my proposals were contracted, so in 2007–2008, my yearly goal planner read like the following:

- October 26: deliver *Baby Blue* Harlequin Historical novella
- Work on new stories
- Revise HH proposal Book #1 (the # refers to the book in a contract)
- November 30: start HH Book #1
- February 29: deliver HH Book #1
- Four weeks to write and revise proposals HH Book #2 and Book #3
- March 30: deliver proposals
- April 1: start Love Inspired Historical (twelve weeks)
- June 30: deliver LIH
- July 7: start writing HH Book #2 (twelve weeks)
- September 30: deliver HH Book #2
- Write proposal for uncontracted LIH

Write Smart, Write Happy

- November 30: start writing HH #3 (Four weeks)
- December 31: deliver HH Book #3

Obviously not every year is organized like this, but some are, and a writer must be disciplined enough to pull it off. A wise author told me early in my career that a backlist is a cash cow. During a lean year, the royalties from backlist books will make the difference. The lesson: Write more books—but always write *quality* books. Never scrimp on quality due to time constraints. The more you write, the better writer you become. Writing is a muscle, and the more you use it, the stronger it becomes. Schedule proposals and work to make those deadlines. While these steps don't promise publication, they are continuous steps in the right direction.

My 2008 goal sheet looked like the following:

- Consistently use planner for deadlines and page counts
- Complete HMBH by March 30
- Book #2 completed by June 30
- Two proposals by September 30
- Book #3 completed by October 30
- Writing improvement: time lines/calendar/built-in conflict
- De-clutter one area (drawer, for example) each week
- Make a decision on a new web designer and act on it
- Four to five pages per day produces a 90,000-word manuscript in ninety days
- Read more fiction

Any goal worth achieving is going to come with challenges. Recommitting to your goals on a regular basis will keep you focused. Add an emotional benefit to a goal to make it more meaningful to you; that is, consider the emotion you'll experience after you have accomplished your goal. For example, if I do the following, I will feel a certain positive emotion:

- **SIMPLIFY AND DECLUTTER:** I will feel less stressed; I'll feel free from possessions.
- **MEET EVERY DEADLINE:** I'll have more time for crafts or playing games to relax.

- **KEEP MY DESK CLEAN:** I won't be flustered in the morning, I'll be more confident.
- **STAY FOCUSED:** I'll make my deadline without last-minute chaos; I'll have time to sew because I enjoy it; I will experience less stress and therefore gain peace of mind.

Show yourself how it will feel to complete a goal and why it's emotionally important. Imagine the accomplishment. Visualize it. See yourself where you want to be.

HAVE A DEADLINE FOR EVERY GOAL

A goal without a deadline is just a wish.

My 2017 goals looked like this:

- Find the joy—daily/monthly
- Submit *Return to Cowboy Creek* #1 proposal before March 31
- Complete *Write Smart, Write Happy* by June 5
- Complete *Return to Cowboy Creek* #1 by July 14
- Update website; add Amazon carousel by end of July
- Write *Cowboy* novella by July 30
- Create and give a webinar
- Propose two stories I love during August
- Write the Aspen Gold story by September 30
- Write and publish *Middles* by December 15
- Read four craft books
- Thin out bookshelves

Break down your deadline projects into bite-size tasks and check them off in your planner with big, bright stickers to show your progress. Something about seeing completed items in a checklist is truly gratifying; it gives you a sense of accomplishment.

No one can tell you the best method to use. What works for one person may not work for you, and what works for you right now may not work for you on the next book, or next year. You have to find your own way, your own pace. Don't get discouraged; if something isn't working, simply reroute.

Congratulate and give yourself credit for every accomplishment. Celebrate every step—small or large. When I finish a book or have a completed manuscript accepted, I bake a cake for my family or critique group. During critiques on Friday nights, my critique partners and I open a bottle of champagne, eat strawberries and chocolate, and take time to acknowledge the accomplishments of our fellow writers.

I'm going to challenge you to take a good look at the people you admire and choose some qualities and habits from a role model (or more than one) as you move forward.

If you haven't already, find someone to be accountable to and to whom you can report your goals and achievements.

When you're setting your goals, think of this person as the one holding the road map to where you want to end up at the end of the year, or in five years.

While developing my calendar, I make writing, personal, and craft goals. Craft goals include one or more areas in which I will work to improve my writing. I advise having at least one current craft goal at all times—we can always improve as writers.

A few suggestions to get you thinking about craft improvement follow:

- Plan adequate preparation time in developing a story
- Character development
- Realistic dialogue
- Develop inherent conflict

And suggestions for accomplishing a craft goal:

- Take three/four classes (online or off) on the subject.
- Attend a conference.
- Read six books on the craft of writing.
- Find books on the writing craft that offer exercises, such as the assignments I created in *Writing With Emotion, Tension & Conflict.*
- Read four books outside my genre.
- Use a calendar for a story time line.

GOALS MUST BE SPECIFIC, CONCRETE, AND MEASURABLE

Goals must be within your power to accomplish.

Here's an example: Let's say one of your personal goals is to lose weight. First, you will need a specific plan; you can't just set the goal without a road map for how to accomplish it. You could join Weight Watchers, or you could buy and read a couple of weight-loss books that include eating plans. Next, you must prepare to make some changes: You'll have to shop differently. You can't fall back into the pattern of picking up a package of Chips Ahoy! and a half-gallon of ice cream during your weekly grocery trip. You'll also have to skip the McDonald's drive-through and keep healthy snacks on hand. You should work in exercise, too, so you'll need a detailed plan for that.

Those cookies are weeds that you need to yank out of the soil by the roots. The problem is that while you're attempting to eradicate those cookie-weeds, your body will put up a fight and resist the change. It won't want to get out of bed early to jump on the treadmill, nor will it want to eat carrot sticks between meals. This is where a support group is invaluable and why companies like Weight Watchers are successful.

One of the most important aids in getting where you want to be is honesty. If you want to make changes and see progress, you're going to have to be honest with yourself. Lying to yourself won't help you get where you want to be next year, or in ten years.

SETTING YOUR GOALS FOR THE YEAR

- Decide exactly what you want to accomplish and make certain you can measure your progress.
- Make a list of the steps you will take to reach each goal.
- Break your steps into bite-size tasks.
- Set appropriate deadlines.

Write Smart, Write Happy

- Use a calendar, datebook, graph, spreadsheet, or some type of schedule to mark progress.
- Reward yourself for each step accomplished.

Set Realistic Goals

Unrealistic goals set us up for failure.

- *I will write* is not specific, nor does it contain a plan.
- *I will write for one hour a day* or *I will write four pages a day* is more specific.
- *I will sell a book* is out of your control.
- *I will research the market and aim for a specific word count* is realistic.
- *I will write fifty pages a week, polish and submit by June* is within your power.
- *I will write 70,000 words by September 1st, hire an editor, and self-publish by December 1st* is a solid, measurable plan, depending on your skill level.

Goals must be things within our control. Instead of setting a goal such as selling a book this year, set your goal for taking all the steps to write, edit, and submit the best possible manuscript. You can't control whether the book is contracted, but you can control the steps it takes to make a publishable product.

Don't set yourself up to fail by making plans that will take twice as much time as you have. Don't set a goal for something you have absolutely no control over: *I want to write and traditionally publish a bestseller* is like saying *I want world peace.*

If we set goals that are nearly impossible to obtain, we're setting ourselves up for disappointment and frustration. We need to expect a lot from ourselves, and we need to expect to continually improve, but a goal that's somewhere in the stratosphere is unrealistic. *I'm going to sell a mainstream novel, and it's going to sell one million copies* is an example of positive thinking, but it's not something *solely* within *your* power to bring about. You can take all the steps, but you can't promise yourself this type of outcome, because you can't control when your manuscript is read, whether the agent wants to represent you, or if a publisher will make an offer. You can't control how many readers will buy your book. Set goals that are within your power to achieve.

Hundreds of thousands of writers participate in National Novel Writing Month every November. They sign up on the NaNoWriMo website, join local and national groups for sprints, and write as many rough draft pages as they can, seeking to accomplish the goal of writing 50,000 words, in thirty days. It's a fun program for those who enjoy participating and can be productive under those circumstances. Some writers make extensive plans for their book before the first of November, so they can charge out of the gate at a dead run. At the end of the month, if the participant has reached her goal, she receives a badge for her website or social media. Group participation and encouragement can be a boon for the solitary writer.

When NaNoWriMo was just catching on, I signed up two or three years in a row. Each time, I became discouraged, and by week two, I knew I'd failed. I was setting myself up to fail. Why? Because I don't write first drafts. I write chronologically, starting at the beginning and going straight through. I end my writing session in the middle of something exciting or when I've run out of steam. The next day, I read back through the previous day's pages and edit, then I move forward. At the halfway point of the book, I go back and do a read-through for continuity and to tweak the characters I've learned more about. Then I write to the end. The book is then finished, ready for a spell check and submission. I've learned this is how I write, and I go with what works.

I still cheer on my friends who are NaNoing. But I don't participate. Doing so is setting myself up to fail, because I don't write in sprints or in first drafts. As long as I'm focused on daily and weekly page-count goals, I'm reaching my goals and making my deadlines. I've learned what works for me and what doesn't, and I'm okay with my method and not writing the way many others do.

I recently read something one writer said about NaNoWriMo that I found interesting. He believes NaNoWriMo taught him to write sloppily, and it's taken him a long time to correct it.

Every writer learns differently. Every writer *writes* differently. It's imperative to learn your method, and then improve it. The only way to learn how you write best is to write, write, write, and then write some more. Make it a goal to learn your writing method. To understand your own process, you have to start somewhere and get experience. You must put a lot of pages under your belt.

What does your goal list look like this year? Is there something you've tried to accomplish but failed? What is your attitude toward it this time? How can you approach it differently? Which bad habits do you need to remove before this new one can take root?

Focus on the things you can control. Focus on taking the steps to make those happen. Here's a list of things you can do:

- You can schedule time every day to polish and finish that manuscript.
- You can find an accountability partner and/or a beta reader.
- You can listen to constructive feedback.
- You can submit your work.
- You can create a daily or weekly to-do list of steps to get where you want to go.

You have power over these things. Therefore, a realistic goal is, *I will write the best mainstream novel I can possibly write and choose three houses to send it to.*

You can have the greatest goals and dreams and intentions, but without commitment, you don't have a hope of achieving them. That's the plain truth. Commitment is a course of action, a pledge to do something. It's the state of being emotionally or intellectually bound to a course of action. New Year's resolutions come and go because we aren't committed to them; we aren't resolved to the action required to follow through. Resolve is the power to make choices and set goals, and act upon them determinedly, despite opposition or difficulty.

Look at the things you want to accomplish and ask yourself—and be honest about the answer—*How badly do I want this?*

Now create your list of goals and the steps to reach them.

I can't make this suggestion strongly enough: Get a journal, note-book, or planner—or all three—to track, take notes, and create lists for your own benefit. Use a binder if you plan to devote effort to your progress and education in the craft. I have several binders I use for craft and study purposes. My planner is for yearly/weekly/daily goals and affirmations. As you read the following chapters, be honest in recognizing behaviors that are holding you back. Make a plan to change those behaviors and redirect your thoughts and actions. Keep track and hold yourself accountable. Only *you* know where you want to be at this time next year. Only *you* have the power to get there. And make no mistake about it—you *do* have the power to make it happen.

Grab Your Notebook

Write down something you want to see come to pass.

Now list three things you will do to see that happen.

Make those three things your *mission.*

If you want the desired goal, you need the determination to take the steps.

Are you willing to act now?

daily & weekly goal setting

Even if your deadline is self-imposed, you must learn to discipline yourself if you want to meet deadlines. This is a skill that will serve you well throughout your career. No one else writes like you, so push yourself to know how many pages you can produce in a session. Realistically consider how many hours you need to work to complete projects. This will help you estimate deadlines that you can achieve.

To achieve deadlines, some writers use a timed writing method. They set an alarm for an hour or two and write until their time is up. Others set a word- or page-count goal. They continue to work as long as it takes to meet their word or page count.

When planning your daily output, you need to decide how many words or pages you can write in a set amount of time. Consider how much time you have to devote each day or each week. Look at the size of your project and break it into manageable chunks. The key word here is *manageable*: If you become overwhelmed, you're likely to give up.

No project is too large when you break it down into steps and accomplish them one at a time. Record your page or time goals and accomplishments in your planner and check them off as you realize each one.

JOKE: *How do you eat an elephant?* One bite at a time.

NO JOKE: *How do you write a book?* One page at a time.

When you're ready, prioritize your day according to when you're most productive. If you write best in the morning, schedule your writing time early. If you write best after waking up and checking your e-mail, work that way. If you have a full-time job, decide whether you will get up early to write, or will carve out time to write in the evening. Think of your writing time as sacred. Reading e-mail isn't writing. Checking Facebook isn't writing. If you're productive in the early morning, then do business in the afternoon or after supper. If you want to check Facebook and keep distractions behind you, set a timer and close the Internet when it's time to write. If you find yourself easily distracted, try turning off the wireless on your computer—so you aren't tempted to surf the Internet.

Sometimes I close the Internet, but most times I leave it pulled up because I know I'll need to do research. For example, I paused here to research a program a couple of friends have mentioned. It's called Freedom.to, and it's used to block specific apps, sites, or the entire Internet. You can schedule it to do its job during your work times so you can't get into those distracting, time-sucking sites.

During my scheduled writing time, I take breaks to change the laundry in the washer over to the dryer, get a cup of coffee, spin through Twitter, post a tweet or a meme. Then I go back to work. An enormous writing community lives on social media and offers the opportunity for writers to check in with writing sprints and daily word counts, or to merely touch base with other writers. If this is helpful to you, join one of these communities. But be careful: It takes balance and self-awareness to prevent these communities from becoming distractions.

As writers, we need to focus, but it's also not good to isolate yourself to the point that you lose valuable friends. My friend Carolyne Aarsen once said that she'd spent so much time alone, focused on her writing, that she'd lost casual friendships. Since that time, she has made a concerted effort to build and nurture a variety of relationships. As a result, she's more motivated to write and is better stocked with ideas. The point is, it's a delicate balance for writers. Sometimes we get so consumed with building our careers and keeping up with deadlines, while trying to keep our families happy, that friends and acquaintances slip out of focus.

Checking your phone isn't writing. We all know how good our phones are at distracting us. I caution you on being so connected that you're not present when you need to be. Remember, checking your phone also is not spending time with your family. I like my smartphone and iPad as much as the next person, but if e-mail, Facebook, Twitter, and LinkedIn notifications take you away from your writing or worse—from your family—I strongly suggest you reevaluate your priorities. Smartphones can mean death to productivity. One quick glance leads to half an hour or more of checking a newsfeed. FoMO or "fear of missing out" is a real social angst, apprehension caused by thinking others are doing something exciting that we're going to miss out on.

In her book, *The Power of Off*, Nancy Colier wrote that most people check their phones 150 times per day, or every six seconds. "Without open spaces and downtime, the nervous system never shuts down—it's in constant fight-or-flight mode," Colier said in an interview. "We're wired and tired all the time. Even computers reboot, but we're not doing it."

It's great to keep in touch with friends, and as writers, we need social media for marketing and promotion, but real-life connections are imperative. The most important thing you can give another person is your presence and full attention.

A couple of years ago I made it a monthly goal to meet one friend for lunch. This type of much-needed break from the world of fiction does relieve stress. It's not healthy to work in a vacuum, and you won't get real connections on social media. Human beings need family and friends. I always come away from lunch with a friend feeling lighter and refreshed. Discover what works for you and the methods that keep you grounded; they will help you find balance and keep perspective about your life priorities.

I polled six authors about how they reach their daily and weekly writing goals. My thanks go out to Peggy L Henderson, author of the Yellowstone Romance series; MK McClintock, the Montana Gallagher series; Kirsten Osbourne, At the Altar series; Hebby Roman, the Snowbrides series; Danni Roan, the Cattleman's Daughter series; and Rain Trueax, author of western historical novels.

WHEN DO YOU WRITE?

- Usually midday, but the best time is late at night when everyone is in bed
- When the kids are in bed
- Any part of the day I can carve out
- Evenings and weekends
- Early morning
- Afternoon

As you can see, the perfect time to write is whenever you can carve out a window and make time for it.

DO YOU SET A TIMER OR AIM FOR A WORD/PAGE COUNT?

- I like to write a chapter a day, my sweet zone is 2,500-3,000 words a day
- I write until my brain and body can no longer function or leave off at a good spot, and I walk around every thirty to forty minutes
- Word count; I don't let myself sleep until I reach it
- Eight to ten pages, but if I'm on a roll, I can get fifteen
- Word count
- I write by scenes, not pages or time

DO YOU WRITE EVERY DAY OR A CERTAIN NUMBER OF DAYS PER WEEK?

- Every day
- Tuesday to Saturday, I spend Mondays catching up on e-mails, social media, etc.; if I get these things out of the way, then the week is less hectic
- Every day
- Five or six days a week
- Mostly every day, but I stay flexible
- Every day, but it's not a rule

DO YOU HAVE A DAILY OR WEEKLY WRITING GOAL?

- My goal is a chapter a day; life at my house changes minute to minute, so I rearrange my schedule accordingly
- I set a chapter goal for each week, and that fits my busy, changing life; with weekly chapter goals, I accomplish more
- Two chapters every day
- Daily page count, plus scheduling what I'll be working on next
- Sometimes to reach a scene, but often a word count
- One scene or more a day; no more than one to two thousand words per day

WHAT TYPE OF PLANNER DO YOU USE FOR ORGANIZATION?

- I'm disorganized, but recently started using a calendar for goals and deadlines
- A physical calendar on my desk with due dates circled
- I don't believe in organization
- My daily planner is my life planner; I've used a legal pad for forty years
- I use a plot map
- Notations on the calendar

HOW DO YOU USE YOUR PLANNER OR CALENDAR?

- I stare at my calendar every once in a while
- I mark due dates for when I need chapters or books ready for the editor

- It all lives in my head, which is scary
- I keep a daily list and check stuff off, keep appointments for the week, and record my monthly or long-term goals down the left margin
- I write out general plot points, the climax of a story, and characters/setting
- I have a calendar for my books where I keep track of where I'm at

HOW DO YOU PLAN AND KEEP TRACK OF EACH PROJECT?

- I just start writing
- I have a dry erase board for works-in-progress and due dates; I also project future books, so I have clear goals in mind; I write under two pen names in multiple genres, so organization is a must
- n/a
- I have a ten-page marketing plan I cruise through with each release, with a checklist for promotion
- I keep notes
- I write one book at a time, so no problem

As you can see, every author's method is different. The important thing is to use the method that's effective for you.

I don't micromanage my time. Years ago, I tried keeping an hourly calendar every week. After a few months, I realized it made me and everyone around me crazy. When you break each day into hours, it looks like you should be able to do more because there are so many slots. The problem is we also underestimate how much time individual tasks actually take. I do not recommend an hourly schedule for anyone (unless you're taking hourly appointments and need a tight schedule). Daily planning is necessary because life is busy, but combining that schedule with your weekly goals makes the most sense to me.

Keeping a weekly goal in addition to daily goals helps relieve stress if you miss a day's work. If you know how many pages or words you need per week to meet your deadline, you have some flexibility in reaching that goal. On the Routines for Writers blog, young mother and writer Jamie Raintree writes, "Yearly goals are great for career goals, and monthly goals break those down into easier-to-swallow chunks. Daily goals are great to have, but they can often get derailed by unexpected grocery shopping trips, family emergencies, or simply not feeling well. Weekly goals create the perfect balance between focus and flexibility."

This observation is spot-on. If you're sick a day or have to take the dog to the vet and miss your writing time, you can make up missed words in the evening or over the next few days and still meet your weekly writing goals.

The last thing a writer needs is guilt for not doing enough, so give yourself the wiggle room to adjust goals around what happens in your life. One of the best things about being a writer is the ability to mold a career around the other things that are important. I've been thankful for many years that I'm not working a nine-to-five job or driving in rush hour traffic. When I start to think my schedule is tight, I remind myself of that. I'm doing exactly what I want to be doing. I'm my own boss, and I try to be good to myself. Determination and perseverance will keep you on track, but flexibility keeps you sane.

IN THEIR OWN WORDS

"I keep track of my life in my planner."

—Connie Crow, author of *All a Lady Wants*

"I track my hours, words, and pages on a simple spreadsheet so I can compare goal versus actual [accomplishments]. It includes a running total. Sometimes I look back at previous stats so I have an idea of whether I'm ahead or behind in my game overall."

—Blythe Gifford, author of *Rumors at Court*

"I write with Scrivener, which has goal-setting built in under Project Targets. It presents a bar graph of progress from start to finish, computed in words written, and allows the writer to set session (daily or weekly) goals. Scrivener will compute a per session target. I check my progress with just a click or I can keep the graph visible at all times."

—Diane Gaston, author of *Bound by Their Secret Passion*

using your planner

A schedule defends from chaos and whim.

—ANNIE DILLARD

I started out as most writers do, writing for the love of writing, dreaming of being an author, but proceeding without much of a plan. I have always written, in some form or another, since I was a kid. Short stories, scrawling ideas longhand, sometimes writing a longer story. When my youngest daughter went to first grade, I decided that would be the year I wrote a book. And I did—by writing the way I liked to write—without forethought—because it was fun. I ended up with a well-researched book with little conflict. Then I wrote another one, and it was better. Eventually I wrote one that sold, and I learned that writing as a profession is labor-intensive and requires plenty of tracking and record keeping—not only in the story, but in the delivery and production of a book.

A unique few can handle everything in their heads without dropping any loose threads. I am not one of them. I need to see where I'm going and what I must accomplish along the way. I want to be organized, and I work constantly to be that way. I can't say what the perfect plan for you might be, but I can show you examples of what works for myself and others.

In the front of my planner, I list my goals so I can refer to them often. In chapter 17, you'll find a list of affirmations I use. When setting up my planner for the year, I write at least one affirmation for each week. Here are some sample affirmations: *I challenge myself to do new things. I take daily steps toward my goals. I don't waste energy on things I can't control.* I refer to my affirmations daily, as a focus for each week. Often I create a Facebook meme with my affirmation for the week as well.

Most often when buying a calendar, I choose a Lang engagement planner. I use the Lang website to see the interior pages and make certain the planner has the features I need. In the front of Lang planners are the previous and following year's calendars at a glance, as well as each month of the year on individual pages. I use these calendars to indicate manuscript delivery dates at a glance. I use the additional blank pages for notes and lists. The weekly pages are where I get down to business.

My planner stands open on my desk at all times. A glance shows me my focus for the week, where I am word-wise, and what's coming up that I need to take care of. I've used this process for eighteen years. I always say, if something's working, don't mess with it. But if you're in a rut, it's time to haul yourself up and out of it. Find a method that works for you.

Before the year ends, I am already listing responsibilities, engagements, and deadlines in the following year's planner. Even though I plan for "life happens," life always happens more abundantly than anticipated, so having a planner to keep me on schedule has saved me many times.

Let's say I have a February 1 deadline for a 75,000-word book, and I plan to start writing in November. First, I look through my planner week by week and see how many days I can truly devote to writing. I don't count holidays or school holidays, and I don't count weekends (until the deadline draws close, and then I pull out all the stops, if necessary), nor do I count any days I know I won't be writing—for example, days I will be at baby showers, weddings, or on a trip. Let's say this averages out to four days of writing a week until the book is complete and the deadline comes due. Then, I divide the target word count by the number of writing days available to me to discover how many words I need to write on each of those days.

To make it simple, let's say it's January 1, and you need a 75,000-word book finished by June, allowing time for revisions and edits.

You're aiming to have a first draft completed in April. We'll say you have sixty days in which to write that first draft. You'd need to write 1,250 words a day to have it finished by April 1. That will give you two months to edit or revise. You decide your daily word goal from January 1 to February 1 is 1,200 words. Now you can mark your planner accordingly and check off the daily goals as you achieve them. This can be done weekly just as effectively, and you would work to a weekly word count.

Of course, this is an example of someone with full days to devote to writing. If you have four hours a day to write, schedule your word goals accordingly. If you want to write with page goals in mind, which I honestly prefer, schedule your planner using how many pages you need per week or day to reach your goal. If you fall behind, simply recalculate. This time you'll have to write more pages per week or day, but you can still make your deadline.

I'm a visual person, so I keep sheets of stickers in the back pocket of my planner and give myself stickers for achieving daily page-count goals. They're bright and fun, and they show my accomplishments and inspire me to continue. If your planner doesn't have a pocket, tape an envelope inside the back cover. I can't picture Stephen King rewarding himself with happy-face stickers in his planner, but it works for me. Encourage yourself and move forward.

My publishers also give deadlines for work I need to complete during the production phase of the book; for example, cover art information is pages long and is filled out online. Filling these out requires writing a brief synopsis; sending photographs in Word files as an attachment; envisioning scenes; describing characters, setting, weather; etc. There is a brief window to finish the work before the art department and marketing teams look at them, so I write that due date for each book into my planner and prepare by collecting the photographs ahead of time. I used to keep physical photos, and then, later, .JPG files, in my book folder on my computer, but now I use Pinterest. I explain my process in chapter 27.

Publishers also require a quick turnaround for line edits and author alterations. The author can only guess at when these will arrive in her inbox, but she has about a week or ten days to turn them around once they arrive. Whatever else is on the calendar must be rearranged in order to fit in these tasks.

I schedule days for guest blogging, too, so I have my blogs prepared or formatted before the date they're due. I also keep track of dates for recording webinars, teaching workshops, hosting book signings, going to retreats and conferences—all together in one planner with the rest of my life, like dentist appointments and kids' birthdays. I keep everything in one planner in one place so I can synchronize my life and know which weeks I'll have more or less time to write.

Your planner is great for tax purposes as well. You can record trips and expenses. When I get my taxes ready for my accountant, who is also my daughter—God bless her—I go through and double-check records, receipts, and mileage for each activity in my planner. The one time I was audited, the IRS auditor was duly impressed with my record keeping.

I don't consider my planner complicated. It's simply facts I need to be aware of to complete tasks on time. I try not to make things any more complicated than they need to be, because life is crazy enough. I remember reading that Mark Zuckerberg, creator of Facebook, wears a gray T-shirt every day so he doesn't have to waste mental energy on deciding which clothes to wear. The idea of keeping the little stuff simple appeals to my logical personality.

Many daily tasks are simply not a big deal. I don't stress over food, though I like to eat. Grocery shopping is a perfunctory task. I don't stress over what to wear as long as I'm presentable. I order most of my clothing, beauty, and household items online, because shopping takes too much time and presents the opportunity to impulse buy things I don't need. Writer friends of mine order groceries online and have them delivered.

The key to your planner is that it fits your life and your thought processes. There are monthly planners, and a look at the entire month might be helpful to some, but it's too overwhelming for me. I can manage one week at a time.

Is there an app for weekly planning? Probably. Will the app work for you? You won't know until you try. I'm not the only one who finds the old-school method of pen-and-paper scheduling the most valuable. Writing things down helps me remember. It's comforting. It's an art form I appreciate.

GET THE MOST FROM YOUR PLANNER

- Record dates and goals for the overall year.
- Create an overview for each month.
- Plan weekly tasks.
- Keep track of daily progress (or lack of).
- Make using your planner a habit.
- Reward yourself for accomplishments on a regular basis.

Similar to planners, but with more adaptability for a writer's creativity, are Bullet Journals and Habit Trackers. A Bullet Journal is basically a planner you create, with a several-months-at-a-glance calendar, an index, and lists of goals, due dates, and tasks. Google "How To Bullet Journal" to watch YouTube videos of how to create and use one. Google "Habit Tracker" to learn how graphs and charts can be created and used. These trackers are a little over the top for me—especially those that record mundane tasks—but you'll never know if they can help you until you check them out and give them a shot. The organization probably appeals to the left-brain thinker, while the colorful pens and creative tracking appeals to the right-brain artist.

When I go on the Lang website, I find a planner I like and usually order it on Amazon with free shipping. You can order Bullet Journals online, as well. Michael's craft store has all kinds of planners and stickers in stock at their stores and online, and they even hold free classes if you want to join one and see how to use a particular planner.

If you're not writing under deadline—whether you're self-published or traditionally published—then you're not a professional writer. I set weekly goals based on current deadlines using an old-fashioned paper-and-pen day planner. I also keep track of monthly word counts.

This method is useful when tracking trends in writing. I consistently write fewer words in December and more words in February. I use these trends to plan my future deadlines.

—Sherri Shackelford, author of the Prairie Courtships series

CHOOSING YOUR PLANNER

Written by *lizzie starr, creator of *6 Month Goals and Accountability Planner for Authors*.

Besides my own creation, I use a calendar-style planner that shows a week-at-a-glance. There's plenty of space on each week for writing and stickers, along with a picture that I enjoy and sometimes take inspiration from. I advise anyone using an engagement planner that has more than spaces for writing (i.e., space for pictures) to choose one illustration that is especially appealing. I use my trusty dachshund calendars every year. I've tried other calendars, but find I'm not as predisposed to use them. Even things I normally would enjoy—like recipes—didn't bring me back to the calendar on a regular basis like doxies do.

I use the blank pages of the planner to record my yearly goals. I record word and page counts when I attend meetings or writer events, webinars, and classes—pretty much anything that's writing related. And stickers. I love stickers. They're the best visual reminder of progress and writing activities.

In the Accountability Planner I created, I break monthly goals into smaller bits, setting weekly and daily goals. Word counts also are recorded there, and eventually I put them on a pretty spreadsheet created by Jamie Raintree because it adds the numbers so much better than I can. The planner includes places for reflection, which a calendar doesn't always allow for. Although I don't always take time for reviewing the previous week's goals, I'm beginning to see the importance of doing so and am making that a personal goal.

In the past, I've kept track of the books I've read and the book reviews I've written in my calendar, but I've now moved those records to my Goal and Accountability Planner.

Right now I make plans for submission goals, as I explore the possibility of becoming a hybrid author; publication goals for self-publishing; and word-count goals to keep me writing.

5

utilizing your strengths

We must have perseverance, and, above all, confidence in ourselves. We must believe that we are gifted for something and that
this thing must be attained.

—MARIE CURIE

We spend a lot of time looking at the things we need to fix about ourselves, but we also need to recognize and utilize the things we do well.
During blissful times of writing, we become lost in our scenes and don't
even realize time has passed. This is because we are using one or more
of our strengths. These strengths are our sweet spots. Take half an hour
or an hour to sit down with your journal and make a list of your talents,
knowledge, skills, and experience. If you get stuck, ask a friend, a mentor, or a family member to share how they see you.

I'll do it for myself right now to show you how to brainstorm your
strengths.

- I'm good at coming up with titles. I've titled many of my friends'
  books and plenty of my own. I can take the premise of a story, consider the hook, and come up with twenty titles, a few of which are
  simply for laughs, but I nearly always end up with one keeper.

- I'm a great speller and good at grammar. I write clean copy.
- I hear passive construction in a sentence from a mile away.
- I naturally write sensory details into my scenes to make them realistic.

Reviews and comments about my writing often describe it as emotional and realistic. A well-known author judged my entry in one of the first contests I entered before I was published. She mentioned the sensory details and compared my work to an author I admire. Ever since, I've used that ability in every proposal and submission I send. Once an editor told me my synopsis made her cry, and she bought the book immediately. Using my abilities to make the reader feel deeply, I can write about a lot of subjects with respect and make the reader care. I know that about myself, so I play it up. One of my critique partners is great with dialogue. She writes natural, yet dynamic interactions between characters. Her first draft of a manuscript is pretty much all dialogue. She writes what the characters are saying first, then goes back and fleshes out the story, setting, everything else—and it works beautifully for her. She understands her strength and uses it well.

Brainstorm the techniques you use well. If you tend toward sarcasm and a jaded viewpoint, you could consider a crime-solving character who always expects the worst, and guide that character through a series of mysteries. Maybe you come up with unpredictable dialogue or find the humor in any situation. If making people laugh is your forte, write humor.

If you feel you have weak areas, ask friends for help. I have a tough time coming up with snarky remarks, but I know someone who makes me laugh without effort, so I ask her to help me figure out what this or that character might say to lighten the mood in a situation. There's a niche for you to fill with your strengths.

The same goes for the business aspect of writing. Every writer has a unique voice and worldview, one that might be a great fit for a blog or group of writers who blog together. Perhaps you're tenacious and can handle criticism and rejection without taking it personally. Maybe you don't get flustered easily and like to speak in front of people, so proposing speaking engagements or book events will be an excellent promotional tool for you. If you enjoy social media, are a natural at marketing, and have a knack for earning followers online, you can build a broad platform and use it for promotion. If you know HTML, you can build and maintain your own website and blogging platform. If you've built up a vast knowledge over your writing career and know how to present ideas and techniques in a way others can understand, you'd be a good workshop speaker. When, how, and how much we use our strengths depends on the individual situation.

There are several tests you can take online to analyze your strengths. Strengthsfinder 2.0 can be purchased at Gallup.com. Myers-Briggs is another choice, as well as enneagraminstitute.com. A free strength test can be found at literacynet.org. Once we know and understand our strengths, we can use them effectively. It's all about discovering and nurturing our gifts to help us grow. The point is not to learn what we do well to say, "look at me" or have others inflate our egos. We want to learn how to use our skills to the best advantage so we can be the best writers possible.

Our careers depend on readers liking our work enough to buy books, so we must focus on writing well, not on pleasing everyone for the sake of approval. It's wonderful to hear complimentary things about our books, but if we need that level of encouragement to continue day after day, and through the difficult times, we will be sorely lacking in tenacity. We must learn and want to give 100 percent, because we desire to do our best, not merely for the accolades. If your self-esteem lies in glowing reviews, you'll encounter plenty of occasions to despair. Our self-esteem must come from a job well done and having given our best.

CONFIDENCE IS CONDITIONED BEHAVIOR

Regardless of how you feel inside, always try to look like a winner. Even if you are behind, a sustained look of control and confidence can give you a mental edge that results in victory.

—DIANE ARBUS, PHOTOGRAPHER

Many years ago, a scientist at the University of Wisconsin tied a mouse's front feet together and placed the animal into the cage of another mouse. The mouse whose cage was being trespassed easily beat up the mouse with its feet tied. After several more times, the scientist put mice without tied feet into the cage. The mouse who'd won repeatedly was so confident by then that it took on and defeated mice even larger than itself. Under ordinary circumstances, that mouse would have run when it saw a larger opponent, but it had been conditioned until it believed it couldn't lose. And it didn't.

Condition Yourself

Writing is a discipline. Writers must be as disciplined as they are creative if they're going to accomplish their goals. Scheduling writing time is necessary to create a routine and make writing a habit. This is something you have to learn about yourself. Look at your other responsibilities, like your family or job. Consider your optimal times for creativity and mental energy; use it wisely. Build your writing muscles by starting out with a regimen. Exercise builds endurance, so make a plan to increase your endurance.

- Set a time limit of thirty to sixty minutes and gradually increase.
- If you're currently writing two days a week, increase it to three, and sustain that for a month.
- Increase to four days a week.
- Write four to seven days a week.
- Envision your reader/know your audience.
- Focus on a technique, like improving dialogue or effectively describing location.
- Make a list of five interesting words and work them into your day's writing.
- Tell someone you trust what you're doing.

If you're just starting out, I caution you not to tell a lot of people that you're writing. Not because you should be embarrassed by any means, but because they will never forget and will, without a doubt, ask you about it each and every time they see you from now until eternity. I can unerringly predict the questions they will ask: *What's your book about? Still working on that book? When will I see you on Jimmy Kimmel/ Jimmy Fallon/Conan/insert current late-night television show host? Has your book been made into a movie yet? Have you done all the stuff you write about?*

These are well-meaning friends and acquaintances, but don't say you haven't been warned about their questions.

Treat your muse like a muscle. You wouldn't expect a couch potato to run a 5K with little or no training. If you've been neglecting your writing for weeks, months, or even years—your muse is flabby and out of shape. Work on conditioning your writing with sprints and don't set yourself up for failure by expecting too much too soon. Good writing takes training and practice.

—SHERRI SHACKELFORD, *A TEMPORARY FAMILY*

You can't learn how you write best without doing a lot of writing. Learn where, when, and how you write best. Creating a work space of your own is one of the most important things—other than putting words on paper—that you can do when starting out or starting over. Not everyone has an entire room or spacious loft to dedicate to their writing, but everyone can carve a space into the area they do have. You can create a writing area on a table pushed into the corner of your bedroom. I know writers who have made private cramped spaces in cold basements or hot attics. Many writers who can work with chaos around them have spaces in the kitchen. The important thing is that you take yourself seriously enough to dedicate a place for your writing. When you respect your writing, you teach others to respect it as well.

You deserve a writing place of your own. A writer's work space can be as simple or complex as needed and as space allows. For years, I used a typewriter. That wouldn't fly today. You need a word processing program, so a laptop or a desktop computer is a good investment. My first computer was an Apple IIc that came from the pawnshop. It didn't even have a hard drive! The operating system was on a floppy disk. I wrote several books on that baby; three that were contracted and published before I could get a better computer. The point is, do what you can afford and work with it.

Make your background wallpaper something that inspires you. Mine is usually a scene or a room from my current work-in-progress. Sometimes it's a character's face. Write positive reminders to yourself and hang them where you can see them when you sit down to work.

If you don't believe in yourself, you can't expect others to. Consider every step toward your writing goals an achievement. Think confidently. Speak with confidence. Expect to do well. Expect to succeed.

Congratulate Yourself

If you write consistently and make your goals, you will achieve something many people never do. Thousands of people claim they want to be writers. Writing means putting words on the page. If you do that, you're further ahead than the rest of the population. You're a writer. Never scoff at your attempts even if they don't seem significant or professional to you.

Give Yourself Incentives

Be creative in congratulating yourself, sharing your success with others, and building your confidence. Make a plan for the year, devising ways to bolster your confidence.

If you have received any good contest remarks or notes from a fellow writer or a judge, post them over your work space.

I mentioned the stickers I place in my planner. Though small, these are daily visual reminders and rewards. It's not the monetary value of a reward from a competition or for an accomplishment, but the psychological effect that's valuable. Perhaps there's something you haven't been able to justify buying; make it the metaphorical carrot before the horse. Do you want a new Keurig or an Amazon Echo but can't rationalize the expense? Promise yourself that reward when you get this book finished or when you sign a contract.

I started out buying myself a gemstone ring every time I sold a book. A ring was something I could look at and be reminded of my achievements. When someone remarked about it, I'd have an occasion to share my accomplishment. I didn't have enough fingers to continue that tradition, and one can only own so many rings, but those rewards served me well for a season. For a long time I had each cover enlarged into an eight-by-ten print and framed it, but I ran out of room and abandoned that tradition as well. My writer's chapter awards a charm for each sale and accomplishment, so I have several bracelets filled with charms I cherish as achievements. Lastly, I have a couple of shelves of my books I can look at as reminders of what I've done and how hard I've worked.

Celebrate Your Successes

I have friends who enjoy a glass of wine after a successful writing day. Many writers go out to dinner with their spouse or friends after they've finished a book. Here's what some of my writing friends do: Barbara Taylor Sanders treats herself to a deep tissue massage because her shoulder and neck are in lockdown after every novel. Geri Krotow spends a day at the nursery, plants flowers, or spruces up the house as a reward. Shannon Lawrence buys herself a Funko Pop figure for each short story she sells. Upon delivering a book, Jennifer Ashley buys dollhouse miniatures. When she hit the USA Today best-sellers list, she bought herself a car!

Open a bottle of champagne, buy yourself flowers—do anything from baking a cake to embarking on a weekend getaway as long as you reward yourself for sticking with a project and completing something to the best of your ability.

Swap Skills with Another Writer

Self-aware writers already know their shortcomings. Maybe you can't make heads or tails out of social media and need to be led by the hand to get started on each platform. In this case, you can trade editing (or whatever you specialize in) for help with technology. Heck, trade meals and chocolate for help with technology!

Nobody can make you feel inferior without your consent.

—ELEANOR ROOSEVELT

Just because you master a technique or become good at something, don't stop there. Never stop learning. My friend MK Meredith always reminds me of the advice I gave her early in her career: "Always be a student. If you think you know everything, you'll stagnate."

Humility is a quality that leads to improving your strengths. I've been writing books for decades, and I still attend workshops, take notes at meetings and retreats, read craft books, and work on improving my craft. There are thousands of books on how to write on the market. You can Google "writing resources" and find an infinite, and overwhelming, number of websites, webinars, and books. I can't recommend all of them, but I can recommend those books I'm familiar with, and those that have helped me or other writers.

Here are some helpful writing resources:

- Robin Perrini and Laura Baker's workshop called "Story Magic" is available online at www.fearlesswriter.com. I was fortunate to attend their live seminar years ago, and it changed my life. Their self-image worksheet for characters is only one of the gems included in their course.
- *Writer's Market*, Robert Lee Brewer (this is an annual edition)
- *Techniques of the Selling Writer*, Dwight V. Swain
- *Building Believable Characters*, Marc McCutcheon
- *Dynamic Characters*, Nancy Kress
- *Characters, Emotions, and Viewpoint*, Nancy Kress
- *Writing With Emotion, Tension & Conflict*, Cheryl St. John
- *Goal, Motivation, Conflict*, Debra Dixon

- *Creating Characters*, the Editors of Writer's Digest
- *Creating Characters: How to Build Story People*, Dwight V. Swain
- *Creating Character Arcs and Story Structure*, K.M. Weiland
- *Creating Dynamic Dialogue*, the Editors of Writer's Digest
- *Writing On Both Sides of the Brain*, Henriette Klauser
- *Breaking Into Fiction*, Mary Buckham, Dianna Love
- *The Complete Writer's Guide to Heroes and Heroines*, Tami D. Cowden
- *Plot and Structure*, James Scott Bell
- *Setting*, Jack Bickham
- *The Fire in Fiction*, Donald Maass
- *On Writing*, Stephen King

If you want confidence, act as if you already have it.

—WILLIAM JAMES

what fits into your life?

Self-discipline is an act of cultivation. It requires you to connect today's actions to tomorrow's results. There's a season for sowing, a season for reaping. Self-discipline helps you know which is which.

—GARY RYAN BLAIR

SELF-DISCIPLINED PEOPLE DON'T MAKE EXCUSES

You've noticed by now that my philosophy is most often "whatever works." There is no one right way to write, edit, be accountable, address social media, study, or self-promote. The right ways are the ways that accomplish your goals. I know a lot of writers, all from various walks of life, of different backgrounds, with different responsibilities and unique family and financial situations. The disciplined writers are the ones who get the most accomplished—the ones who reach their goals and achieve success.

When my local writing chapter's retreat focused on technology and social media, speakers who help companies with social media, websites, and SEO asked each writer to share which social media sites they used and how they felt about them. From the response, it was clear writers either love social media or hate it. There was little middle ground. And a huge percent feel inadequate at promotion and social media, and don't really know what to use or how to use it. Social media in general overwhelms a large number of writers.

How you approach social media is a personal decision. You must be comfortable with the platform, with how much you're willing to share about yourself, and how much time you're going to devote. The best advice is to choose one or two platforms and work them. If you love it all, by all means do it all. If you don't, choose one platform and do it adequately.

Difficult issues for the modern-day writer include the overwhelming abundance of portals for promotion, the amount of posts, a dread of not knowing what to say or of doing too much or too little. Personally, I enjoy social media. Initially, I didn't understand Twitter. Then I took the initiative to figure it out and I realized I could make it fit my needs—and the narrow strip of time I was willing to devote to it—and learning a few tricks made all the difference. Once I weeded out the hoards of free book sites and spam accounts, and made lists so I could find the tweets I actually wanted to read, Twitter became useful. The goal is to search for people and lists that discuss your interests and then follow those people and lists. If you aren't enjoying tweets, or learning something from a person's tweets, unfollow them.

The same goes for Facebook. If you don't enjoy a person's posts, if you don't know them but they post ten times a day, if they promote themselves or their product repeatedly, or if they constantly complain or ridicule others *unfollow* them! Social media—even when used for promotional purposes—is not an obligatory party for work. You are not trapped in a corner, forced to politely listen to the boss's wife talk about her gall bladder surgery. This is your party, your time, and your decision. Make social media you-friendly. Make it your page, your feed, your time line—that means take control.

On Facebook you can unfollow without unfriending. Use that tool to your benefit. I do not follow negative people. I don't follow people who complain. I don't follow people who post photos of abused animals. And I unfriend people who post offensive photos or use vulgar language. There's no place in my day for that. There's no place in my life for that.

Remember the most important parts of social media, though: Respond to readers, interact with writers in your feed, post regularly, and leave comments on other people's posts. To see the feed of the people you enjoy, you must interact with them. If you don't, their posts won't show in your time line. I use a lot of stickers as comments and replies because they're quick and they show that I'm paying attention and interacting. Think of your social media circles as an extension of your writing community. Interact with them positively, and keep positive company.

If you don't enjoy the process, check your page only once a day and interact then. In this day and age, it's imperative for authors to have a presence on social media. If you like it too much or find that it's time-consuming, set a timer before you log on. When it rings, get off!

As an author, you should use social media to reach readers. You may have a profile page or an author/business page, or both. I have both. It's a lot more difficult to get Facebook users to Like your business page, so it takes work and requires a unique hook to build a following.

The following are some general rules and etiquette to follow on social media:

- Do not post the same thing on two pages. Keep your business page strictly professional for those who want to follow that page. Your profile page can be more casual, but always remember that your readers are paying attention. They love to see your family and the color you chose for your kitchen, because they feel as though they know you. They don't want to read a rant about a negative review—one of them may have written it. Readers are people with busy lives, too. They follow you because they enjoy your books and/or they like you. Don't wear them out with negativity or hourly updates. Posts with photos get the most attention. Post a photo or a meme, and you'll get more responses and likes.

- Tread carefully on social media. Don't say anything you wouldn't want friends, readers, your editor, or your Aunt Jenny to read. It's public, and it's forever.
- If Facebook, Twitter, Instagram, Pinterest, LinkedIn, and Snapchat confuse you, choose one and have someone help you set it up and show you how to post at least once a week. You choose how much time and effort to devote to it. I enjoy Facebook, Snapchat, and Pinterest. Interacting is no problem for me, but I understand those who do have a problem with it.
- If you hate it or believe it's a complete waste of your time, don't do it. I've never seen Nora Roberts on Facebook, and she's doing okay.
- Authors must have a professional website with information about themselves and links to buy their books, as well as contact information. Authors should also have a newsletter to alert readers to new books. I know writers whose spouses are gurus at social media and even at building websites. If possible, involve your spouse or your adult children in helping you. If not, and you hate the whole thing, or if the effort causes you stress, by all means pay to have it done. Nothing is worth the hassle. Making promotion fit your life is the important factor.

When asked the best thing about being a writer, I always say it's the ability to fit my career around my family. There have only been tiny windows of time in my life when I've had no children to care for. I raised four children, who are now grown and successful. I've cared for several of my grandchildren, from the oldest to the youngest. I took care of my first granddaughter while I still had two children at home and worked forty plus hours a week at an outside job in the evenings. In more recent times, we had a daughter and grandchildren living with us. One of the best things about being a writer all these years has been the ability to work around my family and church. Writing has had to fit around the other important things in my life.

Two of my daughters had difficult pregnancies, and I was able to help with their other children. I've gone to dozens of musical programs, plays, and awards ceremonies (and cried at every one). I've read books to students, spoken about writing to elementary and junior high classes, attended field trips, and cheered at sporting events. I've driven kids back and forth to school, entertained them on summer and winter breaks, taken them to doctor appointments and extracurricular classes, cuddled them on sick days, watched movies with them on snow days. I've planned weddings and graduations. And around each of those ordinary occurrences and life-changing events, I wrote books.

Looking back on all that, I'm still not sure how. At one Writer's Digest Conference in Los Angeles, an eager fellow approached me after one of my workshops. He seemed incredulous over my bio, and asked, "Fifty books? How did you do that?" I replied: "One book at a time." And he came back with, "Exactly."

I don't think I'd ever looked at those achievements before the way I did that day. We most often see ourselves through the eyes of those around us, and most often I'm a wife, mother, and grandmother. I'm the one with the hugs, the one who makes the stuffing and sweet potatoes for Thanksgiving, the vat of baked beans for graduations, and place orders from Tastees for birthdays. I'm the person with the messy desk and the collection of teapots.

So lest you think I'm Super Writer or more special than you, I'm not going to inflate myself into someone I'm most certainly not. I have asked for my share of extensions on deadlines. I've been stuck in the middle of a book. I've completely forgotten a deadline until unearthing my desktop after a life drama—and then written an entire novella in seventeen days. (It was actually one of the best stories I think I've written, but I wouldn't recommend the last-minute method.)

People who are not my family look at my body of work and ask, "How do you do it all?" Well, I don't. All you see is the finished cake with the pretty icing. You don't see the layers held together with toothpicks or know the first batch was burnt. You see the lovely covers and the Amazon reviews. You don't know how many days I worked in my pajamas or how many times my husband did the grocery shopping or the dishes—or how many times the dishes piled up in the sink. For every workshop prepared and every deadline met, something else fell to the wayside. Sometimes the pile of laundry is so big we have nothing clean left to wear. Sometimes we eat cereal for supper.

What works for another person may not work for you. What worked for you ten years ago may not work now. The seasons of our life are fluid, and if we don't evaluate and flow with them, we'll become frustrated. All my adult life I've heard, "I don't know how you do it all." Just because people don't see me sleeping in, watching TV in my pajamas, and not answering the doorbell, doesn't mean I don't take me-time. I do. I have to make down-time or I'd be a burned-out basket case. Sometimes I go to the antique mall by myself and just wander the aisles, looking, filling the inspirational well. Once in a while I go to a movie by myself and see anything I want to see. Every summer my husband and I take Thursday mornings for garage sale therapy.

There have been times when I didn't know what I was doing, when I was faking it until I made it. And there have been plenty of times I didn't make it. I don't sell every book I propose. I don't land every contract I want. More than once I've fallen asleep at my desk and made myself go for a walk so I could stay awake long enough to finish my word count. In Shonda Rhimes's book *Year of Yes*, she wrote something that echoed my beliefs. She mentions that someone will say, "I want to be a writer," and then they dream of it, they write in their journals, they talk with their friends about it, plan it. She calls it "blue-skying" your life. "Dreams are lovely. But they are just dreams. … Dreams don't come true just because you dream them. It's hard work that makes things happen. It's hard work that creates change."

Rhimes doesn't claim to have everything all pulled together. She writes three award-winning television shows at the same time, including one of my favorites, *Grey's Anatomy*, but she's struggling to be a good mother, terrified of public speaking, and often physically and emotionally exhausted from juggling family, work, and travel. One of the changes she made to get her life under control was to not take calls or e-mails on weekends or after 7 p.m. After all, three hit television shows depend on her completing scripts every week. My deadlines seem frivolous compared to hers, but she keeps her family and personal time sacred. Balance is a juggling act if you have a job, a spouse, children, and parents. A writer's life is never as it's depicted in movies or on television. We must adapt, day to day, year to year. Anne Rice, Harper Lee, J.K. Rowling, Virginia Woolf, and countless others all held down jobs while writing great books. Plenty of people want to be writers. Few can handle the work, the sacrifice, the dedication, or the rejection to make it happen. The perfect time will never come. A convenient window of opportunity will never open. Get a crowbar. Force open that window.

Self-discipline is the key to personal success. It's the key that opens all the doors for your future. You hold the power for success or failure within you. There are no shortcuts to personal happiness or fulfillment. Reaching your goals and achieving your dreams is hard work. Thomas Edison said genius is 1 percent inspiration and 99 percent perspiration. By persevering, you are setting a lifelong habit. Don't make giving up a habit.

Action Steps

Look at the portals available for building a platform:

- Website *
- Mailing list/newsletter *
- Social media
- Blog
- Video blog (vlog)
- Book trailers
- Speaking engagements/workshops

Be selective in choosing which portals fit your time and your technical abilities, and decide how much time you're willing to devote to activities that are not actual writing.

- If you don't know, ask for help.
- Be willing to flow and grow through the seasons of your career.

* At the very least do these; everything else is optional.

PART 2
sharpening your saw

7

positive motivation

It was character that got us out of bed, commitment that moved us into action, and discipline that enabled us to follow through.

—ZIG ZIGLAR

POSITIVE EMOTIONS CHANGE OUR BRAINS

In her book, *Positivity*, Dr. Barbara Fredrickson shares her studies of positive emotions. Her data reveals that negative emotions, like fear, can cripple our ability to function, while positive emotions open us to possibilities and an increased ability to move forward. She lists the top ten positive and helpful emotions as joy, gratitude, serenity, interest, hope, pride, amusement, inspiration, awe, and love.

In Fredrickson's broaden-and-build theory, she believes positive emotions change our brain when we experience them, and they change them for the future as well. Positive emotions broaden our minds, and we become more creative and open to options. Depending on the specific emotion, other momentary benefits include relaxation and feeling invigorated or playful. These feelings propel us to engage in specific behaviors, such as exploring our surroundings or building relationships. Ultimately we learn something new, fashion new relationships, or deepen existing ones. The new feelings and behaviors are building blocks that form beneficial psychological resources.

Low Expectation

On the opposite end of setting unrealistically high goals are those writers who don't set goals or expectations high enough. If just slogging along through the same book you've been working on for the last four years is good enough for you, and you don't plan to change your work habits or improve your skills, well, you're not expecting much from yourself. The problem with that is you're not going to get much either.

Confidence is built on accomplishment, so it can be difficult to be confident when you haven't sold a book, landed a multibook contract, or made a best-seller list. But the writers selling and making those lists are still working on confidence, too. Expect more from yourself. Be willing to do more to achieve more.

What should you expect? You should expect good things from yourself. If you want to keep it simple, just do the best job you can possibly do. And if you've done your best, you should expect good results. Don't let a low image of yourself or your capabilities limit an all-out pursuit of your goals. If you want to write books and sell them, take the steps necessary to get there. Selling is never a guarantee, but you can't sell if you don't write or submit in the first place.

If you're published and still want to break out or change directions, expect more from yourself. Janet Evanovich had published a dozen romances but was frustrated with being unable to write the romantic adventures she wanted to write, so she took a time-out. She spent two years researching and coming up with her own brand of humorous adventures and creating her undauntable character, Stephanie Plum. As of this writing, her series is up to twenty-three books, and *One for the Money* was made into a movie. Janet works fifty hours a week, with her husband, son, and daughter involved in the business. A dream is nothing without action.

At every turn, ask yourself: *How badly do I want this?*

All successful people, men and women, are big dreamers. They imagine what their future could be, ideal in every respect, and then they work every day toward their distant vision, that goal or purpose.

—BRIAN TRACY

The key word here is work, which is what you must do. Don't let fear or insecurity keep you from pursuing a dream. And don't let low expectations keep you from believing in the dream. We tell ourselves we're not talented enough or don't have connections or don't have enough time, when we should be telling ourselves we are capable, talented, and willing to work hard.

Discipline

Ever notice how so many seat-of-the-pants writers—mostly beginners— take pride in being unstructured? Have you ever listened when they talk about their process? "I don't write a synopsis. I just start the story. Planning takes all the fun and spontaneity out of the writing process." That attitude strikes me as arrogant. These writers believe they don't need to set guidelines for themselves because they're creative people, after all, and creative people need their freedom, don't they? Well, it all boils down to, as Dr. Phil would say, "How's that working for you?"

There's nothing inhibiting about planning plot points and conflict. In the long run, plotting saves a heck of a lot of time.

Everyone needs some form of structure. Your structure is certainly not the same as mine, and mine wouldn't work for the next person, but just as we need a plot skeleton to hang a story on, we need structure for our creativity. Even the most impulsive seat-of-the-pants writers need discipline to accomplish their goals. A simple planner will give a writer direction if it's used as a tool and the writer makes it work.

If you're thinking you have enough structure already, and writing isn't your job, here's your wake-up call: *Hello.* If you want to sell books and make money, you want writing to be your job. Treat it seriously. If you respect your craft, others will too. Be disciplined with your time, your computer and Internet use, your free time, and all the hours that make up your day. Time is your most valuable resource. Use it wisely.

Here's where self-discipline serves writers well: We have choices when it comes to feeling inadequate about our writing methods, choices, experience, growth, and accomplishments.

If you have a list of goals from last year, get it out now.

Also pull out this year's list of goals, because you've made that by now, right? Consider these questions.

- How many of last year's goals were accomplished?
- Are there goals that you failed to achieve?
- What held you back? Were the goals not concrete? Unrealistic?
- Are your reasons legitimate or are they excuses? You will know the difference. You're smart like that.

Now, compare your current goals.

- Are any of them the same as last year's? What held you back?
- Evaluate your reasons for not achieving this goal. Is this a problem you have had in the past?
- Is an activity or thought holding you back?

Own up to your bad habits and choose to change them for the better now. You have a bright future ahead of you in which to make better choices.

BRING NEGATIVE THINKING TO AN END

You won't get anything from these chapters if you're not honest with yourself. Just be real. If you can see yourself in one of these examples, if you identify with anything you find here, it's okay. We're all human; you shouldn't feel bad. We're all working on our own stuff. If you see that one or more of these issues are holding you back, own up to it. Be honest enough with yourself to work on it.

Reviews Come with the Job

Some people get bummed when they read the listservs and review magazines; and check the market news and acknowledge the declining market; or read about the achievements of others. If those publications or lists drag you down, unsubscribe from them. Don't read. Don't listen. Don't drag yourself down. Do only the things and be around only the people who encourage you and build you up.

Most books have some bad reviews. J.K. Rowling got scorched for *Harry Potter and the Sorcerer's Stone*. I doubt she lost any sleep. Stephen King's *Carrie* received one- and two-star reviews. He's laughing all the way to the bank, right? Initially he threw that manuscript in the trash himself, but his wife saved it and submitted it, garnering the sale.

Just for the heck of it, I looked at *Anne of Green Gables* on Amazon. You probably already know what the book is about, but here's the description: "*Anne of Green Gables* is a 1908 novel by Canadian author Lucy Maud Montgomery. Written for all ages, it has been considered a children's novel since the mid-twentieth century. … Since publication, *Anne of Green Gables* has sold more than fifty million copies and has been translated into twenty languages. Numerous sequels were written by Montgomery, and since her death another sequel has been published, as well as an authorized prequel. The original book is taught to students around the world. It has been adapted as film, made-for-television movies, and animated and live-action television series."

Add to these credits, plays, and musicals in Canada, the United States, Europe, and Japan, plus an official website and fan clubs. This book is unquestionably a classic. Yet I found this one-star review: "This is the most drippy book I have ever read. … Predictable story line, lots of redundancy and written for a ten-year-old. A waste of time."

I have no words.

There is also a one-star review titled "No Illustrations." Hmm. Wonder what kind of review this person would give *Moby Dick* or *A Tale of Two Cities*—no illustrations there either.

I have friends who never look at their reviews. That's how they handle reviews. Personally, I look. I want to know how readers are receiving my work.

My best advice regarding critical reviews is to do nothing. Suck it up and do absolutely, positively nothing. Do not respond where anyone can see it. Don't post your reaction on social media. Sadly, there are trolls in every genre, and they don't hesitate to label complainers as "authors behaving badly." I have seen trolls get their friends to post additional one-star reviews in retaliation. Too much negativity gets tossed around when authors respond to critical reviews.

One writer cannot please the tastes of every reader out there. Accept that some readers simply won't get your vision of this story, won't appreciate character motivations, won't care for your twist, etc. Yes, books are personal to us because we invest so much of ourselves into them, but to the editors and publishers, to the outlets, these books are merely a product. Every product on Amazon has a range of reviews. I might love a wallet that someone else hated and returned. Does that mean I have poor taste? Does that mean the other person has poor taste? No, it means we have differing opinions of the same product because we're different consumers. If you need convincing, go online and check out reviews of books written by your favorite authors. Not everyone loves the same books, nor should they.

Developing a thick skin will serve you well. It's okay to feel disappointed, to be hurt if the attack feels personal or the words are rude. I've read critical things about my books that have made me either cringe or laugh out loud. To counter the bad feelings, eat some chocolate. Have a glass of wine. Tell your best friend or your critique group—the people who understand—but *hold* everything! *Do not tell anyone who will go post on the review in your defense!*

And remember, many readers seeking to purchase a book are suspicious if there are only scores of glowing reviews. Books that have 99 percent glowing reviews are unrealistic; it looks as though the author put his friends up to writing those reviews. And similar to the adage that says there is no bad publicity, a bad review is still a review. If you've read my book on *Writing With Emotion, Tension & Conflict*, you know my number one rule on writing is to make the reader care. If they feel strongly about my book, good or bad, I've made them care.

Accept that reviewers might leave a one-star review because of poor delivery. It happens all the time. And sometimes these reviews have nothing to do with the book you've written. Sometimes people leave bad reviews because the subject matter didn't turn out to be what they expected, or they received a misprinted edition—both of which are beyond your control. Sometimes the purchaser hasn't even read your book yet, but replies to the auto-e-mail prompt in irritation and scores the book low. If that's the case, you might get some traction by contacting Amazon and explaining the situation. They often work with authors, but if an inappropriate review remains, there's nothing we writers can do about it.

Do your best to make certain all of your reviews are authentic—either verified purchases or reviewers who mention they've received a copy for an honest review. Not all purchases can be verified by the seller, of course, because books are also sold in stores, on other sites, and at conferences in addition to being shared and lent from libraries. Do not pay for reviews. Do not ask your friends to post reviews. Give them books, and if they post one, that's well and good, but don't solicit good reviews. Doing so is obvious. Our focus must be on writing the best book we can write. If there's something to learn, be teachable. If every review says you haven't fleshed out your characters, take another look at your character development and add it to your craft goals.

And remember this: You can't get a good or a bad review if you haven't written and published a book. By publishing, you've done something masses of people only dream of, but never attempt. Be proud of your accomplishments. Wear your badges of honor. And write another book.

Dealing with Critical People

We all know people with negative attitudes. Often they are members of our family or members of the crowd we associate with. We hear that person who says, "If it weren't for bad luck, I wouldn't have any luck at all."

We find these people in all walks of life, in nearly every situation. The weather is miserable, grocery prices are so high they won't be able to afford their next meal, the neighbor is deliberately parking crooked in the street just to make life wretched, the killer bees are coming, our country is going to hell in a handbasket. These people often get caught up in the negativity in the news and anticipate flu season.

Some people can't manage to find anything good in a situation or another person. After an hour in this person's company, anyone would want to jump out a window.

If we allow them to, these people can have a negative influence on our writing and our writing attitudes. They hash over all the bad stuff; they pick apart books and movies critically; they bad-mouth the organization you belong to, the group you enjoy, the industry, the editors, the market. And if you're fresh and new to this arena, you can be negatively influenced. If you're seasoned, that person is annoying at the least and harmful at the worst—as much as you might like them in other ways.

Those people are looking for the bad stuff. And that can get in the way of a lot of good experiences. And sometimes we fall into that trap ourselves.

Creativity and energy are sucked away by thinking about things outside your control, so change your thinking. Seriously consider what puts you in a bad mood or makes you think negatively.

How can you change your thinking?

How can you change your reaction?

We can't change people, and often we have little control over many situations, but we can change how we let people and situations affect us. You can change your reaction.

Perhaps one of the most productive goals you can set for yourself for the rest of this year is *I am going to change my thinking.* For example, *I'm perfectly capable of learning how to navigate Twitter, so I'm not going to be intimidated.* Or, *I've been procrastinating because I let myself believe no one will read this book anyway. I'm changing my thinking right now. I'm going to focus on writing and on the readers who will enjoy my story one day soon.* Jot down three steps to make it happen, and follow through. Make renewed thinking your mission.

Your motivation to take action increases when you picture yourself succeeding.

The bigger, brighter, more immediate, more personal you can imagine the payoff, the greater your desire to pursue your goals.

Try this: When a person speaks negatively, say something positive in response. It almost always works. If you don't join in, or you make a positive statement, people realize what they've done or said. If the negative talk continues, you may have to be straightforward and ask them not to do this in your presence. If you can't confront them, then simply take yourself out of the situation.

Stay away from a person who drags you down with pessimism and disapproval. These people are toxic.

You're Only as Good as Your Next Book

Our books can feel like our babies. We've conceived and given birth to them. We think they're the prettiest babies out there, and we don't want them to lose that new baby smell. But the truth is we're only as good as our next book.

I can't remember where I first heard that philosophy, but I can tell you I took it to heart. I've used it as motivation for as long as I can remember. At first the thought was a tough pill to swallow, but it's a fact. In many genres, and romance in particular, books are here and gone. They're released and the biggest share of buyers purchase them immediately. After that first burst of popularity, sales level out. The advance checks have already paid the bills. By the time a book hits the shelves, I'm well into the next one or have finished another. I actually have to refresh my memory on the recently released book to do interviews and promotion. If I'm fortunate, foreign rights are sold and the book continues to earn out, with royalties coming in. Digital sales make for a continuous trickle that spike each time I release a new book.

If you've self-published, you can go back to edit or improve and update with a new digital and/or print-on-demand edition. It's possible to give your self-published, backlist titles a new life, but it's a lot of work. If you've been traditionally published, that book is pretty much set in stone and is firmly in your backlist. Concern yourself with your next book.

These days, it's unrealistic to think you can stand out from the crowd with one book. You can't promote one book infinitely. You have to be able to move on to the next. If you want that book to sell, write another one. Readers find you and then look for your backlist. New material means sales of the new book and the previous books.

Major Self-Evaluation Time

If you're a negative person, listen to what you're telling yourself and make some changes. You're making yourself miserable. You're making others miserable. You don't want to live like that. Change your thinking. Tell yourself positive things and don't say anything about your writing unless you can say something nice.

Are you a self-involved whiner? Is everything about you, how you're feeling, how your day went, and what's wrong with your life? If you catch yourself in this negative thought trap, *stop* immediately. Put on the brakes and park the Me Bus.

Here's where the rubber meets the road: How much are you willing to invest into your future success, into these chapters, and into self-evaluation? Is it enough to make changes?

Grab Your Notebook

Or get out your pen and journal. Make a list of all the good things that are working for you; count your blessings, in other words. We all know someone who would change places with you on your worst day in a heartbeat. They'd be thrilled to wear your shoes.

Create a list of your good qualities and talents. No, really, it's okay. We tend to be humble and to downplay those things, but we need to acknowledge our strong suits and good qualities to play them up. When I branded myself for marketing, I took a look at what readers said about my writing—that the characters were realistic, the stories true to life, and the emotion engaging—I took those reader observations to heart and used them. When I wrote *Writing With Emotion, Tension & Conflict*, I looked at my strengths and chose how to use them constructively to write a book to help others.

Focus Outside Yourself

The most miserable people are those who sit around focusing on their problems, turning everything inward, focusing on their difficult situations. That type of behavior opens the door to anxiety, physical illness, and depression. When you get down about yourself or your situation, think outside yourself. I challenge you to do something for another person: Take a meal to an elderly neighbor, mow their yard or shovel their walk. Spend an hour a week at an elementary school helping children learn to read. Volunteer to teach English or help someone get their GED. Volunteer to walk dogs or foster rescue pets. Hold babies in the NICU at the hospital. Help out one of the veterans' programs that give homeless veterans food and shelter, and food and clothing. These charities need volunteers to paint, cook, and serve. Take books to the V.A. hospital or the Ronald McDonald House. Start a Little Free Library (if you don't know what this is, Google it).

Can't do something physical? Send a card. Make a phone call. Organize a coat drive or a back-to-school backpack collection. Women's shelters need gently-used business clothing. Clean your closet with them in mind. Write a check to a cause you believe in.

Choose to change your self-defeating behavior. Thinking about others gets the focus away from the negative things in our own lives. The psychological, spiritual, and physical rewards for reaching out will surprise you.

Martin Seligman's book *Learned Optimism* is a scientific, engaging explanation of the benefits of learned optimism. Here are some exercises we can do to increase our optimism:

- Think about how good you will feel when your goal is accomplished.
- Make a list of the things you're looking forward to the next day or the next week.

- Create something to look forward to, like a walk or a chat with a friend.
- Consider pleasant experiences in your past, things that made you feel confident or proud, occasions you especially enjoyed.
- Listen to music that lifts your mood.
- For one month write down three things per day for which you're grateful.
- Journal about your positive experiences.

Conditioning oneself to have more optimistic thought patterns leads to feeling more energized, which leads to increased productivity. Being less stressed is another perk, which also benefits physical health. Studies have found that optimism is related to longevity. The inherent belief that good things will happen is called "dispositional optimism" and has been strongly connected with improved recovery rates after surgery and improved cancer survival rates.

I'm not talking about positive thinking alone, but also about recognizing negative behaviors and pessimism, and replacing those thoughts and behaviors with learned optimism. It is achievable and well worth the effort.

Many years ago, before I was published, I had a job where I was on my feet all day—plus I had children at home—and I was trying to write and submit a book. Every morning, when my aching feet touched the floor, I thought to myself, "This job is killing me."

One morning I heard my own thoughts and called myself out. I still needed to go to work. My family still required love, attention, meals. I still wanted to be a writer. But I deliberately changed my thinking. Instead of the negative thought, I told myself, "This is challenging right now. But I'm not going to be doing this forever. I'm going to be a writer."

My circumstances didn't change immediately. But my attitude and outlook did.

Listen to what you're telling yourself. Make sure it's what you need to hear to set yourself up for success.

Billy Sunday said that more men fail for lack of vision than lack of talent. See yourself accomplishing something great and set yourself on the path to achieve it. Success is motivated by purpose. Don't let the future be that time when you look back and wish you'd done what you're not doing now. All men and women who have achieved great things have been dreamers, so you're in good company. Take a step every day to accomplish your goals. Make decisions and get out of the middle of the road. Ever notice that's where the weeds grow?

One person who is committed always accomplishes more than one hundred people who are interested. Commitment turns your dream into reality.

CELEBRATE TODAY

Review your accomplishments, make note of a breakthrough, take a walk with your dog, or spend time with a child, grandchild, spouse, or call a friend.

EXPECTATIONS AND NEGATIVITY

There was a time years ago when *Romantic Times* magazine was the be-all, end-all—the who's who of romance authors and readers. Often reading through those ads, interviews, and lists of books made me feel like I was lagging behind. It was like everyone was more prolific, made more money, and was more successful. I started feeling inadequate when I read each issue. I unsubscribed and bought an issue only occasionally—usually to see my own review. These days the glut of books and authors on Facebook and Twitter can be overwhelming. Writers we've never heard of before are posting their releases, sales, awards, and Amazon rankings. The excess of information can be overwhelming and make us feel like a fragile petal riding a tidal wave.

As writers, we have the option to pull back from anything that is making us feel badly about ourselves. We can't be ostriches in this fast-paced business, but we can dial it down. Some people *can* handle it all, and if you can, more power to you. But we don't have to do it all. Being Super Writer is an impossible expectation to place on yourself.

Do not compare yourself to other writers, but do develop good role models. I had a role model who was older than myself and more accomplished, but experienced and generous with her knowledge and time. I had another role model who was a peer, a single mom with a career, who was ambitious and determined. Both were strong, smart women who, by example, showed me that with effort and heart, I could become a published writer. We shouldn't imitate a role model's every move, but when we see how well their method is working, we can apply the same techniques. If you see a pattern of work ethic that's panning out for another writer, it can't hurt to see if following a successful example might improve your routine.

Action Steps

Grab your notebook and answer these questions:

- Can you see areas in your opinion of yourself that need to change?
- Are there times you fall into negative thought patterns?
- Is there someone you know who needs your help in this area?
- What would you do today if you knew you couldn't fail? Write it down.
- What would you accomplish in the next six months if you knew you wouldn't fail?
- What are the steps you can take today to change any negative thinking you may have done? Write them down.
- Will you invest in your health and future by challenging your thinking?

When you look back through this chapter and your action steps, can you see places where you can achieve positive and helpful emotions? Don't settle for less.

THE TEN POSITIVE EMOTIONS

Joy

Once or twice a year, I take a month where I focus on joy. For me, it has a lot to do with faith. I add to that a month of Facebook memes, where I post an affirmation or something that gives me joy. We must remind ourselves where our joy comes from. Spending time with a partner, children or family can teach us a lot about simple joys.

Gratitude

Share something for which you're grateful on social media, every day for a month—or challenge yourself to journal your gratitude daily for a year. There is so much to be thankful about.

Serenity

Kick back from the chaos and give yourself free time to think and dream. Remind yourself why you want to be a writer.

Interest

Read things that fascinate you and absorb your attention. Learn something new and work it into your manuscript. Take a true interest in others, in helping them reach their achievements. When they do, it's all the more to celebrate.

Hope

Keep your eye on the goal and don't lose sight of your dream. Without hope, we cannot move forward or find joy in today. Enjoy today, but look forward to tomorrow.

Pride

This isn't puffed-up pride; this is the knowledge of our abilities and gifts we never want to take for granted. It's humble confidence and satisfaction in our accomplishments.

Amusement

Laughter is still the best medicine. Laugh at yourself. Laugh with your friends and family. Watch a movie or read a book that tickles your funny bone. Laugh lines are not wrinkles, they're paths to health and happiness.

Inspiration

Do those things that inspire you. Paint, watch movies, take walks, go fishing, people watch, spend time with those you admire. Be a student, an advocate, a mentor. Inspire others.

Awe

Remember what it is you love about reading, about the swing and sway of musical words and magical images. Read your favorite author, who leaves you breathless and yearning to reach readers with the same impact. Work to capture the same sense of wonder in your stories.

Love

Yes, sometimes a book is merely a job. Sometimes a book is not enjoyable to write. But we love being writers, or we wouldn't do this. We love having written something that will touch and inspire others. We love the magic of stories and creating worlds and people we can manipulate to draw emotions from our audience. We love being writers.

Sometimes it's an effort, but we must remember our first love; we must transport ourselves back to those days when we first knew we had to put those people in our heads on paper and create stories for them. Whenever I've been discouraged or questioned my choices, I've always asked myself the same question: What would I rather be doing?

Even before I was published, I was frustrated and wondered if I should keep pursuing this dream of being a writer. I sometimes wished I could be content to do something else, something with a quicker payoff and a visible reward for the effort. But in my heart of hearts, I knew I would not be satisfied until I'd given writing my very best and written stories that touched readers the way so many books had touched me.

So if you believe you've lost your love of writing or have become discouraged, ask yourself, *What would I rather be doing?* If there's something else that fills that place in you, by all means do that thing. If not, remember your first love. Find the joy, the awe, and the inspiration and discipline to move forward.

8

the price of success

Nothing in this world can take the place of persistence. Talent will not: Nothing is more common than unsuccessful men with talent. Genius will not; unrewarded genius is almost a proverb. Education will not: The world is full of educated derelicts. Persistence and determination alone are omnipotent.

—CALVIN COOLIDGE

Grab a pen and jot down your writing dream. I don't mean your short-term goal or your long-term goal, but your *dream*. When you first started thinking about being a writer, or made the decision to write, what was it you dreamed most of?

Now list how many manuscripts you've submitted this year. How many last year? The year before? Okay, now out of all those submissions, how many do you believe were truly salable short stories or manuscripts?

Sometimes the dream gets a little hazy. Sometimes it changes focus, and sometimes it seems so far away that we'll never reach it. For me, when the house was a wreck, the laundry wasn't done, and no one had eaten a home-cooked meal for weeks, I'd stop and ask myself, "Is this what I really want to be doing?"

How come reaching the dream takes so darned long? Why is it so difficult? How come you're getting all those rejections? And just how long do you hang on to this dream?

Writing is about as glamorous as digging a trench to find a busted sewer line. Sometimes you can't see what you're doing for all the sweat in your eyes. You have to dig a lot of dirt, shovelful by shovelful, to find the break. It helps to keep your tools sharp, but it often seems as though you'll never get there. The whole process often stinks. The labor takes a toll on your body. Nobody wants to do the work, they just want to have the job done. It's a lot more fun and rewarding to have written than to write.

Some of my favorite shows to watch are the programs on how movies are made. There used to be a program called *Movie Magic*, and there are often specials on Bravo or HBO, like *The Making of The Fast & Furious*, *Avatar*, *Jurassic Park*, you name it. Years ago I even went to see *Waterworld* after seeing how over budget the production was and how the blue screen effects were done underwater. No apologies. The creative aspect enthralls me.

I drive my family crazy because I watch the extra material and directors' cuts on DVDs. I stay in the theater to see the bloopers until the employees are sweeping up popcorn and candy wrappers. AMC Online shows how *The Walking Dead* stunts are done, and I always find those riveting. After I watch one of those programs, I have to go see how the special effects, the computer imaging, fake rain and snow, and all that stuff came together into ninety minutes of near-perfect cinematography, sound, and lighting. The process is captivating. And I'd rather know the behind-the-scenes first. Then I can sit and pick out all the places where I know they did a particularly wonderful job—or had an especially difficult time.

I think one reason those shows intrigue me is because everything that looks so polished and perfect in the finished product was actually grueling, laborious, and oftentimes frustrating work behind the scenes. For example, while making the original *Jurassic Park*, every time that huge T-Rex that broke through the fence and came after the kids in the car got wet in the rain scenes, the mechanical parts stopped working.

They'd have to stop filming, dry it down, wait, and start over. Sometimes it took hours to get a few perfect shots.

Not so unlike what we do as writers, is it? Writers and readers see us wearing our good clothes, with our hair in place, signing the glossy finished product. How many hours of unglamorous work went into that finished product? I hate to even think how much I made an hour on some of my first projects. And I hate to tell you, but I'm not dictating to my personal secretary each morning while I get my hair coifed or slip into my pink ostrich feather–trimmed negligee.

When I was sixteen, I wrote my first book on a portable typewriter. I submitted it and got a rejection. I wrote a least four more books through my twenties. I submitted them and received well-deserved rejections. When my youngest daughter went to school, I wrote a book I ended up rewriting six times—on a used Selectric *typewriter.*

In my thirties, I got serious, joined a writers group, learned to write better, and wrote another book from scratch. In doing so I learned sacrifice and discipline. I mapped out my priorities and made choices. I was also working at this time, so I gave up a lot of things. I didn't watch television shows or meet my girlfriends for gatherings. I didn't volunteer at school. I assigned my kids chores, and my husband helped with laundry and grocery shopping. I still made soccer games and swim meets.

That book was rejected once and then agented and sold. I went back and rewrote the one I'd rewritten so many times and sold it as well. But just because you sell a book or two doesn't mean everything falls into place for your career after that. I had two book proposals rejected after my first sale. I had a proposal rejected after my third book. I had three book proposals rejected after my fourth. I still get rejections.

Some authors I spoke with claimed to sell one out of every three proposals. What does this tell us? It tells us why authors are selling—because they're submitting consistently.

We only see the titles that make the review columns and hit the shelves. We don't see the manuscripts on closet shelves, in desk drawers, or file cabinets—we don't see the sacrifice behind the scenes. The more you submit, the better chance you have of selling. The more you submit, the more you sell. I firmly believe it's a direct correlation. The ratio is uncertain. I just keep submitting.

Here's how to know if you truly have the desire to be a published author:

- Your desire to write is greater than your difficulty in getting words on paper.
- Your desire is greater than the disappointment of rejection.
- Your desire is greater than the discouragement of industry hassles.

You may be telling yourself that after a particular stumbling block is removed you'll have more time. *After tax season is over, I'll have more time. When winter arrives, I'll have more time. When I don't have to drive the kids to school, I'll have more time. This summer I'll have more time. I'll have time when I can take a vacation.*

Those times arrive, and with them, more responsibilities and choices. That ideal hiatus from real life when Jupiter aligns with Mars never does happen. Some seasons in life do afford us with fewer responsibilities, but for the most part, time doesn't multiply itself and present windows of opportunity. We make those choices and those opportunities ourselves. We create new habits. We invest in ourselves.

If this is you, and you've been telling yourself there will be more time when X, Y, or Z happens, you've been deceiving yourself. You've been making excuses, but you don't want to look back years from now and finally recognize you could have started writing and made progress by now. Decide right now that you're done deluding yourself and making excuses. If you truly have the desire to be a writer, there will never be a better time. *Now* is the time. Kick fear and procrastination to the curb and stretch toward your dream.

DOING WHATEVER IT TAKES

Very few writers have the luxury of not working while they're launching a writing career. It's not easy, and something must give. Achievement always involves sacrifice. You learn to get up an hour earlier to work on your book or use your lunch hour for edits.

My husband and I made an agreement that he would take the kids to events and family gatherings without me for several months, so that I could devote time to writing. He did the grocery shopping and I did the laundry. I finished the book I was working on in that season. Eventually I cut back my hours at work by a day so I had one full day home alone. I drove an older car for years so payments didn't inhibit my ability to quit my job when the time came. Eventually my writing bought me a better car.

We can't sacrifice our lives or our families for this dream, so we have to learn to make the combination of family, job, and writing work together. We must learn to let go of things that aren't important and nurture those that are. I learned to write no matter what condition the house was in. I still do. These are the decisions that will prove your desire.

SACRIFICES

What compromises are you willing to make? Swap daycare with a young mom and have a morning a week for writing. Let calls go to voice mail. Turn off the Internet—tell yourself it's not forever. (It might be if it works for you, however.) Join or create a group that makes meals together and cook up a month of convenient freezer meals. Sign the kids up for fun classes during summer break. Plan activities they can do together or with another parent during your work time and offer to take all the kids to the zoo or the movies on Friday. If they're little, write during nap time and after the family is down at night.

Realistically, selling one or two books will not support you. But writing more books and selling consistently will. Sporadic or inconveniently spaced advances and royalty checks will not be enough unless you learn discipline now. If your desire is greater than the difficulties and sacrifices, you have much of what it takes to succeed. The techniques and skills of writing are learnable. Talent is a God-given gift, but it's wasted if one doesn't have the desire to make something of it. Authors might be dreamers, but all their dreams are backed by hard work.

BEING ADAPTABLE

During the completion of this book, my life took several turns, with my youngest daughter marrying and moving out. As I am finishing this manuscript, it's summer and our air-conditioning unit went out. In Nebraska, we don't survive in the heat and humidity without air-conditioning. Of course, everyone needs a repairman or a new unit in this weather, so we have to wait nearly a week for installation. My husband and I made a quick run to Costco for window units so we could cool our bedroom and my office. We figured out a plan and carried it out so my work wasn't derailed.

Summer school has started, and the two grandchildren who have lived with us until recently always attend classes, like Lego Technics or other fun things. They thrive on routine and interaction, so I pick them up after school around noon. The teenager is independent, of course, and the seven-year-old entertains herself a lot, but I fix them both lunch. My routine right now is to work in the morning until I pick them up. After lunch, we do an activity or an errand until Mom comes to get them at four. Four evenings a week I work until around eleven or twelve. So I get in about nine hours of work on each of those four days, scheduled around family and meals. It's the summer plan. It's flexibility. It's commitment to my craft without sacrificing my life and the other things that are important to me.

9

put procrastination behind you

I don't wait for moods. You accomplish nothing if you do that. Your mind must know it has got to get down to work.

—PEARL S. BUCK

Many underlying issues may come into play when a writer is procrastinating. We'll take a look at several. If you're having problems with procrastination, you must first acknowledge your behavior. All the writing techniques in the world can't help you if you're acting as your own worst enemy.

Good or bad, behaviors define us, and we often sabotage ourselves with negative ones. Samuel Johnson said, "The chains of habit are too weak to be felt until they are too strong to be broken." We can create habits, good or bad, unconsciously. They sneak up on us if we're not vigilant. We are, after all, creatures of habit. If we're not careful, we tend toward the most comfortable path—because even if it's not in our best interests, it's comfortable.

If we expect to complete a task quickly and easily, we don't put it off.

I'll say that again: If we believe a task is easy, we won't procrastinate. The first step of any process or project is the most difficult. We only put off the difficult tasks. That's why we might clean our desks rather than sit and write. That's why folding the laundry seems more important than grappling with the next chapter in our book.

STOP OVERTHINKING THIS

Trust me, I've done this too. Some problems we have to work on all the time. The important thing is to recognize what we're doing and work on it. The task can look so large, so overwhelming and insurmountable, that we delay the pain. By focusing on the short-term difficulty of getting started, we ignore the long-term stress of falling behind—which is worse!

It takes a conscious effort to create new ways of thinking and doing things. Change is not comfortable, but if we're not working to our potential, it is necessary and worth the effort.

Learn Why You're Procrastinating

Notice that even though this is a difficult subject, I didn't put off this topic until last. It's human nature to put things off; I don't know why that is—probably because we don't like being uncomfortable. We do the easy things first and delay those that require more effort. We make excuses. We justify the delay. *I'll get to it. I'll do it later. I need to think about it. I'll do it when I have some free time. I'm too busy. I can't afford it. I need to prepare first. There's always tomorrow.*

It's an illusion that we'll do the work tomorrow. Tomorrow will be the same as today. And the next day and the next. There's always next week. Next month. Out of sight, out of mind. Avoiding something difficult causes us more pain and difficulty in the long run. Avoidance leads to guilty feelings of inferiority. In the long run, delay causes stress.

I read an article that said those who procrastinate, and then write the book in a panic before the delivery date, teach their brain that this method works. So they do the same thing the next time. I've worked hard to keep this from being my method. I want my brain to learn that chipping away in increments and not working furiously in the last few weeks is the most effective and least stressful method. It's a constant process for me.

If it's not important enough to handle right away, we're subconsciously telling ourselves it's not as important as what we're doing right now. And, sure, there are plenty of things that are equally important, but again you need to prioritize.

Procrastination is often caused by fear of emotional discomfort. If you're procrastinating, it may be that at some point along the way writing stopped being so much fun, and became work. Now you have to stretch yourself. Our initial love of writing is based on ignorance. When I began writing, I was thrilled with the excitement of producing a story. I could spend hours lost in the euphoria of putting words on paper and just writing, writing, writing—blindly in love with the characters and the book. Eventually, however, I learned I needed a plot and conflict, and that there were actual techniques to sentence structures and chapter beginnings and ends. And with that new understanding, the task became infinitely more difficult. It wasn't pure fun anymore. A lot of work was involved.

As a result, I had to learn discipline. Writing can be extremely difficult. Those who say differently are lying or hopelessly misinformed.

Acclaimed regency romance author and Spur Award–winner Carla Kelly, author of *Courting Carrie in Wonderland*, told me, "I suspect many novelists hear this at book signings: 'I'd like to write a novel.' I smile and say, 'Go for it.' What I really want to say is, 'Be prepared for an adventure that is grueling, grinding, exhilarating, and rewarding in turn. … There's no magic pill to make your words all sparkly and fit for instant acclaim. It never gets easy. What makes subsequent books possible is that once you've written a novel, you know you can.'"

Carla said that during those moments when writing is hard or she loses interest, she reminds herself to be patient with the process. "I keep writing, always with the goal of 'The End' on that final page."

Redirect Tendencies to Procrastinate

If you look over your list of household chores for this week or your goals for this year, do you find that you're picking and choosing, completing the easy things first? That's our natural tendency. If the chore or goal is too big to accomplish while working toward a deadline, move it to your "after the book is finished" list. If it's just difficult, but needs your attention now, do it first and get it out of the way. Completing a difficult task is empowering. Look at your lists now and resolve to accomplish one difficult thing today.

We must deliberately and consciously choose to move forward. We must be emotionally and intellectually bound to our goals. Without this resolve, we become victims to our own habits and comfort zones. Never forget you alone have the power to move your goals from thought to reality. Our choices determine our actions, and our actions determine the results.

When you find yourself stuck, or feel like you're about to give in to the powers of procrastination, ask yourself these questions from George A. Ford, MD, a Fellow of the American College of Physicians: "Where do I want to be at any given time? How am I going to get there? What do I have to do to get myself from where I am to where I want to be? What's the first small step I can take to get moving?"

Multipublished author Ruth Logan Herne, author of *Back in the Saddle*, suggests writers "give up the easy ways out. The easy ways are the things you allow to steal your time, the things that implode your work ethic. How many times have you lamented the lack of good things on TV? Forget the television and write."

Herne also advises that we, "turn off Facebook and e-mail notifications, and focus on the story at hand. I finish every project because my reward is a new project. But it is work, and you have to truly want to do it, despite the odds, because the only way to tip those odds in your favor is to finish the book."

I love Ruthy. She's intelligent, cheerful, and energetic; she's prolific, and though she produces award-winning books, she makes time for family, friends, church, baking, and running a truck garden. She obviously does not allow distractions to sway her work ethic. Want to be more like her? Ask yourself the following questions:

- Am I ready to take control of my writing career?
- What am I doing right?
- What do I need to do differently?
- How can I make the needed change?
- How can I block the distractions that spoil my work ethic?
- Am I committed to change?

Write Smart, Write Happy

In her class "Defeating Self-Defeating Behaviors," writing instructor Margie Lawson says, "High achievers know how to delay gratification."

Most modern-day people are accustomed to instant gratification and immediate results. If we want to watch a specific movie, whether it just came out on video this week or was in the theaters twenty years ago, we can turn on Amazon Prime, Netflix, or Hulu, and very likely find it. If we're hungry, we can pop a dinner in the microwave or order take-out. When we need an answer, we text someone and hear back within seconds. Want to verify a fact? We have Google, Alexa, and Siri for that.

As writers, too, we want instant feedback. I've seen beginners so eager to see their book published that they don't take time to perfect their craft and end up self-publishing products that aren't ready. As a rule, fast results aren't a writer's friend. Lawyers don't read a couple of books and hang a shingle. Doctors don't take speed courses and practice medicine. Neither should we attend a few workshops and think we're ready to launch a writing career.

As you read earlier in this chapter, Ruth Logan Herne says her carrot for getting to the end of a book is that she can start a new story. We do need to give ourselves incentives. I, too, have things I look forward to once each book is finished. As I mentioned before, I celebrate the achievement with my critique group. But I also clean my office. (Don't laugh! When I'm bearing down on a deadline, I don't stop to tidy my desk or the room. So, I really look forward to cleaning my desk.) Doing so is delayed gratification. When the book is finished, I'll go to lunch with a friend, take a trip, or paint a room.

Giving yourself promises of shiny rewards will inspire you to write the book.

Success is a finished book, a stack of pages, each of which is filled with words. If you reach that point you have won a victory over yourself no more impressive than sailing single-handed around the world.

—TOM CLANCY

I especially like that Clancy quote because it says the determination of completing a book is a victory over one's self. We can either be our own worst enemy or our own cheerleading squad. Be the latter. Tell yourself, I can do this! I'm going to do this!

We all have the same number of hours in our day as Tom Clancy, Stephen King, Agatha Christie, Sue Grafton, or Debbie Macomber.

Be Accountable

If you commit to a critique group or a partner, you're accountable. This is where that accountability partner or group will serve you well. If you feel a responsibility to report your actions and page counts, you will be more likely to hold yourself to them.

Maybe not every book is the book of your heart.

Maybe some books are just plain hard work. This happens. Remind yourself why you want to do this. Remind yourself of the options.

Maybe there's pressure to be brilliant and the pressure weighs on you, so you put it off.

A couple of years ago, a friend I spoke to about perfectionism gave me a wake-up call. I was stressing over coming up with a brilliant submission package. When editors love a particular story, they want you to write another one just like it. That kind of expectation adds up to pressure. My friend said to me, "You don't have to be brilliant. You just have to be you. That's why readers buy your books and that's what they like about your writing. Just do what you do."

Her wise advice allowed me to stop trying too hard.

Thank goodness for friends who can be honest with us, who have the perspective to see what we're doing to ourselves and point it out in a caring way. We put a lot of pressure on ourselves to be brilliant, to be the best, to write the next bestseller, to write a better book than the last one. It's not a bad thing to want to excel and to expect a lot from yourself, because you're capable of a lot. But sometimes we forget that we're unique and valuable, that we have something important to say in a way that no one else can. We could give twenty writers the same plot premise and character, and each one would come up with a completely different story. We all have our own backstories, our own unique history that brings us to our worldview. No one else can tell the same stories we tell. We each have something special to offer, but sometimes it's difficult, scary, or we feel we're not up to it.

If this is you, challenge yourself: Start every day, project, or time period by doing the most difficult tasks first instead of last. When faced with an unpleasant task, take care of it right away instead of stressing yourself by avoiding it. Doing so will free up your attention and allow you to be more productive in the long run. If it has to be done eventually, start now.

If your only excuse for not getting your project done is that you're busy, you need to ask yourself if you're procrastinating—and why. If you're avoiding something difficult or if a new challenge is pushing you out of your comfort zone, your feelings of nervousness or insecurity may lead you to procrastinate.

Break It Up Into Manageable Chunks

When we look at a whole book or series as a goal, the undertaking looms so large that it's easy to procrastinate; which only leads to a real emergency later on.

That's why it's so important to plan the small steps of any project and to find pleasure in the parts of the job that you enjoy. Consider how easy it was not to procrastinate when you first started writing. You wrote for the pure joy of it. Capture that again by getting excited about a story—by concentrating on one or two small bits: one scene, one chapter, one character, one plot thread. Find a warmup exercise that works for you, maybe ten minutes of writing or sketching out a scene of dialogue only. Generate some momentum to get you going. For me, it's going back over the previous day's writing and seeing where I can improve the narrative or inject emotion. My goal is to make the reader feel, so if I see I've done that effectively, it's enough to propel me forward.

Always remember that you don't have to write the whole book today. Looking at how many pages you have ahead of you may be daunting. Even though those first pages are the most fun for me, I get to about chapter four or five and realize how much I have yet to go. The bigger the goal, the more daunting it appears. Divide the number of pages or words by the number of days you will be writing, and look only at those daily and weekly goals. Looking at your planner offers assurance that you're going to reach your page count when it's due.

If you're intimidated by the size of the project or the day ahead, set a timer for thirty minutes and tell yourself you can stop after thirty minutes if you want to. When the alarm chimes, most likely you'll be in the middle of a scene or will have captured some inspiration and won't want to stop.

Another option is to set a goal of three pages, a hundred words, or one scene. Tell yourself you can stop after that if you want to. Seriously, if I'm at my desk with the computer on and the file open and fingers on the keyboard, the pages come. It's sitting there that is the trigger, so I talk myself into the chair any way I can.

When I'm exceptionally tired and have a lot of work to do, I tell myself I can take a nap in the afternoon if I want to. I really could take a nap. I'm here in my office and my bedroom is down the hall. In all these years, however, I've probably only napped one or two times (unless I was under the weather). But I could nap if I wanted to—and sometimes that's what motivates me to get to work. Do whatever it takes to convince yourself to write those pages.

Create a Routine

Good or bad, habits are things we do without thought or decision. I never put off brushing my teeth in the morning because it's a habit. I don't have to think about whether or not I'll floss my teeth, get dressed, or eat breakfast. I don't need a chart to congratulate me on tying my shoes. When we develop habits, the tasks are, then, simply our lives. Before I'm even dressed, and usually before breakfast, I start my computer. Once I've done the rest of the routine, brushing my teeth, getting dressed, eating, making coffee or tea, sometimes putting in a load of laundry, I sit at my desk and open my files. Because it's become a routine, I'm less likely to put it off or think about it. I simply do it.

Action Steps

- For one week, keep a record of every time you recognize you are procrastinating.
- At the end of the week, evaluate how many times you procrastinated.
- Look at the reasons why: Did the task seem insurmountable? Did you feel you weren't good enough?
- Did you report to someone? If you've been putting off an accountability partner, find one now.
- Did you move past the avoidance? How? Record what worked, or what didn't.
- Using this information, come up with a plan for next week.
- Review your deadline and adjust as necessary.
- Analyze the cost of continued inaction.
- Stop trying to be perfect.
- Visualize where you want to be and how it will feel when you've accomplished your goal.
- Work on developing your writing-time routine.

DISCOVER YOUR EXCUSES

Do you need to recognize these excuses and find ways to deal with them?

- Fear of not being good enough
- The task looks insurmountable
- Distracted by Internet
- Distracted by research
- No accountability
- Staying in a comfort zone
- Not developing a writing routine

Creative clutter is better than idle tidiness.

—UNKNOWN

10

your energy flywheel

You can't wait for inspiration. You have to go after it with a club.

—JACK LONDON

APATHY/LACK OF MOTIVATION

Apathy is a lack of feeling, concern, interest, or motivation, or simple indifference. As much as aspiring writers claim they'd be more motivated if they had already sold their books, I confess that a deadline doesn't even do it for me every time. Fear is not a good or healthy motivator. Ambition is helpful. Career growth is good. A paycheck is better motivation to produce. But in our line of work, you can't always force quality production.

I heard someone say once that high-energy people have a flywheel. I wish I'd heard more of that talk, whatever it was and whoever said it, because I kept coming around to this idea. I didn't know anything about it, so I researched the flywheel. A flywheel, I learned, is, in essence, a mechanical battery. It's a heavy wheel attached to a rotating shaft used to smooth out delivery of power from a motor to a machine. The inertia of the flywheel opposes and moderates fluctuations in the speed of the engine and—here's the important part—stores the excess energy for intermittent use.

Stick with me for a minute: When an electric motor increases the speed of the spinning flywheel, energy is stored. The system releases its energy by using the momentum of the flywheel to power the motor/generator. Think about storing writing energy as you hear the following explanation.

In car engines, the flywheel smooths out the pulses of energy provided by the combustion in the cylinders and provides energy for the compression stroke of the pistons. During the longer nonactive period, a comparatively low-powered motor builds up the speed of the flywheel slowly. The flywheel stores energy mechanically in the form of kinetic energy. Flywheels are one of the oldest and most common mechanical devices in existence. They're better than batteries, because they're not as limited in the amount of energy they can hold. Generally speaking, the stronger the disc, the faster it spins, and the more energy the system can store.

I've explained all of this simply so you can understand the concept and compare it to the idea that *we writers store creative energy.* I know it's a fact for me.

Probably quite a few of us experience a form of apathy brought on by another factor, like rejection or depression. There's no shame in needing or asking for help if your negative thoughts are more serious than those I've mentioned.

Sometimes we can bring ourselves out of a slump, and other times it takes an external force to do it for us. An excellent book or a weekend workshop can inspire us to write. During these difficult times, it might help to remember that the desire to be a writer is inside you. When you're not writing, it's because you're not feeding or nurturing the desire—or perhaps it's because you're not getting positive feedback.

Sometimes we have to be our own positive feedback.

Since the seventies, behavioral theorists have believed that *depression* was indirectly a result of inactivity. According to Noam Shpancer, Ph.D., on the *Psychology Today* blog, "After many failures and disappointments, people stopped trying and withdrew from the world; withdrawal and inactivity, however, decrease the possibility of positive interactions or experiences, hence isolation and passivity increase, hence depression."

If you didn't care about being a writer and improving yourself, you probably wouldn't have picked up this book. The desire to improve and succeed is an inherent part of you. If you recognize apathy as something that's been holding you back, it's probably secondary to one of the other problems I've mentioned and can be addressed as such.

First, recognize or learn the activities that get you fired up—those things that motivate you—and do more of those things. For me, it's reading or watching movies; it's being creative in ways other than writing or taking a class, like baking or browsing a flea market. For you, it could be freeing your mind by taking a walk, painting, meditation, exercising—whatever works. In *The 7 Habits of Highly Effective People*, Stephen Covey calls this technique sharpening your saw.

Grab Your Notebook

Ponder the times when you've been so energized that you couldn't wait to get words on paper. What prompted that writing energy? If you know right off, that's a plus. If you don't, take time to figure it out. Here are a few ideas:

- Your favorite movie
- A new movie and popcorn at a theater
- A favorite book
- Watching the latest episode of your favorite TV series
- A new book by a favorite author
- Reading the current bestseller
- Writing prompts
- Yoga
- Cooking or baking
- Painting or sewing
- Enjoying the outdoors/nature (fishing, walking, biking, hiking, running)
- Exercise
- A class, workshop, conference, or retreat

- Looking at inspirational photos or photo books
- Prayer or meditation
- Being around other writers
- Brainstorming in a group
- Brainstorming characters, plot, or conflict
- Driving
- Learning how others approach writing and overcome setbacks
- Listening to instructional workshops in the car

How can you capitalize on the enthusiasm when you find it?

- Remember what it was that got you fired up.
- Make a list to refer to later.
- Create a routine.

In the fourth episode of season one of 2016's television show *American Housewife*, titled "Art Show," (find it on Hulu) history professor Greg Otto (played by Diedrich Bader) is writing an article he's sure will earn him tenure. He poses like Wonder Woman for two minutes to raise his testosterone, listens to jazz to activate his right brain, and eats six almonds for energy. Finally, he has a glass of port to loosen up. Greg's belief in this ritual is exaggerated, of course, so comedy ensues when he's repeatedly interrupted and ends up getting sloshed. But it's true that creating rituals can help stimulate creativity.

Some writers light a candle, others play a specific soundtrack. Some want background noise so they leave on the television. Perhaps it sounds silly, but even using a particular coffee mug might be part of a writer's ritual. I'm not the only one who uses a favorite—and my favorite changes from time to time.

WAITING FOR INSPIRATION IS FOR AMATEURS

Sitting around waiting for inspiration doesn't get a lot of books written. Just sayin'. Inspiration is fickle. You have to go after inspiration, chase it down, and tie it to your chair.

I know the things that prompt me to write: Watching movies that inspire strong emotion, being with other writers, reading excellent books, deadlines, desired income. It's up to you to figure out what gets your juices flowing. It's up to you to learn that the juices don't always flow, and if they don't, you need to *write anyway*.

In an interview with Chuck Close published in *Inside the Painter's Studio*, he says, "Inspiration is for amateurs—the rest of us just show up and get to work. And the belief that things will grow out of the activity itself and that you will—through work—bump into other possibilities and kick open other doors that you would never have dreamt of if you were just sitting around looking for a great 'art idea.' And the belief that process, in a sense, is liberating and that you don't have to reinvent the wheel every day. Today, you know what you'll do, you could be doing what you were doing yesterday, and tomorrow you are gonna do what you did today, and at least for a certain period of time you can just work. If you hang in there, you will get somewhere."

Close's quote reinforces what I mentioned about teaching our brains what worked before will work again. We have to do whatever it takes to convince ourselves we're writers and that we will write today. If it's going to a coffee shop and working on your laptop because that atmosphere is conducive to work, then by all means get to Starbucks. If it's fixing your hair and putting on makeup, if you're a female, or shaving, if you're a guy, looking and feeling like you're ready for the day, then do it. If it's sitting in your chair in the familiar position with a cup of tea and a cat on your lap, then grab the cat. If convincing yourself this is your writing mode means lighting a candle and reading your daily affirmations, get on it.

Show up.

Action Steps

Grab your notebook and make another list.

- What are the things that inspire and motivate you to write?
- What did you do to motivate yourself this week?

- What have you done to sharpen your saw in the past few months?
- What do you need to do more often?

    - Read a book by a new author.
    - Read a book by an author who inspired your love of reading.
    - Read a classic.

Create a Collage

Collages are great tools for story inspiration as well as for motivation and as visual reminders of your goals. I mentioned I made a collage when I was a beginning writer, cutting and pasting best-seller lists, awards, things I saw myself doing, and achieving.

> In creating my collages, I go through magazines and cut out photos that represent my writing dreams, scenery that represents my deepest yearnings, and words that evoke emotion, challenge, and motivation, particularly those that elicit the emotions I want my readers to experience. I look for anything—be it pictures, words, or colors—that inspires me, anything that reminds me why I write, why I continue without hesitation after rejection, why I can't imagine doing anything else. I glue these clippings to a poster board, frame it, and hang it on my office wall directly across from my writing space. If I'm ever feeling low or stuck, I gaze at the collage to find inspiration to continue writing.
>
> —MK Meredith, author of the On the Cape series

11

right feelings follow right actions

Talent is something that you're born with. It doesn't evaporate or drain away. Skill is an element you build, out of work and study and expierience. It can't vanish in a puff of smoke.

—DWIGHT V. SWAIN

I learned early in my career—thank God—that just because I'm not feeling passionate, my life is in turmoil, or I'm facing family challenges, my talent doesn't up and desert me. It's still there.

If I open a Word file and place my fingers on the keyboard, words come to me. The work doesn't always *feel* inspired, but after an edit, a good story is still there. Sure, the process is better when it feels wonderful and I'm enthused, but I've learned something that applies to almost everything: Right feelings follow right actions.

I've learned that doing the right thing changes our thinking and emotions. Don't deny there's a problem; instead, decide to correct the behavior. John Maxwell said, "The decisions you will regret in life are the ones you never made."

You might not feel like being kind. Be kind anyway. Even if you don't feel like saying you're sorry, say it. Right feelings follow right actions. Even if you're not feeling inspired, write.

I've also learned that when I don't make time to do the things that allow me to build up energy and create excitement, I'm less creative and more apt to avoid the work or to get stuck. You might not feel like motivating yourself. Do it anyway.

We all have something—no matter how simple or eccentric—that is important in that it gets us going, motivates us, and stirs our energy. It could be cutting out recipes from a magazine, cooking, shopping, gardening, painting, decorating, searching for fossils, bike riding. It's that special something that fills you with kinetic energy and keeps the flywheel spinning until you sit down at the keyboard. It took my husband years to understand that whether I'm shopping at a flea market, watching a movie, or making him change the color of the bathroom for the third time, I'm actually doing something writing related, because in the long run, I'm a better writer for the time spent building momentum.

Like that power press, during the nonactive or nonwriting periods, those activities slowly build up the speed of the flywheel—or my writing energy—and loosen my creativity. Allowing myself to assimilate and not produce, gives me the freedom to burst into action when I'm ready.

In 1971, researchers led by psychology professor Philip Zimbardo randomly divided undergraduates into two groups, labeling them prisoners and prison guards. They created a scenario in which the students carried out their assigned roles in a mock prison in the basement of the Stanford University psychology building.

It didn't take long—only days, until the "guards" took on strict and demanding attitudes, to the point of deliberately humiliating the students playing prisoners. The "prisoners'" attitudes became passive, with many of them becoming depressed. After only six days, the experiment got out of hand and was called off. These students were only posing as inmates and guards, but their actions took control of their emotions. This experiment shows how social roles shape behavior, as well as demonstrates how behavior affects feelings.

We're conditioned to believe motivation and reaction extends to human behavior: I love the person, so I'm kind to him; I don't care for the person, so I ignore or am rude to him. A relationship is reciprocal, however, and actions can shape emotions. Look how many actors fall in love doing a movie together. Kurt Russell and Goldie Hawn fell in love filming *Swing Shift*; Kelly Ripa and Mark Consuelos fell for each other on the daytime soap *All My Children*; Johnny Depp and Winona Ryder met during *Edward Scissorhands*. The list goes on and on: Angelina Jolie and Billy Bob Thornton, Angelina Jolie and Brad Pitt, Jennifer Aniston and Vince Vaughn, Jennifer Aniston and Justin Theroux, Ben Affleck and Jennifer Lopez, Ben Afflek and Jennifer Garner.

Ginnifer Goodwin and Josh Dallas are star-crossed lovers in two fairy tale time zones in *Once Upon a Time* and married in real life; Blake Shelton and Gwen Stefani met on the set of *The Voice*. Look how often an actor is even married to another at the time, but falls for their costar. Why? They're speaking sweetly to each other, professing love, touching, imitating lovemaking, staying in close proximity, and encouraging each other. Actions and behavior lead to feelings.

Research in clinical psychology proves the fastest way to change an emotion is to change the behavior attached to it. If I'm struggling with a situation like procrastination, I need to change my behavior.

THE WAY THAT WORKS FOR YOU IS THE RIGHT WAY

If you find a writer whom you trust and admire, if you know her work ethic and aspire to it, and if her advice about writing, professionalism, or the business connects with you, by all means heed her wisdom. If you don't know this writer by reputation or experience, check her out. It's possible that a well-meaning person might steer you in the wrong direction. If a piece of advice from a beta reader or an editor doesn't ring true, and you can't corroborate the information with another experienced person, let it go. This goes for my advice as well. I never tell anyone that my way is the only way to do something; I strongly suggest each writer discover and adhere to effective methods that work best for him.

I can't tell you how many times I've heard a speaker in a workshop say, "A writer writes every day." When I was inexperienced, I took that advice to heart and believed I was lazy or not dedicated enough because

I didn't write every day. Every time I didn't follow through, I thought I'd failed. Well, I now have enough experience to say, "Phooey!"

Don't tell me writers write every day like that advice is the Holy Grail. Maybe you do write every day, and that's great, but not all of us do. I sometimes go a week or more without writing. Are you shocked? If writing every day works for others or for you, that's well and good, but don't bulldoze everyone else to do the same. You should never feel pressured to write the way someone else does just because you admire her drive or skill. You should never feel like "less" because you don't follow the same methods another person follows.

Sometimes creativity is more effective when it's not forced. Ever notice how great ideas come to you in the shower? Or in that twilight sleep just before drifting off, or when just waking up? There's no secret ingredient in your water or the fabric softener in your sheets; the right side of your brain was simply free to create while the left side eased off and didn't compete for dominance.

There was a time when I didn't believe I was a professional writer. Mind you, I had sold several books, but because I had listened to a myriad of workshop speakers say that "a real writer writes every day," I subconsciously thought my method was inferior. I didn't recognize my negative thought pattern until I read Henriette Klauser's *Writing on Both Sides of the Brain*, and it became clear to me that writing the way I write is okay; I don't need to operate on the same schedule others use.

In her book, Klauser writes about a student in her first-grade writing class who never participated, didn't do assignments, and didn't seem to pay attention. As long as he wasn't disrupting the class, she gave him the freedom to play on the sidelines, while she despaired over his final grade. She was frustrated, feeling she wasn't getting through to this child.

However, when the end of the term came and she asked if he'd like to tell her a story and offered to write it down for him (she doubted he could even print), he grabbed the paper and wrote an entire story in cursive, using every technique she had taught—similes, metaphors, and alliteration! All that time he'd been processing with the luxury of silent time and no pressure to write. Later, he even had a story accepted and published in a children's magazine.

I haven't told this story with nearly the same eloquence as Klauser's firsthand account, and I strongly suggest you get a copy of her book and read it yourself. That story and the author's revelation set something free inside me. I realized, perhaps for the first time, that my brain doesn't function in orderly, scheduled time slots, but it creates like mad in impulsive bursts. And that's okay, because my method works for me. Crazy that someone had to tell me my way was okay, isn't it? And then I had to reassure *myself*—that's the imperative part. Telling yourself positive things—programming your brain with positive information—is one of the best things you can do for your writing.

I Don't Procrastinate; I Incubate

Real writers aren't real writers because they write every day. Writing every day works for some. I don't write every day, and I'm a real writer. Real writers produce books, no matter the method. Writers write, period.

Klauser's story set me free. I understand now that my time spent away from the keyboard is not unproductive time. Don't get me wrong: If you want to finish a book, you need to apply yourself and put words on paper. I'm a firm believer that you should finish every book you start. If you don't finish your book, you'll never learn to push past the middle or how to tie the end to the beginning or prove to yourself that you can follow through. We all need to set deadlines and have strategic goals. But I don't believe everyone works the same way or dances to the same drum. Appreciate your differences. Use them to your advantage.

Anticipating a weekend activity or a midweek break can get you up every morning and get you through otherwise mundane tasks. Refuse to feel guilty, silly, or wasteful of time when you know that you're setting the flywheel in motion. Make up your mind to generate creativity by getting that fun haircut or buying an outfit, shoes, or purse in a color that makes you happy. These things aren't life changing, except in how they motivate you.

Change Behavior to Change How You Feel

I may not feel like writing today. I may not feel particularly inspired or motivated. I may not even feel talented in this moment. But if I take the steps to follow through, if I use all the techniques I've learned and the routine I've developed, if I sit in my chair and place my fingers on the keyboard, my training and instinct will take over. I will become caught up in the characters I've developed and in the story I'm telling. Right feelings about my work and my commitment will follow the appropriate actions.

Noam Shpancer on the *Psychology Today* blog said, "Recent research in clinical psychology has shown that the fastest way to change an emotion is to change the behavior attached to it."

He goes on to say, "Withdrawal and avoidance reward us in the short run by eliminating discomfort, but they punish us in the long run by preventing us from learning how to obtain rewards in the environment. The correct reaction to failure is not to give up and shut yourself away, but to learn to act more skillfully and purposefully so as to reintroduce positive reinforcements into your life."

By procrastinating, we avoid the discomfort of hard work and perhaps some frustration or confusion. The wrong response to those feelings of inferiority or discomfort is avoidance. The correct response is to tackle the big stuff, to jump into the project with both feet as though we know what we're doing. If we act as though we're confident and empowered, our emotions will follow. I believe it.

Action Steps

If you're skeptical, test out the power of positivity this week. Instead of thinking, *I wish I could shake off this bad mood so I can be nice to others and enjoy myself*, do it the other way around. Be nice and behave as though you're enjoying yourself. Pretty soon you will be. If you find yourself in the doldrums or feeling cranky, consciously redirect your thoughts and behavior as though you're having a good time, as though you're in a good mood. Say something nice. It won't take long to change your feelings.

Am I saying you can never have an off day? That you can never get angry, grieve, or mope? Not at all. I said we were going to take an honest look at ourselves. Writers are real people. Situations and people affect us. We all have our moments. But we can't camp out in the negativity. We can choose to turn situations to our advantage.

12

job or passion?

Opportunities are usually disguised as hard work, so most people don't recognize them.

—ANN LANDERS

Each January when I set my goals, I choose an overall theme to help me focus. Many writers I know select a word, like *determination* or *discipline*, which is an excellent way to zero in on the year ahead. A couple of years ago, after a particularly difficult stretch in my personal life, my singular plan for the upcoming year was to *find the joy*. I wrote it on every week's page in my planner. I found quotes to inspire me. I shared quotes about joy every day for a month on my social media.

In 2017, I chose the same focus. To me, if we find the joy in our families, our faith, our writing, our everyday tasks, then discipline, peace, determination, and focus all fall into place.

There is so much to stress over in this business. Contracts are never a guarantee. Sometimes months—or a year—pass without a sale. Sometimes we have so many books contracted, we don't know how we'll finish them all. The market fluctuates, and it's no secret book sales are down. That means the average writer must write more, write faster, or take on a second income to make the same living he did ten years ago.

Being self-employed has its benefits (my boss is really good to me), but there are down sides as well, like paying taxes and finding health insurance.

I'm just going to be frank now. I've been called painfully honest in the past because my thinking is why not tell it like it is so others don't think they're the only ones with these feelings? Sometimes editorial input, in the way of a particular edit or revision, changes the story so much that the story no longer feels like your own. These editorial requests are difficult to work through, because we feel we have to compromise a story we love for a story that sells. Sometimes that line edit looks so bad it makes a writer feel as though he doesn't know what he's doing. If you ever find this to be the case, it's always best to be up-front with your editor. Often a discussion can bring the story back where you need it to be, and occasionally your editor can rein in an overenthusiastic copyeditor. It happens. But when that overzealous edit or story-changing revision does happen, it can suck the joy from a project.

I can look back on the majority of my books and remember exactly what was happening in my life at the time I wrote them. I remember editorial input, praise, criticism, and reader reactions. I have written books from my heart that didn't get good distribution or weren't received well. I've written books that I wasn't crazy about but that found popularity in genre niches. We have no way of knowing ahead of time which books will be successful and which will be less so, but we need to write each one as though it's the most important—the one with the most possibility.

Writing isn't glamorous. Behind the scenes, it's messy desks and coffee rings on paper, sweat pants, and floor filing. It's the T-Rex breaking down in the rain in *Jurassic Park*. When the average person looks at a newly released book, he sees the glossy cover, smells the pages, and admires the author's name appearing in a distinctive font. He doesn't see the months of intensive work, extensive revisions, editing, and the marketing plan. He has no idea that midway through that memorable scene he loves so much, the author took care of a sick child, bathed a dog that rolled in who-knows-what, handled fraud on her bank account, and called the plumber to fix a leak.

So how do you find the joy in all this? Where do you recover your passion?

When the writing process becomes too stressful, it's a good idea to pull back and look at what we're doing, where we want to be, and weigh our decisions. I've known writers who couldn't balance the negative with the positive and for their own peace of mind, quit writing. It boils down to being okay with your choices. I will admit to you, there have been times I've thought about throwing in the towel—more in the beginning of my career than the latter. Now those thoughts are more easily handled and dismissed, because even when I struggle, I weigh my options and ask myself, *What would I rather be doing?*

Not every book is a book from my heart. Some books are simply hard work to get to the next step. You'll find it the same in your career. But stories are my passion, so I can wade through the mire until I get to the other side, because I've proven it to myself time and time again. There is always another side.

A lot of people say they want to write a book. Once someone learns you're a writer, it's common to hear, "Oh, I want to write a book, but I just don't have the time." Guess what? I didn't have the time either. I made the time. Everyone wants to write a book. Few actually want to do the work involved to actually write it.

I never want to discourage anyone from their dream; in fact, I believe in just the opposite. We can't know what we're capable of until we put ourselves out there, until we push past our own limits and wade through our own muck and see just how badly we want this.

People—and more so writers—talk about finding a "passion," about writing the books of their heart, but for me something so exalted can often end up more draining than energizing. Let's face it, some days writing is just a job.

There, I said it. The sky didn't fall.

The passion for writing comes from within. Being happy, passionate, or content doesn't come from external situations. If it did, happiness would evaporate like a puff of smoke as soon as you had to stop writing to take your sick pet to the vet and put an unplanned three hundred dollars on your credit card, or as soon as you read a critical review of your work. Look inside for positive resources of energy. Redirect negative thoughts.

If today you feel that writing is just a job—and a difficult one at that—remind yourself why you're doing this. For me, I am reminded why I write every time I have to drive in rush hour traffic, which thankfully isn't that often. I'm reminded every time I put on my jeans and T-shirt and sit at my desk with a cup of coffee. I remember why I love being a writer when I'm able to schedule my work around Girl Scout field trips or being home with a little one who's not feeling well. I remember every night when I snuggle into bed with the satisfaction of having done something I loved doing that day.

If writing feels like a job today, and you're wondering where the passion went, remind yourself that right actions follow right feelings. Don't say negative things about your writing, your lack of enthusiasm, or your current project. Take all the necessary steps to get in the zone. Make coffee, light the candle, clear the desktop, eat six almonds and drink the port—whatever your routine might be—and then open the file and put your fingers on the keyboard.

It's a great idea to take photos of our readers when we meet them. We're usually efficient about taking names and addresses to add to our newsletter lists, but how about gathering photos to remind us *who* we're writing for? I discovered this years ago when a few readers included their pictures with letters. I pinned the pictures on the board behind my desk. When I was having a difficult time or struggling, I'd glance at those photos and remind myself of the readers who enjoyed my stories. It's easy to take photos with our phones at signings and events and print a copy later for inspiration.

So if you have a few photos of readers, tack them up near your work space. When the writing feels like a job, remind yourself why you're doing this, and for whom.

Sometimes a writer loses his passion because of burnout. Burnout is not writer's block. Writer's block is looking at the blank screen and not knowing how to fill it or what to say, which is actually fear or procrastination, or any of the numerous roadblocks I've mentioned. Burnout happens when a writer is stressed and overworked for too long. It's being frustrated, exhausted, and sick of the whole process. It's not caring any longer and not wanting to write.

Authors can function and produce at the onset of burnout. We keep going because we have deadlines, responsibilities, and a lot to accomplish. We often adapt to the pressure without even realizing we are doing so. This isn't healthy, and eventually the burden will catch up with us. We can only continue on reserves for so long, before the signs start showing up.

Ray Bradbury gives us a different perspective in a talk he gave at The Sixth Annual Writer's Symposium by the Sea in 2001: "I've never worked a day in my life. The joy of writing has propelled me from day to day and year to year. I want you to envy me, my joy. Get out of here tonight and say, *Am I being joyful?* And if you've got a writer's block, you can cure it this evening by stopping whatever you're writing and doing something else. You picked the wrong subject."

What causes burnout?

- Having no time for yourself
- Not relaxing or taking days off
- Feeling underappreciated
- Taking on too much responsibility
- Feeling overwhelmed
- Not seeing growth or improvement
- Not challenging yourself
- Not nourishing friendships
- Guilt over ignoring relationships/family
- Working too many hours
- Having no support
- Expecting perfection of yourself
- Thinking or speaking negatively about yourself
- Not delegating tasks or asking for help
- Needing control over everything

HOW DOES BURNOUT MANIFEST?

Burnout manifests itself in various ways, and we must learn to recognize the signs and take action to correct what we're doing. It's good to know these signs if you spot them in a friend as well. Offer to talk it out and let them vent.

- **PHYSICAL:** Headaches, trouble sleeping, tiredness, getting ill or feeling sick, wanting to sleep all the time as an escape, inability to concentrate
- **EMOTIONAL:** Depression exhibits the same physical symptoms listed above, with lack of energy, irritability, lack of motivation, decline in productivity, loss of passion, frustration, cynicism
- **BEHAVIORAL:** Withdrawing socially, having trouble making decisions, feeling angry toward others, feeling angry toward yourself, missing deadlines, feeling a lack of concern for consequences

How Does a Writer Keep from Burning Out?

Don't allow the demands placed on you—or the demands you're placing on yourself—to be greater than the resources you have to complete them. Time and energy are resources. Guard them like the precious and valuable commodities they are.

You are your own tolerance meter. I learned my max a long time ago: Four books a year is too many for me. I can do it, but the writing becomes more drudgery than passion. At that rate, my life and attitude suffers. I know authors who write six or more books a year and they don't suffer during the process (nor does the quality of their work). Others tell me they're doing their best to write one book a year—or one every two years. That's absolutely okay. Don't compare your output to anyone else's—unless they're managing something you truly want to do and know that you're capable of doing, and so you're using their work ethic as inspiration.

Writing is what I do, but it's not who I am. I always remind myself of that. I'm a wife, mother, grandmother, sister, friend, worship leader, volunteer, teacher, and more. I want to be present and excel in each one of those positions, but prioritizing is the only way to manage it all without resenting one or more of my obligations or the ways in which I serve.

Every year I do an evaluation and consider what I will do in the upcoming months. This can be done more often than yearly. The important thing is that you don't find yourself taking on more responsibilities, because you don't want to disappoint people or let someone down. It's *your* life. You need to be in charge of it. I consider this process "laying down my tools" and deciding which ones to pick up again and which to set aside for a time. For example, I like to travel and teach workshops. It requires that I do a lot of flying and staying in hotels, which is fun—and I love meeting people—but traveling can grow wearisome. For this reason, there are years I don't accept any offers to teach workshops if I plan to focus elsewhere.

WHAT TO DO FOR BURNOUT AND TO PREVENT BURNOUT

- Prioritize and be selective with commitments
- Keep a healthy balance of family, friends, and work
- Exercise, walk, get up and move often
- Get at least six hours of sleep a night
- Give yourself days off
- Take a class or learn to do something new
- Limit caffeine and alcohol
- Hydrate
- Unplug for an afternoon or a day—no Internet or phone allowed
- Be kind to yourself
- Attend to mechanical tasks, like mowing or cleaning, that allow your right brain freedom
- Talk to a friend or family member in person
- If you feel depressed, see a doctor
- Read your favorite book
- Binge watch something you've been wanting to see on Netflix or Hulu
- Plan time off over the holidays to enjoy the season and family

Some of these things might seem obvious, but when we're caught up in deadlines and responsibilities, we forget to take care of ourselves and do the obvious.

Discipline and willpower alone won't carry you through the length of a career. A healthy balance between writing and the rest of your life will help you hang onto your passion and continually cultivate your love for this crazy profession. Determine to find the joy in writing on a yearly, monthly, weekly basis, and then you'll be able to share the joy with others through your stories.

For me, writing smart means taking care of the important things first. That includes my health and happiness. Because I write five days a week, with weekends off unless I'm on deadline and the finishing line is quickly approaching, I make good use of the time I'm not at my computer. I take two hours off in the middle of the day to either walk a three-mile mountain path we have right out our front door or ride my elliptical for fifty minutes. The time passes quickly and that's where some of my best ideas are born. I limit my intake of sugar and not-so-healthy foods (that are oh-so-good) plus eat organic and fresh. I'm blessed to have a retired firefighter husband who enjoys cooking, so that ball is in his court every night, giving me more time to write.

I believe writing the next book is the best tip in the business [for staying focused and avoiding burnout]. I don't let myself get bogged down with what everyone else is doing. That said, I do a limited amount of advertising. When it comes to social media and Facebook, I do my own posts because I enjoy connecting with readers and friends, but I make sure to limit my time there. It's amazing how fast an hour can slip away. I have a talented young man who knows a lot more than I do [about marketing] who takes care of my advertising. I explain what I'd like, and he works his magic. Keeping up with this ever-changing business scene can be a stress factor in itself, and one I'd rather not have. I love to write—and so that's what I do!

—Caroline Fyffe, author of the Prairie Hearts series

PART 3
winning the struggle within

13

overcoming self-doubt

Our doubts are traitors and make us lose the good we oft might win by fearing to attempt.

—WILLIAM SHAKESPEARE

Research on long-term space flights has revealed that astronauts experience the most physiologically difficult leg of their journey at the midway point. The travelers report more lethargy, irritability, and homesickness halfway through the mission. Compare this to the journey of writing a book: The initial excitement has abated, and home isn't yet within sight.

You've probably been on a long car trip with children. Which stretch would you say was the most difficult? No, really, you have to pick *one*. The middle perhaps? You probably had to come up with some creative ideas to keep your kids from killing each other and to save your sanity. Before long trips with my youngest, I would go to the used bookstore and buy bags of books. At restaurants and rest stops, we would leave the books she'd already read for someone else. The middle of the trip was always the longest. Excitement about the destination hit a lull, just like the middle of a book usually does.

Everything after chapter three until you reach the black moment and resolution is the middle. Had you realized that before? You spend three chapters introducing your characters, setting up the conflict, creating a dynamic hook, showing your setting, hinting at the backstory, and teasing the reader with the promise of adventure. That's a whole lot of finesse, fine-tuning, planning, and execution. And now, you've walked into a gray area, the twilight zone, the unknown, and perhaps even uncharted, center of the story. *Gulp.*

Here's where self-doubt raises its ugly head.

- What if this writing thing is a fluke, and I can't really do this?
- What will my family think if they read it? *Yikes, there's sex!*
- What will my friends and fellow writers think if I show this to them and it's not good?
- What if it's not good?
- What if no one ever wants to publish it?

You're the one who's going to have to tune out those doubts and do some self-talk. Seriously. If you want this badly enough, you're going to have to challenge your thoughts and start thinking more positively about your ability to accomplish your goals and learn in the process.

- **WHAT IF THIS IS A FLUKE?** Then you haven't really tried or given yourself a chance. You're allowing fear to stifle you.
- **WHAT IF I CAN'T REALLY DO THIS?** What if you *can*? All the techniques of writing are learnable. The storytelling gift is one you've been given, and you have the desire inside you or you wouldn't be doing this. The only one who will stop you is you.
- **WHAT WILL MY FAMILY THINK IF THEY READ IT? *YIKES, THERE'S SEX!*** This is a logical consideration. You have to decide whether or not this worry will disturb you enough to hinder you. If you're not comfortable with an aspect of your book, maybe you need to consider another genre. More likely than not, however, your family and friends won't be shocked. Or they will simply choose not to read your work. Not everyone loves everything we write (or do for that matter).
- **WHAT WILL MY FRIENDS AND FELLOW WRITERS THINK IF I SHOW THIS TO THEM AND IT'S NOT GOOD?** Your fellow writers will think you're brave for being open to their opinions and evaluations. Even if it's not good, you will open yourself up for help to grow and learn.

And those friends? I've learned they like it all, even if it's not good. They're not editors or reviewers.

- **WHAT IF IT'S NOT GOOD?** Congratulations. You don't think every word you write is gold. And you're willing to be coached. With that attitude you will succeed.

- **WHAT IF NO ONE EVER WANTS TO PUBLISH IT?** If you never sold anything you wrote, would you still want to write? Is it a desire you can't turn your back on? Taking classes and writing are more than many people accomplish. Plenty of people like the idea of being a writer, but not the work involved. Those willing to do the work are those more likely to sell. That fact seems obvious, but sometimes we let fear blind us.

You're the only one who governs your future in publishing. Have confidence in your ability and gift. If you submit something and turn around and say, "I hope I get rejected quickly and get it over with," you're shooting yourself in the foot with your attitude. And yes, I've heard writers say that. Don't let it be you.

So you've got three chapters written, all spiffy and shiny. Now what? You've just figured out who these story people are. Any time during the chapters that follow, you might need to go back to the beginning and adjust for the growing knowledge about your characters. Stay open to their development. But don't go back and get bogged down in rewriting the beginning because you can't seem to go forward from the middle.

Thinking this is too hard? Wondering if you can do this? Speaking from experience here and talking to myself: *Yes, you can. Stop whining.*

I know people who have never moved past the beginning of their first book. Some don't move past the beginning of their second book—or third. What is stopping them? Lack of confidence. Fear of failure. *Fear of success.* Yes, fear of success is real. If this book is published, I'll be expected to promote it, to write more, to know what I'm doing. I don't know if I am ready for my career to take off. What will be expected of me?

I know people who have written the first three chapters of several books, and then flailed and floundered and didn't finish those projects, but started another. Why? Fear. Laziness. Writing a book is hard work. Maybe they didn't plan the book well enough in advance and there really is nowhere to go now. Perhaps they wrote a great first character introduction and everything was downhill from there. Maybe they weren't listening to the part about needing conflict to sustain the middle—or missed that class altogether. Are you one of these writers? If so, there's help for you. Recognize and choose to fix the problem and finish the book you are writing no matter what.

There's nothing wrong with going back and rereading the beginning to recapture your initial excitement. Read the synopsis. You do have a synopsis, right? If not, you should. Even if you're a write-by-the-seat-of-your-pants novelist, you should write a two-page synopsis so you can ensure there's sufficient motivation and conflict to sustain the story. Read over the notes you made and the character sketches, if any. Figure out what it was about this story that caught your interest and made you want to tell it. Read all the way to where you've stalled, but then keep moving forward.

Finish the rough draft. If you don't think it's perfect, you can always go back and fix it. You can fix crap, but you can't fix nothing.

Holly Jacobs, author of *Just One Thing*, told me, "One of the ways I get over writing hurdles, whether it's the story or life itself that's getting in my way, is to give myself permission to write complete and utter crap. Some days my writing is less than the sparkling prose I hope for. I can go back and fix crap. I can't fix a blank page. And sometimes I need to just make myself write a crappy scene as a bridge to getting to a part of the story that really excites me. Later, I can either cut or spruce up that crappy bridge."

BE CONVINCING

Convince the reader to care about your story and your characters. Convince yourself you care about this book.

Use all the tools you've been given in workshops you've attended. Read and apply *The Techniques of the Selling Writer* by Dwight V. Swain. If you've read the book before, read it again. I still refresh myself with it in the middle of writing a book. If you've never read it, order it now and study his advice. You have to do whatever it takes to move forward.

Once we understand how we learn and perform best, we're better able to stick with tasks and perform them with less frustration. I have enormous appreciation for the public school systems in the state where I live. There have been many changes since I was a child, plenty of changes since most of us were children. Many of us were raised in a competitive and comparative environment, where our achievements were profiled and graphed into percentiles; where we were matched up against our peers as a gauge to see how we were doing. Remember the skills tests where we were placed in categories? And whoever thought up the distribution curve? One person can get an A only if another gets a C.

Not that long ago, left-handed children were expected to cut right-handed with scissors they couldn't manage, and forced to learn flowing penmanship with the "correct" hand.

It's no wonder so many of us have self-esteem issues and doubts about our abilities. Thank goodness teachers, counselors, and parents have learned to work in teams to choose learning methods suitable for children of all capabilities. Now children with forms of autism, and even brain injuries are in classrooms with children of their own age. Finally, schools have teams that include the parents, who, with teachers, counselors, and professionals, aid in decisions about how the student can learn best. As a team, they plan methods. Students are treated as individuals and encouraged to learn at their own speed and in the manner best suited for them. These individualized programs help those kids succeed, rather than lumping all students together and expecting cookie-cutter results. I have high hopes for the future generations of students and young adults receiving recognition for intrinsic value. We should all know that our value lies inside of us, not in our performance.

Some things just can't be measured. What makes one book better than the next, or one writer better than another? Only perspective. Only the reader, when you get right down to it. Because storytelling can be so subjective that one reader might enjoy a book another can't finish, what one reader thinks is drivel can land on the other's keeper shelf.

A mind troubled by doubt cannot focus on the course to victory.

—ARTHUR GOLDEN

After I'd been writing and educating myself on the craft of writing for what I considered a lengthy time, I became frustrated. I had a burning desire for someone to just tell me whether or not I could do this. If I learned that I was an awful writer, I would have just quit and moved on to something else—or so I thought from time to time. I often wondered why I wasn't happy cross-stitching or creating craft projects like the other young moms I knew.

It's normal to seek endorsement or approval, but no one can tell you whether or not you're going to sell a book, publish fifty more, or be a success. Another writer can read your work and assure you it's good, but that's not a guarantee. There are no guarantees when you start writing, and that can be frustrating.

We all wonder if we have the stuff it takes. As beginners, we wonder if we have an inkling of talent. Once our talent is validated by others, we still wonder if it's good enough—if we have what it takes. It's good to acknowledge that we don't know it all and to have a desire to learn and grow. But sometimes doubt holds us back. Yes, we do shoot ourselves in the foot by creating and feeding feelings of inadequacy.

I know someone who has written several books but has rarely shared them with another writer. This person has never submitted any of her finished projects to an agent or editor. Because she's unwilling to stick her neck out there, show her work, submit it, open herself up to criticism or rejection, she has guaranteed she won't sell.

YOU HAVE TO BE WILLING TO MAKE MISTAKES

Some writers never get started because they're always planning, plotting, and talking about the book instead of putting words on pages. Some writing students (not actual *writers* yet) read every book on the craft and attend all the workshops and conferences and ask questions and take notes and plan, plan, plan, but never get down to the actual writing.

Of course, it's a good thing to be eager to learn. But you can't learn to write until you put words on paper. The people who don't get that far want everything to be perfect before they put words on the page—

or they want the words to come out perfect on the first try, so they wait until they're good enough. Guess what? It ain't gonna happen.

You have to be willing to make mistakes. You have to be willing to write badly to learn to write well.

I was asked to cut cake at a fancy anniversary celebration, which a congressman and former mayor attended. My dear friend said to me, "I'm so thankful you're doing that. I'd never be brave enough to cut that beautiful cake." This woman does more than cut cakes. She's a force to be reckoned with behind the scenes at functions. She's faithful, insightful, and she's also a teacher—she's multitalented in her own right. I told her that when I'm faced with something intimidating, I always ask myself the same question: *What's the worst that could happen?*

I have subscribed to this philosophy for years and it has served me well. I might cut the first few pieces of cake a little sloppily until I get the perfect knife for that particular frosting and develop a rhythm, but no one cares. They're eyeballing that inch-thick butter icing and those white frosting roses. So I've cut a few sloppy slices of expensive and beautiful cake. I learned from my mistakes and improved. If I attempt to write in a genre that isn't my thing, what's the worst that could happen? I get rejected. The world doesn't come crashing down. I'm not blackballed from ever submitting again.

If I write a scene that my editor doesn't think fits the story or that she wants changed, she'll tell me, and I'll change it. If my friends and I come up with what we believe is an innovative idea for a series, and we go for it, what's the worst that could happen? It flops. When I was starting out, I sent really amateurish manuscripts and proposals to agents and editors in multiple publishing houses. When I say amateurish, I'm not exaggerating. I put manuscripts in three-punch folders because I didn't know any better. I mailed them in boxes, rather than secured with rubber bands in envelopes—in other words, all the no-nos. I was rejected. I deserved to be rejected. I've been rejected by the best editors at the biggest houses in publishing. And you know what? That was the worst that could happen. I survived. I rallied. I sent better manuscripts.

OVERCOMING SELF-DOUBT

No one can tell you whether or not you're going to sell a book, publish more, or be a success. We all wonder if we have the stuff it takes. As beginners we wonder if we have an inkling of talent. Once other writers and readers validate our talent, we still wonder if it's good enough, if we have what it takes. It's good to acknowledge that we don't know it all and we must have a desire to learn and grow.

But sometimes, doubt holds us back. We inhibit ourselves by creating and feeding feelings of inadequacy, by being unwilling to stick our necks out and show our work. Submission requires opening ourselves up to criticism and rejection.

Confidence comes with practice and maturity.

Take, for instance, a man with a desire to run a one hundred meter race. He buys a pair of Nikes, goes out, and gives running a shot, but he doesn't do very well. Why not? He didn't practice! He didn't study how other runners achieve endurance through diet, exercise, and training. He doesn't know how good he really is until he trains for a time, eating properly in an effort to maximize energy and muscle development. After he's prepared, by stretching to limber up and then by actually running, then he must run again and again and again until he's as fast as he can be, and he's confident that he's fast, and he's ready to compete.

In many ways, submitting a book is a similar endeavor. Your manuscript will be compared to all the others that cross an editor's desk. It will be scrutinized for its ability to make the publishing house money in the marketplace. The bottom line in this business is, will your manuscript make an editor look good if she buys it? Will your book make money for the publisher? The only way you can have the confidence to know you're submitting something with a chance of making it past that test is to learn your craft and practice, practice, practice. Write, write,

write. Work at writing until you get better, until you hit your personal stride. Then share your work and get feedback from people you trust.

Sure, sometimes self-doubts are rooted much more deeply; we carry inadequacies from childhood and our past relationships, hurts, and experiences. But there's help for such things, too, ways to work them out and work on our self-confidence. First we must recognize our uncertainties and seek help, if need be. You're a valuable person. You're worth it. You deserve to give yourself the gift of improving yourself and reaching for your dream.

Confidence Comes with Practice and Maturity

So how can you grow your self-assurance? Confidence is gained by successfully completing a task and recognizing the accomplishment—repeatedly. By acknowledging a success, your brain processes, *I can do this again.* We can't nurture confidence if we don't recognize or even appreciate what we've done.

Don't ever demean an accomplishment by saying or thinking, *I was just lucky,* or *Anyone could have done it.* Anyone could not have done what you did in the same way and with the same heart.

Celebrate Each Success Along the Way

Have a Chapter One Achievement Award Party or treat yourself to something special for milestones reached. Give yourself fun stickers or hearts on your calendar—something visual to note your progress.

Learn from your mistakes. This might sound ridiculously simple, but if one method doesn't work, try a different one. *You can't expect a different result from the same behavior.*

Ability is what you're capable of doing. Motivation determines what you do. Attitude determines how well you do it.

—LOU HOLTZ

---

learning from the past, living in the present

It is not possible to go forward while looking back.

—LUDWIG MIES VAN DER ROHE

In the past few chapters, I've spent a lot of time encouraging you to overcome inadequacies and negativity, but to be healthy you also can't ignore your feelings. If you've received multiple rejections or have had bad experiences on your journey to publication, those experiences are yours, and they're real. Don't pretend they didn't happen. Don't ignore the pain or frustration. No one is immune to these feelings. Understand why you're upset, fearful, or untrusting. After a rejection I will usually give myself one day to wallow, where anything goes—whine (really whine), eat chocolate, eat fast food, whatever.

In his book, *The Rejection Syndrome*, Charles R. Solomon writes: "At the core of rejection is this message: 'You don't measure up. Either you're not tall enough, you're not strong enough, you're not pretty enough, you're not smart enough.' Verbally or non-verbally a message you got was, 'You're a mistake, you were an accident, we don't want you.'"

Everyone has been excluded at some point in life, in some form or another—being chosen last for the softball team in grade school, receiving harsh words from parents or teachers, engaging in failed relationships, being neglected, being overlooked. Our pasts instill a belief system within us. Words of rejection about our writing are filtered through our experiences, and those experiences can make us believe we're not good enough, we don't measure up, we're not smart enough, good-looking enough, or talented enough. According to the definition in *Webster's Dictionary*, being *rejected* means the material is worthless, useless, or substandard. That's harsh.

First, we have to recognize what rejection truly means in this business. It may mean quite a few different things. First, it might mean the material is less than adequate. But that's what the learning curve is all about; it's what contests, critiques, and edits are for—making our work better. That's why writers are always learning. But not all manuscripts are rejected on the basis of inferior work. Sometimes the publisher recently bought a book on the same topic your book covers and simply doesn't have room for another one on the schedule. Other times the editorial department is looking for something specific, and your story doesn't fit that criteria.

Publisher's marketing departments perform research in an effort to determine what's selling and what isn't. There are times when all they want are mystery and suspense, because these genres are selling like hotcakes. When that niche becomes glutted, they may look for Amish romances and paranormal themes—or Amish paranormals. Follow editors and agents on social media to see what they're looking for. I'm not recommending you follow the trends, because once you discover one, it often changes too quickly to act on—but it's wise to know what publishers are looking for and what they don't want.

Consider that hundreds of manuscripts might cross an editor's desk the month yours reaches her. And there are only so many slots to be filled in the lineup. Publishers and authors fight for space in retail stores. The shelves are narrow and double-pocketed all the time. Executive editors are responsible for choosing only the books that have the best chance of making the company money. Period. They want a sure thing.

The confusing thing for writers is that publishers want something new and different, something that blows them away, while at the same time wanting something like *The Handmaid's Tale* or *The Girl on the Train* or *Any Best-Selling Book*, all wrapped into one. They want you to figure out what that is. They'll know it when they see it.

So your book may have been rejected because it didn't have that elusive, magical element the publisher was looking for. Maybe dystopian fiction is hot, and you wrote a World War II story. Or vice versa. It's a fickle business.

And then a dark horse book fitting none of those criteria catches on and becomes a bestseller. That's when the publishers wish they'd bought it, and all the writers wish they'd written it. That's the nature of publishing. Sometimes it's writing the right book at the right time and sending it to the right editor at the right house when the moon is in the seventh house and Jupiter aligns with Mars. Most of the time, however, it's doggedly working at your craft, refusing to be discouraged by the market and its rejections, and persistently submitting until you and your book break through.

So rejection doesn't always mean your manuscript isn't adequate or that you're not a strong enough writer. You have to decide how many times you'll try, how long you'll persist, and how you'll encourage yourself to do better next time.

Share your experience with a friend or counselor. Write down your feelings in your journal. Feelings are real, so acknowledge them. Because rejection wrongly communicates that our work is inadequate or that we're unworthy, we need to remind ourselves of our worth. *Rejections don't define us. How we respond to rejection defines us. Our actions today define us.*

In my critique group of six members, we share our rejections and frustrations. We allow ourselves a period of anger or disappointment. It's okay to vent, cry, rant, or do whatever it takes to get the feelings out. When we get together after a rejection, we open a bottle of champagne and eat chocolate and strawberries to share our support and understanding. You might think rejection doesn't call for champagne, but we believe it does. No one can receive a rejection unless they've submitted. No one can submit until they've done the work, put in the time, and had the courage to try. A rejection means you gave it your best effort, and this time it didn't work out. That's okay. Failure is not trying at all.

Notice that this advice runs parallel with the philosophy that says, "right feelings follow right actions." And I'm not suggesting you pretend something didn't hurt or affect you deeply. We face a lot of broken dreams in life. None of us had idyllic childhoods, none of us made perfect choices. If you had a perfect writing life, you wouldn't have even picked up this book, because you'd already be writing smart and happy. While you were writing your first piece, you were dreaming of publication, accolades, sales, and bags of money. Again, we're defining success for ourselves. Does writing in-and-of-itself mean success? Is self-publishing/small-press publishing considered a success? Is simply having a reader enjoy our stories success? Are our dreams fulfilled even when we don't make *The New York Times* best-seller list? Am I okay with not making the best-seller list? Am I broken by the loss of that dream?

Maybe you reach midlife and haven't had a bestseller. That's a broken dream, because you wanted to be there by now. So many times we push away disappointment and don't really deal with it. We move on, stuffing frustration, fear, and loss. It's a big mistake to lie to ourselves and act as though we don't care. We have to deal with the issue because dysfunction can grow out of denial. This goes for all areas of our lives, not only rejection. We have choices:

1. Let the disappointment break us. Lose all confidence in ourselves and quit. Decide writing is just too hard and we're not willing to experience the rejections anymore. It happens.
2. Stuff down the hurt and go on as though it never happened. Blame someone or the situation. Lie to ourselves about being disappointed and shuffle on, status quo.
3. Deal with it by acknowledging our disappointment. Have the courage to face our part in the rejection and grow from the experience.

If you select the third choice, you will have to face that you may have had some unrealistic expectations about your happiness. If you believed getting a contract, selling a book, or making a best-seller list would make you happy, you weren't being realistic. Millions of successful people are unhappy. Your self-worth does not depend on selling books.

Of course it's great to sell books and get contracts! It's satisfying and rewarding. Those are accomplishments to be proud of. But if the deal falls through or the editor passes on your project, you must remember that you are the same person you were before.

HOW TO DEAL WITH DISAPPOINTMENT

- Acknowledge the pain. *I'm disappointed. I had hoped this would be the one. This is difficult. This is where I'm at right now and it hurts.*
- Share your feelings of hurt and frustration with someone who understands.
- Consider all the factors that might have caused the rejection. Choose to fix those you can and release the ones you have no control over. Changes can only be made in the present.
- Move on. The past is over and done. Go for a walk, play with your children or pets. Listen to music and sing. Wear something that makes you feel good. Treat yourself.
- If there is anything to be learned from the experience, learn it and put it to good use the next time around. If all you learned was that rejection sucks, leave it behind. Living in the past robs you of your power to create in the present. You can't change the past, but you can learn from it. Make the most of this moment.
- Focus on writing a new project or fixing the old one. Plot a book you love. Throw yourself into it with renewed focus and determination. Come up with a better strategy for the next time.
- Appreciate the people who traveled through the valley with you. They're the ones you want beside you when you reach the mountain peak.

In *The Power of Now*, Eckhart Tolle writes, "All negativity is caused by an accumulation of psychological time and denial of the present. Unease, anxiety, tension, stress, worry—all forms of fear—are caused by too much future and not enough presence. Guilt, regret, resentment, grievances, sadness, bitterness, and all forms of nonforgiveness are caused by too much past, and not enough presence."

Not every venture is successful. Writers sometimes start out in genres where they think they'll have a better chance of success, only to learn it's more difficult to write something they don't necessarily love. Some writers try several genres before they find something that clicks and falls into place.

Market trends skyrocket and plunge unexpectedly. Years ago, when the historical fiction market dropped, a big portion of its writers reinvented themselves as contemporary authors. Each time a new trend comes along, plenty of writers spring to the challenge, applying themselves to the latest thing. Publishers fold, editors leave their positions (and orphan writers), entire lines are dropped. Sales numbers decline and authors need to recover, or they get bored writing the same genre for years and years, and decide to take up a new challenge. A great many things may cause authors to reinvent themselves in new genres—often with new names.

The usual way of doing things isn't called a *comfort zone* for nothing. Unfamiliarity and uncertainty cause us discomfort. On the other hand, doing something new and challenging presents the optimal conditions for outstanding results. We don't do our best work on autopilot. We do our best when we're pushing the boundaries. The rewards and benefits are bigger when we're stretched. A new personal best involves the risk of missing the mark or being rejected.

On the worst possible day, I still have the best possible job.

—LENORA WORTH

15

taking responsibility

The happiest people in the world are those who feel absolutely terrific about themselves, and this is the natural outgrowth of accepting total responsibility for every part of their life.

—BRIAN TRACY

We hear a lot of excuses. We make a lot of excuses. No one wants to take the blame for something gone wrong or an effort that misses its mark. Remember this: The only person responsible for your career is *you*.

Define what kind of writer you want to be. A flourishing career requires a plan. You need to know what is important to you and where you want to go. Knowing your priorities will aid you in decision-making.

Know where you want to be in ten years. Keep close track of your goals and base every decision upon them. *Will attending this conference help me finish this book by February? Which books shall I read to accomplish my craft goals?* When your goals are clear, you can take responsibility for every decision based on where the action is taking you. If an action will move you closer to your goal, take the necessary steps. If an action delays your goal, chose not to do it. You decide what to pursue and what to avoid.

Don't blame others. Blaming others is a cop out. Blame is the lazy way out. Why? If it's not your fault, you don't have to do anything to rectify the situation.

Blaming others is an attempt to shift attention away from our actions and toward another person or even a situation. *The Internet was down, so I couldn't research. The air-conditioning was out, so it was too hot to concentrate. The phone kept ringing, and I couldn't focus with all the distractions. The roofers were hammering so loud, I couldn't think.* I've used at least a couple of these. (We went over the list of excuses we make to ourselves in chapter 1.)

We also shift blame, so it takes the heat away from us. Complaining about things we can't control is an exercise in futility. But we complain anyway, to throw up a smokescreen. *It's not my fault I couldn't write.* Wait, what?

I've heard people say all kinds of things about why editors rejected their project. *He's a dog lover, and I wrote a book with a cat. She's having personal problems. She was having a bad day and took it out on me.*

If you're saying these kinds of things, you're taking the rejection personally rather than professionally. Second, give editors more credit than that. They're professionals who have degrees in literature, English, languages, history. They're good at organizing ideas, remembering details, working within deadlines, organizing material for clarity, thinking logically, visualizing stories, and working with teams. Editors want to like your book—they want to love it. They want to find a gem and help shape it into the best product possible.

That editor didn't reject your book because she was having a bad day. Your book simply didn't meet the requirements she needed to make an offer. Maybe she took six months to evaluate it and then she used a rubber stamp in place of a personal note, but she wasn't trying to hurt your feelings. She is overworked and looking for something specific. Blaming her might make you feel better for a moment, but it won't help you send a better product next time.

Blame doesn't change the situation. It only highlights your insecurity. Taking responsibility gives you the power to change your situation.

Negative feedback can be difficult to accept. First, you have to trust the person giving the feedback. Next, you must decide if any suggestions will make a better story, and whether or not you're willing to work with the ideas. If the feedback is from a friend or an acquaintance, weigh the source. Hopefully you trust this person's opinion or you wouldn't have shown them your work.

But sometimes a reader's thoughts are simply not on track with yours. Be confident enough to recognize that and know their ideas are not compatible with your vision for the story. If the suggestions are about plotting or characters, get another opinion. Editors have personal preferences, like readers. Be open to improving technique. Go with your gut when it comes to editorial feedback. Ninety-nine percent of the time editorial suggestions and changes have helped me develop a stronger book. To rectify a problem, you need to take responsibility, identify what went wrong, determine what you can do differently next time, and put your plan into action.

My first editor taught me so much, and I'll always be grateful for the time she took to groom and teach me. She was the first person to tell me I had a "voice." I'd never heard the term before. She once said she appreciated my "Hemmingway-ish style" and it took me a while to figure out what she meant. Now I know she was referring to my straightforward way of saying things. I don't use flowery language or purple prose. My honest and practical nature is revealed in my writing style—but I had never realized it until she pointed it out to me.

We all strive to be the perfect writer, but I doubt such a thing exists. An editor once told me that the passage of time was blurry in my stories. I work on this element in my storytelling to this day, using blank calendar pages for the months during which my stories take place and noting the passage of time, day by day. I previously missed a lot of opportunities to say, "after a week" or "the following day" or "it had been two weeks since," all of which let the reader know how much time has passed. By knowing I needed to work on this element and taking ownership of it, I improved my writing. Even though it takes a concerted effort for me to stay focused on the passage of time, recognizing and changing the way I do things has given me more confidence.

I have friends who, after learning they used certain words repeatedly, made a list of those words and use the find-and-replace tool in word processing programs to eliminate or change them. After doing that enough times, their writing has improved and their confidence has grown.

It is impossible to live without failing at something, unless you live so cautiously that you might as well not have lived at all, in which case you fail by default.

—J.K. ROWLING

Don't Blame Yourself Either

No one needs to be punished for a mistake or missed mark. Take responsibility for your part in the problem, identify the changes you need to make, and make them. Everyone was a beginner once. And even writers who've been published for decades make mistakes.

Be Honest with Yourself

Take responsibility for your career and forget the excuses.

Think You're Too Old?

Colonel Harland David Sanders was sixty-two when he franchised his first Kentucky Fried Chicken.

Think You're Too Young?

Mark Zuckerberg launched Facebook at the age of nineteen and was a billionaire within three years.

Think You're Too Busy?

Busy isn't the same as productive. Busy people say they don't have enough time. Productive people make time for what is important. Lack of time is not an excuse. Success is measured by output, not by blocks of time.

Believe You Can't Afford It?

We all choose where, when, and how to make the sacrifices that make our dreams happen. If it's a conference you want to go to, plan ahead. Research travel options. Find a friend to share a room and expenses with. Stay at a less expensive nearby hotel, rather than the conference hotel. Use travel points. Propose a workshop and get a registration break. Drive and take your own snacks and drinks.

Think You Have Quirks, Issues, or Flaws that Hold You Back?

Peter Roget had obsessive-compulsive disorder (OCD) and calmed himself by making random lists. He came up with an infinite list of synonyms and created the thesaurus at age seventy-three. Roget's *Thesaurus of English Words and Phrases* has been in print since its first publication in 1852. Each of us probably has one on our desk or on our computer.

You're Deciding Right Now

We can either make excuses or use every resource available to help us move toward our goals. Taking responsibility starts with a sense of purpose and a desire to make something happen. You'll be faced with decisions every day, every week, every year of your life. Doing nothing is a decision. Taking no action is choosing to stagnate, to let life pass you by. If you choose this path, you'll miss out on opportunities for reasons of fear, insecurity, lack of motivation, and lack of purpose. Decide to do something now.

16

finding perspective on offense

It's not that I'm so smart; it's just that I stay with problems longer.

—ALBERT EINSTEIN

It seems that criticism and taking offense has detonated into an art form. The population is angry, entitled, sensitive, and offended about everything. You can't listen to the news or check your Twitter feed without running across someone's rant. On the flip side, offenders are stacking up aspersions like cordwood, many of them gleefully proud to be offensive. For the most part, the writing and publishing community is supportive and encouraging, thank goodness. But unprovoked attacks and insults occur in every walk of life, and publishing is not immune. Often the most innocent slight is misunderstood and leads to hurt feelings. It's well and good to advise writers to develop a thick skin, but how does one acquire said hide?

TAKING OFFENSE/GRUDGES

It happens, even among the most well-meaning people. Somebody's idea wasn't considered. Someone said something thoughtless, or someone made a comment about your work that you didn't like. You took offense.

You can do one of two things: Either separate yourself and nurse that wrongdoing until it eats away at you—or give the person the benefit of the doubt and ignore it. Consider telling the person how he made you feel, get it off your chest. Maybe he doesn't even know he stepped on your toes. (Note: This advice does not pertain to reviews and is only wise if you personally know the person who offended you. Don't respond to negative reviews on Amazon or Goodreads. Ever.)

Sure, there are rude people who sometimes do deliberately hurtful things. But you know what? Everybody knows those people are rude, and you're the bigger person if you don't let them get to you. All you can control in this situation is your reaction. I've seen people let one person who rubs them the wrong way keep them away from an entire group that's otherwise helpful and beneficial.

Get over yourself. Seriously. You don't have to make that one person your best friend, but you certainly don't have to let her have an immense measure of power over you. Whatever we focus on becomes magnified. If we focus on what was said or done and what we *should have* said or done, we end up heaping fuel on a negative situation. Sometimes it's something that happened a year ago or five years ago, and yet when we think of it, we refresh ourselves on every last detail. In refreshing it, the incident becomes as good as new.

In such cases, we need to process our feelings, learn to let go, and move on. Here are a couple of tools for processing and releasing offense:

- Go ahead and vent—to the right person. Not on Facebook or any social media, not in a group of friends, not to just anyone who will listen. Share why you feel wronged with a trusted friend or partner. Or, write it down for your eyes only, if you want to. Express the hurt and frustration.
- Try, try, *try* to look at the situation through the other person's point of view. You should be able to do that, right? You are a writer who concerns himself with viewpoints and getting into other people's heads. You may look at things with that person's viewpoint and still find her inexcusably rude or offensive, but at least you tried. On the

Write Smart, Write Happy

other hand, you might see where she's coming from and be able to cut her some slack.

Finding compassion for people we believe have wronged us shows strength of character. We all have a backstory and motivation. We can recognize that each of us is the product of our lives, aspirations, relationships, dreams, and hurts, and we can even consider what may have provoked a person to lash out, withdraw, or attack. That person may never recognize it or admit it, but he's probably hurting, feeling inadequate, or threatened. We don't have to counsel or question him. If you really want to, however, you can talk to the person in a nonconfrontational manner. Let her know how her words or behavior affected you. Or don't bring it up and simply let it go. For our own sake, we need to forgive and show kindness.

I could write a book on forgiveness, and perhaps one day I will, but for now I'll stress that holding grudges and clinging to an unwillingness to forgive is not hurting the other person—it's hurting you. Forgiveness is not condoning or excusing. It doesn't require anything (like regret) from the offender. We simply grant forgiveness without expecting anything from the offender.

Sometimes we don't want to forgive. We want to hang onto that wrongdoing like we'll never let go, as if doing so is somehow a form of payback—as if our refusal to grant forgiveness is hurting the other person. We can cling to the offense until we make ourselves sick, emotionally and physically. Forgiving is an action, not a feeling, therefore right feelings follow right actions in this instance.

I've learned to write offenses I've suffered in my planner. *On this date, I forgave so-and-so for whatever hurtful thing.* I draw a box around it and put a sticker beside it. Tomorrow or next week or next month, when I think about it—and I will—I'll pick up my planner and flip back to that day. Then I put my finger on it and announce, "Nope. I forgave them for that."

This might not make sense to you right now, but when a time comes that you need it, I hope you'll remember and apply the technique. Doing so has released me from depression, illness, and insomnia.

Yes, our feelings get hurt. We're human. We're intelligent and intuitive. We know when someone's deliberately yanking our chain. We cry. We get mad. We get over it. But anger and hurt are different from being offended. An offense is a deep wound that will fester if it's not treated so it can heal. Holding onto an offense leads to bitterness. Allowing an offense to take root is allowing it to grow bigger and bigger. Recognizing offense right away and taking care of it will spare you bitterness, as well as reduce anger and stress.

What if the person is not sorry? What if he believes he's in the right and won't budge? Forgive him anyway.

What if you'll never see the person again or the person is no longer living? Forgive her anyway.

What if the person has done or said the same thing more than once? Forgive him anyway.

In all of these cases, forgiveness is for you, not for the other person.

I didn't say forgive her and be her best friend. I would never suggest you enter a situation in which you allow yourself to be abused or taken advantage of. I don't suggest you excuse, entertain, or encourage a toxic person. Rather, protect yourself from all situations and persons who deliberately aim to hurt. But for your own well-being, I believe you must forgive.

I've had plenty of opportunity to hold onto offense, but I chose not to. Why? Because I would have ended up miserable.

It's human nature to want the last word, to prove to someone that we're worthy and good. Instead, acknowledge the wrongdoing and forgive. Let it go and move on.

Sometimes we unconsciously offend others. Other times it's a conscious decision. Usually it happens when we're dealing with our own issues—we snap at people because we're stressed. Stuff happens. And then we want people to give us the benefit of the doubt, don't we? So it makes sense that we should give others the benefit of the doubt.

You probably know the minute something leaves your lips that it was unkind or rude, but sometimes you don't realize it until you see the other person's reaction.

I saw this happen between two people: One was focused on a challenging problem and trying to think. The other kept offering suggestions and didn't realize she was irritating her friend. We do this all the time without thinking. The frustrated person snapped. The offended person was hurt and reacted. The person who snapped tried to apologize—but the offended friend didn't want to listen and defended her reaction.

The person who makes the first attempt to right a situation is the most mature. The person who doesn't forgive does himself an injustice. The person who forgives can sleep well at night.

Work on improving your confidence regarding your writing and your desire to write, so you don't easily take offense.

- Write more; write often.
- Write something for sheer pleasure.
- Follow through and finish projects.
- Remind yourself why you want to be a writer.
- Make writing a habit.
- Don't compare yourself to others.
- Forget perfectionism.
- Read books on the writing craft.
- Find a mentor.
- Read your work to other writers and ask for feedback.
- Read in multiple genres.
- Offer to help a beginner—you'll be surprised how far you've come.
- Offer critiques the way you expect to receive them: point out strengths; give constructive ideas for improvement; be kind.
- Set and meet goals.
- Understand not everyone likes the same stories or styles, and that's okay.
- Give yourself credit for how far you've come.

17

self-talk & affirmations

> Just as your car runs more smoothly and requires less energy to go faster and farther when the wheels are in perfect alignment, you perform better when your thoughts, feelings, emotions, goals, and values are in balance.
>
> **—BRIAN TRACY**

THE POWER OF NEGATIVE WORDS HOLD US BACK

There is power in words—more power than you might expect or imagine. Words can construct or destruct, and they've been taking root in our minds since childhood. Words shaped you into the person you are. Your mother and father's words, the words of your teachers, pastors, friends, bullies, even acquaintances, and people you heard on television. Each word has had an effect on you.

The subconscious mind doesn't think or reason. It simply does whatever we program it to do. And it thinks what other people program it to think, as well.

If you don't believe me, consider your body image. Your self-image has been developing since your childhood when your mother said you needed to drink your milk to grow strong and tall, and that sixth grader laughed at your ears, or you watched a commercial and heard that facial hair was unsightly. Did your father ever ask you to get off your *lazy butt* and take out the trash? My dad used to say, "You'd complain if you were being hung with a new rope." (Well, yeah.) Well-meaning parents say things that negatively shape our identities, too: "I'm ashamed of you." "You don't want to be a chubby girl." "Don't cry, you're okay."

Unfortunately, more negative programming makes its way into our minds than positive.

It's no wonder we end up thinking things like, "I'll never get the hang of this," or, "I've always had a terrible memory." We say these things to ourselves and to others. And we continue to believe the things we say and hear until we recognize what we're doing and reprogram ourselves to think and speak differently.

Poor Self-Talk Makes Us Believers in the Negative Stuff

Have you heard people say things like, "I sent my first three chapters to a contest, but I know I'm not going to win." If you are convinced, you won't win, why did you bother to send it?

Or this one: "My manuscript has been at X publisher for three months. I wish they'd just hurry up and reject it." When I heard that statement come from someone's mouth, I think my ears rang for a full minute. I wanted to get her attention and wake her up to the negativity she was projecting. Those types of fatalistic, pessimistic statements blow me away.

That self-defeating talk is representative of what's going on *inside* a person.

Ever heard this? "Prepare for the worst, but expect the best." That seems counterproductive to me. If I'm expecting the best, I'm not going to prepare for the worst! I'm not saying a backup plan isn't a good idea. I'm just saying, don't close the book before you've read the end. Don't count on the worst when you're hoping for the best. You can't trick yourself, you know. Just because you say, "I'm expecting to get rejected," doesn't mean you're not going to feel disappointment when a rejection letter comes.

And when you speak negatively, you're *listening to yourself.* That means you can convince yourself of the opposite, if you're persistent enough.

Many years ago I attended a Romance Writers of America conference with a group of friends, and a couple of us attended a positive-affirmation workshop by the late Rita Rainville. Her advice and suggestions made perfect sense to me; I'm a positive full-cup kind of gal to start with. We took our affirmations to an extreme the rest of our trip, and on the way home we said things like, "My nails are long and pretty," and we laughed. But seriously, I made a list of positive affirmations and stuck them up above my monitor. They said things like, "I'm writing a book that I'm going to sell," and "I'm doing my very best work." And lo and behold, an amazing number of the confessions on that sheet came to pass—and it didn't take all that long.

We convince ourselves the same way. We all talk to ourselves on some level—either aloud or silently—when making decisions, driving, or searching for something we lost. We give ourselves little pep talks to handle stressful situations like job interviews, difficult meetings, and important presentations. And it works. I talked to myself frequently while I was getting sick and in severe pain in the hospital after a surgery. I said every positive thing that I could dredge from my memory— and thank God those things were planted there so I could draw upon them. To reap positive thoughts and words when you need them most, you must have planted them sometime in the past.

Self-deprecation seems like humor, but it can be an extension of low expectations and negativity. *I'll just put myself down now before anyone else can do it.* Or it can come from a person who's just so humble that they're actually prideful in reverse.

- *I'll never be any good at this.*
- *I was born this way, and that's just me.*
- *You'll just have to accept me the way I am.*
- *I've tried, but I'm too old to learn new tricks.*
- *If someone's going to get the ax, it's me. It's always me.*

Saying things out loud reinforces them because you're *hearing them* as well.

You can convince yourself of anything. Why not convince yourself you're capable and successful? While you're at it, get your family and friends onboard by being an example with your speech. We have a note on our fridge that reads, "If you say so." When one of us says something negative, the other replies with, "If you say so."

A nutritionist will tell you, "You are what you eat." Well, I say, "You are what you say." Shad Helmstetter has written a couple of books on this subject, and if negative talk is a problem for you, I recommend reading *What to Say When You Talk to Yourself* or *365 Days of Positive Self-Talk*. There's also a book titled *The Art of Self Talk*, by hypnotherapist William W. Hewitt. I don't necessarily subscribe to all of their theories and techniques, but I do firmly believe that changing our talk can change our lives for the better. Make a list of affirmations and read it out loud in the morning.

If you are tempted to say, *I know this manuscript is just going to come right back rejected.* Then my question is, why did you send it out in the first place? King Solomon, believed to be the wisest man who ever lived, said the power of life and death is in the tongue. We can create and destroy with words. When you picture and speak failure, you lose your motivation to succeed. You focus on avoiding mistakes, rather than striving to do your best.

You need to see yourself working hard, selling your books, getting glowing reviews, and accepting awards. Visual aids are helpful for positive reinforcement, too. Make yourself a poster of all the things you want to happen. That's a visual affirmation. Before I was published,

I created a poster of the things I aimed to achieve. In those days, Waldenbooks had a weekly best-seller list, and I printed one and added my own name and book title at the number one slot. Eventually, I made that list. In my genre, the top award has always been the RITA, named after one of the founders of RWA. I printed and cut out a picture of that golden statue and included it on my board. I've been nominated several times but am still waiting for a win. I have friends who create mock covers of their books as affirmations.

Before he ever sold a cartoon, Scott Adams, the creator of the cartoon *Dilbert*, wrote down every day that he would be "a famous syndicated cartoon artist." Henriette Klauser wrote a book titled *Write It Down, Make It Happen: Knowing What You Want and Getting It*. I find the principles helpful. We're book people; we all have a lot of books. We're all searching for methods that work for us. We take a little from this and a little from that to come up with a plan that fits us. Do whatever it takes to motivate yourself with positive energy.

Consciously Listen to Your Thoughts and Words

I did my share of whining and feeling sorry for myself when I was working, raising my children, and attempting to get my first book published. I was determined not to work at my then job for the rest of my life. I wrote every available minute around work and family. My children took turns fixing supper. My husband—who had never turned on the washer in his life—learned how to do laundry. Together, my family sacrificed a lot.

Thoughts of throwing in the towel crept into my head, but I knew in my heart I would never be happy with myself if I didn't give this thing every last ounce of energy I had. When I was working a job that kept me on my feet all day, getting the kids off to school, and handling all that being a mom entails, I can remember dragging myself out of bed first thing in the morning. It was still dark, and I'd barely slept enough hours to combat exhaustion. Something has to go when there's that much pressure and frustration.

It's the closest I ever came to quitting. I had to talk to myself to keep from giving up on writing. "This day gets me one day closer to my goal. I can do it. I can make the best of it. I'm not going to be working at this job much longer."

I changed my confession, and with that, I changed my thinking.

Speak with Confidence

When you talk to yourself, be convincing!

Speaking out loud is more focused than silent talk. If you want to memorize something, don't read it silently; read it out loud, over and over again. If you're getting results, seeing your situations change, do you really care that it may seem a little strange at first to talk to yourself?

Read your goals list. Make a second page, listing the benefits to staying on track with goals, and read that. By reminding yourself often, you encourage yourself to stick to the schedule. Read your list out loud at least once a week.

To reprogram your negative thoughts and talk, you have to make a change and speak positively to yourself and others. Start by recognizing what needs to change.

I'm tired of having to run the dishwasher twice on Monday morning, so I'm going to do dishes and ask for more help on Sunday afternoon.

Not giving myself enough time to get to work and running out in a rush is not working for me. I don't need the stress, so I'm going to set my alarm a half hour earlier from now on. Tomorrow I'm getting up at six.

Have you heard or said this one? *I just don't have the time.* Everyone on earth is allotted the same twenty-four hours a day. We can all find time to do what we really want to do.

Talk your way to a new schedule. Creating writing time means something else has to go. That could be e-mail listservs, television programs, or sleeping in.

I want to be a successful author, so I'm going to take the steps necessary to make that happen. I will write twenty pages a week. I have the discipline to do it. Say it now!

Get Out Your Pen and Journal

Create a list of the positive things you want to say to yourself. Tape it to your mirror and read it out loud, if you have to. Post a few positive statements over your monitor. Print your favorite quotes and read them to yourself regularly.

Several years ago, I printed an encouraging e-mail that a friend sent me regarding my writing. I had it on my monitor so long it turned yellow, but it gave me confidence every time I looked at it. I have a folder in my office drawer labeled "warm fuzzies." It's filled with notes people have written to me over the years. Once in a while I get out those slips of paper and notecards and read them for encouragement.

I've heard it said that using affirmations sometimes ends up masking a deeper problem without getting to the core issue—that affirmations allow a person to create a lie without resolving the trouble. Rest assured, I don't want you to gloss over a deep inferiority problem. We're not lying to ourselves when we speak positively. We're not denying anything except failure. My hope is that you will improve your self-image and gain confidence, remove labels from past experiences, and develop new beliefs about your self-worth. Self-confidence is learned.

To get you started on your positive self-talk, here is a list of affirmations I use and revise occasionally. When I prepare my writing planner at the first of the year, I get out my colorful fine-point felt pens and write one or more on each week's page. Feel free to adapt the following writing affirmations to pertain to you and your goals, or develop your own. It's best to make them short and simple; stick to the point. Affirmations must be present tense.

Here's a sample list:

- I am working every day at improving my craft and becoming a better writer.
- I'm accountable for my own work ethic and practices.
- I set attainable, measurable goals and achieve them.
- I give myself realistic deadlines and consistently work toward them.
- I'm guarding my time and energy.
- I'm determined to reach my goals.

- I don't allow the negative opinions of others to affect my writing.
- I balance my family and writing in a healthy manner.
- I'm a creative person.
- I have a God-given talent.
- I'm working toward success and expect to see results.
- I learn from rejections and accept criticism with confidence.
- I have enthusiasm for my writing.
- I'm getting better every day.
- My enthusiasm is carrying me through this book.
- I like being organized and efficient.
- I'm not waiting for inspiration; I'm a professional.
- I'm proud of this book and my accomplishment.
- I'm willing to try new things.
- I stick with projects and issues until I succeed.
- I'm in the process of becoming a published author/best-selling author.

Affirmations

Your problem is not your ideas. Your problem is you don't act on them.

—MEL ROBBINS

- I find the joy in every day.
- I revisit and clarify my goals.
- I take daily steps toward my goals.
- I take action and don't procrastinate.
- I am thankful every day.
- I let go of idealism and negative things around me.
- People don't have to be perfect.
- I don't have to be perfect.
- I do things I'm passionate about.

- I challenge myself to do new things.
- I congratulate myself.
- I understand all things, good and bad, eventually come to an end.
- I persevere and pick up things I'd previously given up on.
- I get enough rest.
- I stick to my sleep schedule and am productive.
- I acknowledge my feelings.
- I choose to do the things that make me happy.
- I spend time with friends.
- I tell people I love them.
- I hug family and friends.
- I surround myself with people who build me up and encourage me.
- I'm a good friend and make time for relationships.
- I enjoy giving unexpected gifts.
- Sometimes I spend a day alone.
- I forgive people.
- I live in the moment and have joy.
- Thank You, Lord, for blessing the work of my hands.
- I embrace the fact that I'm not the same writer I was five or ten years ago.
- I don't waste time feeling sorry for myself.
- I am in control of my own emotions.
- I don't waste energy on things I can't control.
- I strive for perfection in everything.
- I take the best and make it better.
- I don't worry about pleasing everyone.
- I don't fear taking calculated risks.
- I don't dwell on the past.
- I don't make the same mistake over and over.
- I spend it all! Play it! Shoot it! Right away, every time. (Note: If you don't recognize this Annie Dillard quote from *The Writing Life*, you really should look it up.)
- I'm passionate about storytelling.
- I don't give up after the first failure.

- I don't fear alone time.
- I don't feel the world owes me anything.
- I don't expect immediate results, but I expect results.
- I don't compare myself to others.
- I don't resent other people's success.
- I don't let the achievements of others intimidate me.
- I'm genuinely happy for my friends' success.
- I socialize for connections and friendship.
- I love others, and my joy is full.
- No one can steal my joy.
- I make healthy decisions.
- I am sure of my ability to do what is necessary to improve my life.
- I am fortunate to work at what I love to do.
- I possess the wisdom, the power, the motivation, the inspiration, and the passion to accomplish anything and everything I choose.
- I'm a good writer, and I'm taking the steps to become even better.
- I'm serious about my craft, and therefore I make the time to work at it.
- I'm serious about my craft, and my family and friends respect my time.
- *Doggone it, people like me!*
- I look ahead, not behind, but I live in the moment.
- I find joy in every day's work.
- I'm prepared.
- I'm proactive.
- I'm kind to myself.
- I strive to make people fans of my books, and of me.
- I challenge my thinking and don't stagnate.
- I make every deadline early.
- I expect a great day!
- Something great is going to happen to me today!

Really listen to yourself and hear what you say when you speak these affirmations.

If you hear another person say something negative, care enough to challenge his thinking. Don't criticize—empower!

change your thinking

> Just because someone stumbles and loses their path, doesn't mean they're lost forever. Sometimes, we all need a little help.
>
> **—PROFESSOR X, THE X-MEN**

WRITER'S BLOCK IS AN EXCUSE

I don't believe in writer's block. To me, calling a problem "writer's block" is another excuse for stalling—for not writing. I find that putting my butt in the chair, opening the file, and placing my fingers on the keyboard, makes the words come. They don't always flow like sparkling gems, but words come, and words written are words that can be edited. Coming to a snag in a scene is like finding an unexpected detour while driving. You're forced to take an unplanned turn, which makes your navigation system recalculate.

A technique I use when I'm stuck in a scene is to type a couple of asterisks and move on to a place where I know what's going to happen. Forward motion is the key. Later, after I've had time to think (and I've put some space between myself and the page), I come back and reevaluate it. Usually by then I'm ready to move forward. Often I come up with solutions in the shower or while driving—but sometimes I realize that the reason I can't figure out where to go is that I'd reached the end of the scene. In that case, I move on to creating the hook and end the scene.

There might be one hundred different reasons the words don't flow. Maybe you didn't plan the story well enough, so you don't know where you're going. Maybe you failed to create enough inherent conflict to sustain the plot. If the story isn't working for you, take it apart, analyze it, and put it back together. See it as a challenge, a place to improve the story. If it's the middle, muddling around like this is normal for most writers. It's time to find a helpful craft book or to Google writing techniques that can get you moving forward again. It's not time to stop simply because it's hard. Writing is always hard.

Do I sound unsympathetic? I'm not. I'm saying the hard things, talking to you like a mentor. I *am* empathetic because I've gone through it more times than I can count, but I want to encourage you to keep going when it's difficult. Every once in a while, we tell our kids, "Life is hard. Try harder." We don't *want* to tell them, but we have to.

Fill the well. Take time for you. Be kind to yourself. Do something that relaxes you or gives you pleasure. Go to a movie. Go on a date. Paint. Sing. Listen to music. Refinish a table. Do something fun with your kids, grandkids, or the neighbor kids. Read out of your genre, and read something that's not research or instructional. Buy a book for children and read it to them, seeing it through their eyes.

The summer before my youngest granddaughter started kindergarten, my daughter enrolled her in a phonics class. I took her to the classes and watched the kids act out stories like *Where The Wild Things Are* and *Caps for Sale*. I also took her to the library once a week and, from a suggested reading list, we checked out and read dozens of classics, like *Mike Mulligan and His Steam Shovel* and *Strega Nona*. It took me back to my first experiences with books and my love of reading. Teaching a child to read and seeing his enjoyment in the process is a rewarding way to remind ourselves why we love stories.

Write something longhand to get your head out of the current project and jog your creativity. Have your journal handy? Make the following lists:

- Interesting words you're going to use in your book
- Your favorite childhood books
- Your favorite Christmas movies

- Movies you want to put in your Netflix queue
- Potential titles for your work-in-progress or books you want to write
- The positive things about being a writer
- Street names you like and will use in a project
- Metaphors that describe a good writing day

Write a blog, whether it's writing related or not. Pick something that piques your interest, that you have an opinion about, that you're curious about, or in which you can instill some humor.

Topics to consider:

- A funny travel experience
- A hobby
- A product review
- Review a recent movie
- Your favorite movie characters and why
- Share something people don't know about you
- A memory involving a holiday, like Mother's Day or Christmas
- What you would say to the sixteen-year-old you
- An embarrassing moment
- Share a music playlist
- Share a behind-the-scenes look at your story or work space
- Share a fascinating bit of research

Getting stuck or losing focus isn't always cut-and-dried. Maybe you've truly lost focus. Life is happening all around you, and you're in no state of mind to be productive. The latter is not writer's block. It's an emotional issue, and it's a serious situation. Give yourself permission to take a hiatus during periods of emotional distress. Sometimes writing is therapeutic and carries you to another place for some much-needed distraction; other times it's the last thing you need to concern yourself with. Learn the difference. Don't beat yourself up during difficult times.

What I want to make sure you know is that there are legitimate roadblocks. There are valid reasons for getting behind or missing the mark. Life happens—in a big way. In unexpected ways. Emotion, tension, and conflict make for a compelling story. They aren't, however, conducive to writing.

I've gone through situations where writing was a catharsis. I dealt with the circumstance on one hand, while on the other I shut out the world and wrote. I've also gone through situations where writing a book was the last thing I could think about, even if I wanted to.

A financial emergency, a medical emergency, an illness, caring for an ill parent or child, the death of a loved one, depression or anxiety, a relationship in crisis, children in crisis, the nation in crisis—all of these are legitimate roadblocks to concentrating on the fictional world of a story. Being unable to focus on your work is yet another stress to add to the strain of the situation. You've cashed the advance check. You have a deadline. Your editor has a schedule to keep. All of this adds to the pressure.

After dealing with cancer for years and enduring radiation and chemo, my mother eventually needed full-time care. (I've just reduced years and months into one sentence that boils down to a full-fledged writing roadblock.) Take it from me, when something like this occurs, a writer couldn't care any less about the book. Day-to-day survival, grief, mental and physical exhaustion will take over. In my own experience, there came a point when I knew I would not be able to work on the book I'd contracted—and I had no idea when I would be able to. I called my editor to explain the situation.

Editors are caring, feeling people with families of their own. They understand life crises. My editor was kind and expressed her sympathy. She told me not to give the book or the deadline another thought, to focus where I needed to focus, and when I was ready to work on it again, to let her know. My books are scheduled as soon as they're contracted, so she removed it from the lineup, freeing me of that additional stress at a difficult time.

My mother lived longer than the doctors predicted, giving us more time together. I was able to focus on her, her care, make arrangements for her, and eventually learn how to move forward after the loss. To be honest, I lost track of time for a while and much of that year is a blur in my memory, but it was months before I went back to that book and picked up where I'd left off.

As fate would have it, the book I'd started is about a young woman who left home at a young age, and when she eventually returns, she learns her mother has died. She has to grieve after the fact and must learn to forgive herself. When I reopened that file and read what I'd started, I remember thinking something like, *Seriously? This is the book I'm writing?* I plugged away for a while and wrote chapter after chapter. Then I came to a place where I went back to the beginning and did a read-through, only to discover I'd written a dreadfully depressing book. *Dreadfully.* Well, duh, right? So for only the second time in my career, I tore the book apart, took out an entire thread, and rewrote a character's viewpoint in its entirely.

I still don't know how I had the wherewithal on my own to realize where I'd gone wrong or how I had the aptitude to rewrite the book. But I did. And it turned out well. I loved the story when I'd planned and plotted it, and I still love the story to this day. The story reminds me that when I nurture my gift, I can accomplish a good thing. The experience reminds me that sometimes we have to give ourselves permission to take a break, so we can experience life—and loss—and figure out how to be okay in the end.

I'm reminded of Cher's character in *Moonstruck*. After Nicolas Cage's character, Ronny, confesses he's in love with Loretta, she slaps him and demands, "Snap out of it!" It's a funny line. But we can't shout solutions and expect instant recoveries. There's no snapping out of emotional turbulence. If you become overwhelmed by a life circumstance, give yourself permission to take a break. If you need kindness and patience, be kind to yourself, and be patient with yourself. Give yourself time and space. Ask for help when you need help.

Roadblocks happen. If you do get derailed, give yourself permission to re-evaluate. Then set new goals. It's always a good idea to revisit goals. If you're on track, well and good—have a party. If you're behind or took a dirt road like I did, don't beat yourself up. One roadblock, mistake, setback, or failure isn't a reason to give up. Neither are two—or three. You're allowed a do over. You're always allowed a do over.

Write Smart, Write Happy

19

nurture confidence in your abilities

What humility does for one is it reminds us that there are people before me. I have already been paid for. And what I need to do is prepare myself so that I can pay for someone else who has yet to come but who may be here and needs me.

—MAYA ANGELOU

Writing newbies share a common misconception: They think that if they can only sell a book, their struggles will magically disappear. I'm here to tell you that the struggle does not disappear. Not by any means. After an author has published five or fifty books, the struggle only evolves.

THERE IS NO SECRET HANDSHAKE

Writers buy a lot of books, watch a lot of webinars, and go to a lot of conferences, looking for the secret handshake. This misconception is that published authors know something we don't know, that they're holding (or withholding) the key to success. I've been in the shoes of both the unpublished and the published writer. Many issues we face are the same. Other issues are unique to the current situation.

I enjoy meeting new writers. They're enthused. They can't wait to know everything they need to know to get their books published and see their names on the covers. If you're an enthusiastic new writer, you probably belong to a writers' group, attend events and lectures, and take classes—as you should. To you, published authors seem to have it all together. They've been where you are, made the right moves to break in, found a publishing home, and are now thriving. Obviously, the multi-published authors know the elusive answers to writing the best query letter and a shining synopsis, and finding the perfect agent and editor. You expect them to be able to pass along that information. Maybe you've asked a couple of published authors to read your manuscript.

Most published authors remember those feelings vividly. I remember exactly what it feels like to want someone to tell you whether or not you can do this. Sometimes asking an author to read your material pays off. Other times it's just awkward. *Really* awkward. Not that the author doesn't wish you well, or won't offer tips and advice, but if an author read everything that was thrust before her, she'd never have time for her own work.

I'm not saying don't approach an author for a conversation or never ask for advice. But please don't believe they owe you anything. They did their time. They put in the work. Personally, I believe what goes around, comes around. Plenty of more-experienced writers mentored me along the way, and I'm forever grateful. I can't repay them, but I can pay it forward and help others in the same way. But not everyone believes that. A small percent even think teaching writing is like training replacements for their job.

You're not entitled. Nice will get you a long way. Being humble will get you further. The fastest ways to alienate yourself in a writing community are 1) be a know-it-all and 2) feel entitled. Sometimes new writers are so eager to reach their goal that they can't be bothered to learn to write well. They want to see actual query letters and synopses that landed contracts. They'd like to be provided with lists of publishers and agents, along with guidelines and details of the process. They want to understand contracts, hear explanations of the publishing and editing process, hear how much they can expect to be paid—in other words, they're looking for The Secret Handshake. I heard this compared eloquently to a carpenter who made one table leg and now wants to sell the whole table. You must first take time to learn your craft.

My writing organization, Romance Authors of the Heartland, a local chapter of Romance Writers of America, teaches all that and more. Not all at once obviously. We are respectful of the time and willingness of our hardworking authors. There's nothing wrong with knowing what you need and going after it, but expecting another person to do the work for you is unacceptable and probably the most likely way to earn yourself the reputation of a person to avoid.

FACT: Sometimes simply going to lunch with published authors and listening to their conversation is as informative as a day-long workshop.

LEARN TO BUILD SELF-CONFIDENCE & REHEARSE VICTORIES

A majority of published authors are sympathetic to the beginner's struggle and are willing to share their experiences and advice. However, we're also busy with deadlines, copyedits, cover art fact sheets, newsletters, speaking engagements, our sales rankings, and answering questions about margin widths. So how can we graciously offer help to new writers, still make our deadlines, and keep our sanity?

What do we do when approached with unreasonable demands? It's good to have ready responses for eager writers. This is the information age, after all. Newbies can Google a lot of information. It's a good idea to have standby advice ready, perhaps even to prepare handouts. What is reasonable advice?

- Do your research.
- *Writer's Market* is a solid resource too look for editors and agents.
- In the U.K., Society of Authors vets contracts.
- Join a group/critique group.

- Science Fiction and Fantasy Writers of America has a Writer's Beware section on their website: www.sfwa.org/other-resources/for-authors/writer-beware/.
- Critters Workshop lists scams and gives publisher advice: critters.org/c/pubtips.ht.
- Log into the following to see warnings of the pitfalls of vanity publishing: www.sfwa.org/other-resources/for-authors/writer-beware/vanity/.
- A free database of agents exists on Agent Query: www.agentquery.com/resource_ww.aspx.
- Author Brenda Hyatt does a yearly survey of income by traditional and indie publishing: brendahiatt.com/show-me-the-money/traditional-publisher-survey/.
- Join online communities selectively. They can be a time suck, and your time is valuable. Always align yourself with writers who share your vision and support each other.

There's no reason to reinvent the wheel. The information is out there if writers look for it.

Create a simple list of beneficial books for aspiring writers. You might include the following:

- *Techniques of the Selling Writer*, Dwight V. Swain, University of Oklahoma Press
- *Writing With Emotion, Tension, & Conflict*, Cheryl St. John, Writer's Digest Books
- *GMC, Debra Dixon*, Gryphon Books
- *Creating Story People*, Dwight V. Swain, Writer's Digest Books
- *Building Believable Characters*, Marc McCutcheon, Writer's Digest Books
- *Break Into Fiction*, Mary Buckham and Dianna Love, Adams Media

If you're an unpublished writer, hopefully you've been reading the previous chapters and keeping a notebook in which you've taken action steps. In chapter 16, I suggested ways to boost your self-esteem and confidence. I advised you to create your own affirmations and speak positively about yourself and your writing.

When you're starting out, it's important to have realistic expectations about your time or abilities. Start where you're comfortable. If you're a short story writer, plan your goals and write to your intended word count. Do that faithfully until it becomes habit.

If you plan to write a full-length novel, stretch your writing muscles with prompts or exercises. Write a scene that you'll use later. Write character sketches.

EARNEST ADVICE: LEARN TO WRITE A SYNOPSIS

If you want to be a career writer, you will be expected to write a strong synopsis to land a contract and get an advance. Just like storytelling, there are techniques to writing a synopsis. Number one: *It's more important to show why the characters are doing what they're doing than to show what they are doing.* You'll need to remember that bit of knowledge for the rest of your career.

Find or Build a Writers' Community

You can try a couple of items to form a writers' community for yourself (and others!):

- Check your local libraries: They often know the area authors and writers groups.
- Ask your local bookstore: Booksellers may know the writing groups and authors.
- Community colleges often have writing classes; instructors or other students are likely to know of groups.
- Attend book signings and readings to meet other writers.
- Go to Meetup.com and search for writers' support groups.
- Check online for organizations in your area or nationally. Here's a sampling:

- Horror Writing Association: horror.org/
- Science Fiction and Fantasy Writers Association of America: www.sfwa.org/
- Society of Children's Book Writers and Illustratorsz: www.scbwi.org/
- The Author's Guild: www.authorsguild.org/
- American Society of Journalists and Authors: www.asja.org/index.php
- Romance Writers of American: www.rwa.org/
- The National Writers Union: www.nwu.org/
- National Association of Writers: www.nationalwriters.com/page/page/1963103.htm
- The International Women's Guild: www.iwwg.org/
- National Novel Writing Month: www.nanowrimo.org/
- American Christian Fiction Writers: www.acfw.com/
- Mystery Writers of America: www.mysterywriters.org/
- Western Writers of America: westernwriters.org/

Check for Facebook groups by searching for "authors" or "writers" by "groups." These closed groups can be extremely helpful for finding writing partners and critique groups.

Check Yahoo! groups for "writers" and "authors." There are private listservs for indie authors, as well as for genre writers, writers of fan fiction, and for traditionally published authors. Most have archives of previous Q&A sessions that can be a treasure trove of great information. One such group is Marie Force's group for independently published writers. She has a Yahoo! group and a Facebook group.

Remember when joining these groups to read the rules and regulations for posting. Some of these have hundreds or even thousands of members, and there are moderators who keep the posts regulated and orderly. Also remember to check the archives before asking a question. All those hundreds of people who've been there forever don't want to read or answer another question about margins or fonts.

If there's nothing in your area, join a group online or start a group of your own. The important thing is to hook up with like-minded creative people—people who understand you. Writing can be lonely, and you'll go nowhere fast if you work in a vacuum. It's life changing to meet people who don't think you're wacky for having characters and stories in your head. Having others to share your excitement and enthusiasm, and discussing fictional people as though they're real—because to us, they are—can create an incomparable high.

At family gatherings and social events, someone will politely ask, "What's your new story about?" If you actually tell them, their eyes glaze over, and you know you've lost them. In a writers group, when you explain your plot and characters, the listener gets it—they ask questions, make suggestions, they're involved—they get you!

In chapter 23, I will share with you how I found my local writers' group. I don't believe I'd be published without them. We need others who understand us, who encourage us.

Be an encourager yourself.

My own experience is that there is no real effort in life that is not done better under encouragement and approval of our fellow men.

—CHARLES M. SCHWAB

PART 4
emulate
success
while
being
yourself

20

friendships & relationships

> Comparison is the fast track to unhappiness. No one ever compares themselves to someone else and comes out even. Nine times out of ten, we compare ourselves to people who are somehow better than us and end up feeling more inadequate.
>
> **—JACK CANFIELD**

YOUR ORDINARY LIFE VS. THEIR FACEBOOK REEL

A bright new day dawns all shiny and new. You wake up eager to get to your work-in-progress. Sitting down to your desk with your morning cup of coffee, you start your writing program and check in on Facebook to see the latest happenings in your writer's world. Meghan Megastar has another book releasing today. How many is that so far this year? Three? Oh look, it's been released for about four hours and there are seventy-six reviews. Savannah Sellout is celebrating her recent book being on the Amazon Top 100 three days in a row. Brock Blockbuster signed a six-book contract and his agent sent him steaks. Cynthia Celebrity's big news, which she hinted at for weeks, can finally be shared: Her book was optioned for a movie. *Let's see, shall I post something this morning? Here's my cat.*

Wanting the same thing another person has isn't jealousy. It's natural. We don't wish we had that measure of success *instead* of them. We can be happy for them, proud of them, admire them. Sometimes acknowledging how hard a person worked for his achievement makes all the difference. Sometimes we do see that and still let our inadequacies get in the way. We have to acknowledge all of our feelings and make plans to reach similar goals.

Everyone feels inferior sometimes. But when we let those negative feelings influence our behavior, inferiority becomes a problem. Self-confidence is learned when we condition ourselves to believe we're as worthwhile and capable as the next person. It's time to break the cycle or, in other words, right feelings follow right actions. Behaving in a confident manner will slowly erode the negative beliefs you harbor about yourself. Acting confident gives our subconscious new feedback, negating those negative beliefs about ourselves.

Jealousy & Envy

Jealousy and envy are not the same. Jealousy is a negative emotion based on a person's fear that he's losing something, like time or attention from another, because of an activity, interest, or other friendships or relationships. This is how a friend or spouse might feel about you focusing on your writing, writing friends, conferences and travel, etc.

Envy is the desire to have another person's qualities, success, or possessions. Envy is the feeling that you lack something that could bring you happiness, fulfillment, or admiration. It's feelings of inadequacy that stem from comparing ourselves to others. Envious people often devalue the accomplishments of others.

Undoubtedly, you've experienced this type of devaluation in the form of petty criticism. Even if I don't enjoy another published person's writing, or if I think their skills need improvement, I give them credit for their success. Just because I think someone is a less-than-stellar writer doesn't mean they haven't found an audience and figured out how to sell their books. We all want that. But envy is destructive. We have to work on self-worth and not feel inferior in light of another person's achievements.

Write Smart, Write Happy

With whom are we competing? Sometimes it can seem as though we're competing with everyone. Before we're published, it seems as though we're competing for a spot in an agent or editor's stable of authors. We're entering contests and competing for approval from our peers. Others are getting the call, while our manuscripts are languishing on editors' desks for months. After we're published, we're competing for slots on publishers' schedules. We're competing for shelf space. We're competing for spots on the best-seller lists. We're competing for the reader's approval and dollar.

Perhaps we should change our thinking about yet another thing and complete only with ourselves. Challenge only our personal best.

Actress Marlo Thomas said, "Thoroughbreds run their own races."

I had friends who published ahead of me, and I was genuinely happy for them. We had critiqued together, and I knew how hard they'd worked and how good they were. I was still new enough that I didn't recognize others' envious reactions to those sales until later.

How do other writers' successes affect you? If you're feeling bad or resentful about someone's sales, earnings, or popularity, I recommend you find a new perspective. Another person's success doesn't take anything away from you or me. I don't write like that person in the number one slot. They don't write like me. But I understand that with dedication and the right story, it's possible for me to achieve the same recognition.

Understand this: There's nothing wrong with wanting the same thing someone else has. In fact, another writer's achievements can spur us to do better. Begrudging them success is a different thing. When I sold my first contemporary romance, one of my best friends said to me, "I'm envious as hell, but I'm so happy for you." She wasn't envious in a negative, bitter way; she just wanted the same thing for herself so badly she could smell it, taste it. We've all been there. And she was honest about it: honest with herself and honest with me. We're still close.

When I got a RITA nomination (the RITA is Romance Writers of America's prestigious published authors award) for that same book and told a different friend, one who had been a mentor to me, she said, "Oh, that's all just a good old boy game; they score the people they like high. If you're not popular, your book gets passed over. You're just lucky someone likes you." Coming from someone I considered a good friend, that devaluation of my achievement was hurtful. I understood her insecurity and forgave her, but sadly, the friendship fell by the wayside.

Jealousy and envy can destroy relationships. The bitterness is hurtful to the person envied—and for the person experiencing the envy, it can lead to shame, withdrawal, preoccupation, anger, and offensive behavior. True friends are happy for each other's achievements. Success doesn't threaten secure or sincere people. It's an unfortunate fact that success in this business quickly separates true friends from the others. Sometimes even the successful people see new writers' successes as a threat.

Once I started publishing regularly, I had a difficult lesson to learn: While I hadn't changed, others' perceptions of me and their attitudes toward me had. Being published can change the dynamics of a relationship. I wish this wasn't so. All we can do is learn to deal realistically with the envy that's directed toward us and understand it's not because of anything we did, but because of the other person's lack of confidence. What we can do is make sure we never fall into this pit ourselves.

We can all look at someone else and see something we want. That's normal. It's okay to want the same thing as your friend or that person in your writers group. Success is something to admire and strive for. It's something we all aim for and desire. But envy is bitterness, and bitterness will eat a person alive.

Remember: That successful author didn't sell a book or win a contest instead of you.

Publishing is a competitive business. Some authors believe teaching or mentoring is a threat to their livelihood. I see it as The Golden Rule. I believe with every fiber of my being that what goes around comes around. A lot of people helped me when I was starting out. Even if I shared every last thing I know about writing with another person, it wouldn't make them me. I've never hesitated to help someone improve her craft, because I know what that hunger to learn and improve is like.

I entered my share of contests before I was published. And sometimes I enter the RITA, and I've had a few books make the finals. It's okay to feel disappointed when you don't place or win in a contest. It's okay to feel disappointed that your manuscript was turned down. Disappointment is perfectly natural. But disappointment is not resentment and envy. Those are other things.

If your friend or chapter member has more success than you, you can still be genuinely happy for him. If you're on the *USA Today* bestseller's list and Nancy Nice is on *The New York Times*, give her credit for earning that position. She wouldn't be there if readers weren't buying her books in droves. Sure, you want the same status, but don't let her achievement keep you from working toward yours by entertaining a green-eyed monster. She earned those accolades. Congratulate her, and mean it. Then, move on. Plenty of people have successful careers without ever winning an award. Sometimes the ultimate satisfaction is in hearing from a reader who was deeply affected by your story. Sometimes the satisfaction is in accomplishing the task in the first place.

And somebody will always be doing it better—and with more skill, flair, or natural poise and style. We can't compare ourselves to others. If we do, we're asking for disappointment.

The world bombards us with visions of everything that will supposedly make us happy: an expensive car, a bigger house, an exotic trip or a cruise, a bigger income. In this age of social media, it's so easy to assume everyone else is zooming along at a million miles an hour, winning awards, effortlessly getting the right agent, landing the coveted multiple-book deal, having their books promoted in the publisher's catalog, seeing their book turned into a movie. But the more we want to be like that other person, the less confidence we have in our own strengths and abilities.

EMULATE SUCCESS WHILE BEING YOURSELF

If you've ever felt overwhelmed or experienced a lack of confidence, if you thought someone else was doing it all better or wondered what the heck you thought you were doing … you are not alone. In fact, you are in the majority. While writing this book, I discussed this topic with my tolerant and wise friends, and their input was honest and revealing. I used much of what I learned from them to address in this book the issues we all experience.

Throughout these chapters I've often mentioned my writer friends, critique partners, writing group—my friends. The act of writing is a solitary business. Writers probably spend a lot more time in their heads than they do with other humans. Books are mostly written by getting it wrong the first and second times and reworking them until we hope it's right. There's no measurement or scale to identify when a story is right. There's no feedback until it's out of our hands and with the editorial team—and eventually in the hands of readers and reviewers. We need the camaraderie, support, and encouragement of other writers, working relationships, and people who understand and think like us—people who are vulnerable, too, and really truly get us.

Your writing community can be your lifeline to sanity, and often to success. If you don't live in an area where there are local, like-minded writers who gather together, there are a multitude of online groups where you can find support and encouragement. Try a few until you find one or two that work for you.

Being confident is not the same as being conceited. People might mistake confidence for conceit at first, but true confidence is quickly revealed.

A confident person recognizes and credits those who've helped him reach his goals. Confident people know they have what it takes to get through any situation.

Conceited people are overcompensating for their insecurity. They crave praise and recognition to build up their low self-esteem. Conceited people let success define them, rather than defining themselves by the journey that developed character. A conceited person hasn't necessarily worked hard to get where she is, but she takes all the credit anyway.

Develop Strong Friendships & Relationships with Writers

My critique group formed nearly thirty years ago. Over the years, members moved away (I live in a city with an air base and military families) and others joined. One of our founders, who was like family, passed away a couple of years ago. After all these years of sharing our lives, dreams, disappointments, of helping each other, sharing meals, celebrating birthdays, encouraging each other and traveling together, we've grown very close.

Ideally, a writer should find other writers he trusts to share this journey with. It helps if you know their work ethic and their career goals, and believe they're committed to their writing and the group. Ideally, a beginning writer wants to find a mentor or a group with more experience than he has, but that's not always possible. There's nothing wrong with learning together. The group should have guidelines in place, a set schedule, and a location in which to meet.

It's easy to meet and develop relationships with writers online, as well. My rule for authors on social media is to be *social*. Authors who only post when they have a book out and want to promote it do not win friends or influence people. No one—not even loyal readers—want to see *Buy my book! Buy my book!* posts all the time.

This is exactly the reason I DVR everything I want to watch. I detest commercials and advertisements. I buy what I need and what I want, not what aggressive marketing wants to sell me. In fact, if you're a *Buy my book!* author, I've probably unfollowed you by now. These writers will say it's their page and they can talk about whatever they want—which is true—but we don't have to follow them and see it all the time. Turning you off and following someone else who's more interesting is as easy as *click*.

Trust me, I have hundreds of author friends and acquaintances. Those I enjoy and follow are the ones who interact, make a concerted effort to leave comments and likes, post pictures of everyday life, and engage readers. If I've followed and interacted with you and enjoyed your posts, I'll buy your book when you have a new one out.

You probably know some people who do this well, but here are examples of my author friends who do a great job of posting on Facebook:

- **DEBORAH RANEY:** Deborah posts photos of trips and grandchildren, but she also shares her home decorating, which is always in progress, and sets her posts apart from the hundreds of posts by other authors. She and her husband visit garage sales each week, and she posts the items she finds, then shows how she uses them in her decorating themes.
- **HOLLY JACOBS:** Holly has a glee theme, and posts about glee every Monday. She loves all things rustic and posts about her cabin

renovation, her gardening, cooking, and baking with homegrown ingredients—and her wood-chopping skills.

- **COLLETTE CAMERON:** Colette shares all things romantic, such as Victorian homes, vintage-style dresses, and quilts. She posts near-daily photos encouraging readers to choose their favorite items between jewelry, rooms, porches, and gowns.
- **MARY CONNEALY:** Mary's wit and self-deprecating humor keep readers chuckling. A rancher's wife, she shares photos of newborn calves and posts about life in the country. Her memories of growing up in a large family are touching.
- **RUTH LOGAN HERNE:** Ruthy exudes cheerfulness and energy all day long. Her posts of daycare children, grandkids, early morning writing sprints, farming, baking, and faith demonstrate her zest for life and love for people.

Interaction is the key. Read your time line and take an interest. Comment on posts. Commenting or liking keeps that person's posts in your feed—and it's social. It's friendly. Ignoring others but wanting attention is not social. It's arrogant. Do you remember that saying, *to have a friend, be a friend*? This philosophy should be your rule of thumb on Facebook or any other social media platform.

Writers are everywhere. It's not that difficult to find them and form relationships. Be a friend. Be yourself.

IN THEIR OWN WORDS

"Many years ago I met Stephanie Bond and Beth Harbison at a local writers' group. We recognized a spark in each other that drew us into a lifelong friendship and career-focused support group. We met in food courts, in libraries, and in homes every week without fail. We accepted no excuses for not bringing fresh material every meeting. We attended writers conferences together and educated each other on the business of writing as much as the craft. It took more than a year of this, but one by one, each of us sold our first book.

Our critique group had some basic rules: Write to publish. Rewrite to make your work the best you can. Always be honest with each other about the work. Always listen to what is said (there was a strict no whining, no arguing, no trying to explain why during a critique) and even if you don't agree with it, respect the opinions of others.

These things prepared us for the good and bad of a lifetime of creative success.

All of us went on to be best-selling authors and remain supportive of each other to this day. My best advice is to find someone who shares your passion for the goal, keep at it, learn and share what you learn, be honest, listen, and write, write, write.

Good mentoring can come from a person or a team but either way, it can make all the difference and serve you your entire career and beyond."

—Annie Jones, author of *The House on Dream Away Bay* and The Christmas Sister series.

What You Can Do Today

- If you recognize any negative behaviors or attitudes in yourself, make a decision now to remove them from your life. Don't let anything hold you back from being the best you can be.
- Make a list of the people you admire.
- Include the behaviors and talents you recognize that helped the people you admire get where they are.
- Make a list of thoughts and behaviors you want to change.
- Make a list of why you want to change. This is even more important to figure out.
- Make another list of how an improved attitude will advance your writing, your energy, and your ambition. Writing things down and referring back to them helps you check progress and hold yourself accountable. It also helps you remember your objectives.
- Take time to meditate on how you're going to think differently about the successful writers you know. Write it down.
- Make yourself note cards as reminders of the above and place them on your mirror or above the sink or at your desk.
- Use self-talk to encourage yourself.

21

using others' success as your catalyst

Audrey Hepburn is revered for both her acting skills and her philanthropic efforts as a UNICEF ambassador, making her one of the most notable female role models. With a life devoted to kindness and compassion, Audrey devoted herself to being a mother, a wife, and a humanitarian.

—CHRIS HAIGH, ON LIFEHACK.ORG

ROLE MODELS

We don't want to compare our lives or our careers to anyone else's, but it's helpful to develop good role models. We won't imitate a role model's every move, but when we see how well their method is working, we can apply the same techniques. We might see a pattern of work ethic that's panning out for another writer, so we try it out in an effort to improve our own routine.

Looking to my community of authors, I see many who have proven methods that they've shared. Inspiration is one of the great things about networking and sharing information. It's great to be inspired and to find motivation.

Years ago, one of my chapter members decided she was going to write to sell. In our group, we study and teach *Techniques of the Selling Writer* by Dwight V. Swain. But beyond her dedication to the craft, she set herself on a track to accomplish the things she wanted to see happen. She researched imprints and editors, and their guidelines, and came up with list of agents and editors to target. To make the time for all of this, she dropped extraneous activities from her life. She worked a full-time job, writing on weekends and editing during her lunch hours. With so much intense determination focused on her goal, it wasn't a big surprise that she got a book contract and continues to sell books. She always used her weekends for writing, often at the expense of fun activities. She has since retired from her day job and remains every bit as focused.

Another good friend joined my chapter having never written a word. But she had done her research, and by that I mean she had familiarized herself with the writing industry, educated herself on editors at specific publishing houses, knew word counts for various imprints and publishers, studied what publishers were looking for, and set out to find a niche.

Over a year or two she tried a few things that didn't work for her. She submitted manuscripts and was asked to revise them. Eventually she sold a book and continues to sell well. She could write a book on self-discipline and be the shining example. I admire her tenacity, energy, and focus. Even with setbacks and frustrations like imprints folding, illnesses in the family, and other life circumstances, she consistently and deliberately moves forward, beyond the challenges. She replans, replots, and rewrites with her final destination firmly in her mind.

Because we reach and move through different stages in our writing life, it stands to reason we will want to change our role models as we progress. A role model should reflect the level of self-discipline or success we want to reach. Learn enough about your chosen role model so that you can emulate her actions. Your role models can come from anywhere and aren't restricted to writers. Maybe you admire an athlete or a teacher. The point is to study the actions of someone who is focused and moving forward in her thinking or career, someone whose performance makes you want to stretch your own. And remember, you're not comparing yourself to this person or her work. You're simply looking for a similar dynamic that works for you.

If you have the opportunity, talk to writers who have careers of the sort you desire. Ask about goals and work habits. If you can't speak with authors you admire in person, you can still learn about their careers and study their books. Watch their presentations and talks online, if they've done that sort of thing. Read the author's entire body of work, in order of publication to see how their writing has evolved. Don't copy their books, but do copy their work ethic. Create goals and a time line for how you will achieve similar accomplishments.

You're reaching for self-discipline, and self-disciplined people focus on their goals. They concentrate on one task at a time. And this is a hard one: self-disciplined people set aside instant pleasure to attain the long-term achievement. It's always easier to kick back and watch television than it is to write 500 words at your desk. But you can certainly reward yourself with your favorite shows once the words are written. Once we have our priorities set, we need to keep them in front of us.

Laura Landon, a successful writer friend of mine, doesn't even own a television because she doesn't want the distraction. Now, that's discipline! Self-disciplined people don't make excuses.

Standing desks have become popular for improving posture and productivity, but Hemingway did it first. It seems there is nothing new under the sun. Though Ernest had a perfectly good desk in his large upstairs bedroom, he wrote standing before a cluttered bookcase on a chest-high typewriter.

In 1958, George Plimpton interviewed Hemingway, who said, "When I am working on a book or a story, I write every morning as soon after first light as possible. There is no one to disturb you and it is cool or cold and you come to your work and warm as you write. You read what you have written and, as you always stop when you know what is going to happen next, you go on from there. You write until you come to a place where you still have your juice and know what will happen next and you stop and try to live through until the next day when you hit it again."

Plimpton's article also says, "[Hemingway] keeps track of his daily progress—'so as not to kid myself'—on a large chart made out of the side of a cardboard packing case and set up against the wall under the nose of a mounted gazelle head. The numbers on the chart showing the daily output of words differ from 450, 575, 462, 1,250, back to 512, the higher figures on days Hemingway puts in extra work so he won't feel guilty spending the following day fishing on the Gulf Stream."

A multitude of writers admire Stephen King's writing and his career, and I'm one of them. I think the man is a creative genius. I've read my favorites of his books multiple times. *On Writing* is on my desk right now. King said, "You cannot hope to sweep someone else away by the force of your writing until it has been done to you." I don't write like him, and I don't aspire to. I don't even write in the same genre. But his writing has swept me away, and I aspire to sweep others away in the same manner. Therefore, his creativity and his writing process are influential.

In a 2010 interview, Ray Bradbury said, "My passions drive me to the typewriter every day of my life, and they have driven me there since I was twelve. So I never have to worry about schedules. Some new thing is always exploding in me, and it schedules me, I don't schedule it. It says: *Get to the typewriter right now and finish this.*

"I can work anywhere," Bradbury continues. "I wrote in bedrooms and living rooms when I was growing up with my parents and my brother in a small house in Los Angeles. I worked on my typewriter in the living room, with the radio and my mother and dad and brother all talking at the same time. Later on, when I wanted to write *Fahrenheit 451*, I went up to UCLA and found a basement typing room where, if you inserted ten cents into the typewriter, you could buy thirty minutes of typing time."

Now that's a driven writer. I admire that drive and his excitement over getting the story down.

Huffington Post did a slideshow on the writers and books that influenced successful authors. J.K. Rowling was a voracious reader as a youngster. Her favorite stories included *The Little White Horse* by Elizabeth Goudge and *Manxmouse* by Paul Gallico, the latter being a story about a creature with a mouse's body, rabbit's ears, and monkey's paws. She also appreciated *The Lion, the Witch and the Wardrobe* by C.S. Lewis. Not difficult to see those influences in her books, is it?

We have choices when it comes to feeling inadequate. Desiring the same thing another person has isn't jealousy, it's a natural inclination. We don't begrudge that person's accomplishment. We can be happy for her, proud of her, and admire her. We should acknowledge all of our feelings and make plans to reach similar goals. Sometimes we see others' achievements and recognition and let our inadequacies get in the way. But acknowledging how hard a person worked for their accomplishment makes all the difference.

If you want to pursue a career similar to another writer, there are a few things you should consider. First, make sure this person is writing the same type of books you are, in the same genre, and that their audience is the audience you desire. Don't follow in the steps of a romance writer if you want to write westerns. Find a western writer who is doing what you want to do and learn from their methods. There are listservs and Facebook groups for every genre of writers. Seek them out and listen in. Every listerv has an archive of all the previous discussions. Search and read topics in the archives that apply to you.

The Good Mentor

A good mentor is willing to share his knowledge and experiences. He remembers what it's like to be a newbie. He takes the time to read and evaluate your material. A good mentor respects your ideas, feels invested in your vision, and doesn't try to change your story to one he would write. He points out the things you do well and gives constructive feedback without being critical.

A good mentor has a positive attitude and is a positive role model. You respect his body of work and the way he interacts with others. He has solid relationships with other writers and publishers. He's well respected in the writing community. He's walked the road ahead of you and is willing to warn you of the curves and drop-offs.

A good mentor communicates techniques in a way you can understand and does so kindly. She empowers you to develop your strengths, your voice, and momentum without being discouraging or wanting you to write the way she writes.

A good mentor is excited about your genre. Someone who writes in another genre can read your work for content, advise on sentence structure, grammar, pacing, and techniques, but if he doesn't share your love of your specific genre, he may miss things or not understand specific nuances. This relationship will work, but remember he's not reading or critiquing with the same eye as someone who loves—and is thoroughly familiar with—your genre.

A good mentor makes a good example by being a lifelong student of the writing craft himself. He continues to stretch his abilities, and to improve and grow. He sets both personal and professional goals.

A good mentor values other writer's and instructor's opinions, accomplishments, and ideas. He doesn't criticize to puff himself up. Your success is his success. Don't copy the work of someone you admire; do emulate their steps to success by figuring out how they came to be in that place.

How to Find a Mentor

A mentor works with you hands-on, makes an investment in your education and craft improvement. If you want a mentor, you want a writer whose work ethic you admire, a person you trust to give you solid advice. A mentor who shares your same values as well as overlapping interests is valuable.

If you want someone who will read your pages and give you critiques, a time commitment is required. It's a big commitment, so it's no wonder good mentors can be difficult to come by.

To find a mentor, you must become connected.

- Join a writing organization.
- Facebook and Yahoo! Groups have places to share writing and find contacts.
- Courses at community colleges are led by writers who know other writers.
- Attend workshops and conferences.
- Join NaNoWriMo and locate the forums.

IN THEIR OWN WORDS

"I've had many mentors over the years, some in person, some on-line, and some through workshops or writing how-to books. The first author I ever met in person became both a mentor and great friend. We hit it off right away, and through her example, through long talks about this crazy business of writing fiction, through sharing our struggles and triumphs, she helped me navigate this winding road of publication.

"Some people have mentored me without even being aware of it, as I have read their blog posts, visited their websites, read their books on writing, and sat in on their classes. James Scott Bell, Debra Dixon, and Margie Lawson come to mind. Each has had a hand in mentoring me by sharing their hard-won knowledge online and in books on the writing craft.

"I've also been mentored by authors who write great fiction. By studying their work, I've learned what I liked and didn't, new techniques, and the subtleties of characterization. Great mentors abound, and if you can't find one in person, 'adopt' one or more online or through their writings."

—Erica Vetsch, author of *The Cactus Creek Challenge*

"Several people have greatly influenced my writing life. I used to be a book reviewer. When Julia Quinn got started, I reviewed her first book, *Splendid*. She thanked me for writing a 'splendid review' (pun intended), and she complimented my writing and told me I should, and could, write novels. So I did and then promptly stuck it in a trunk for fourteen years. When I pulled it out, it was published (a time travel written under the pen name, Geralyn Beauchamp) with a small press owned by Peter Honsberger. Peter taught me to believe in myself and to just keep writing. 'Tell yourself you deserve everything your hard work produces. Always strive to improve your craft, and you'll make it, kid,' he used to say.

"Author Julie Lessman loved that same book enough to give it to her agent, who read the book and told me she had no doubt one of the big five publishers would pick me up one day. She also said I had raw talent that needed to be honed and a lack of self-confidence that needed to improve. Lack of self-confidence, more than anything else, held me back.

"So, what did those people teach me? That you can be the best writer in the world, but if you don't believe in yourself, what good is it? You can have talent, but if you don't believe you deserve the rewards it can bring you, then what? In essence, you become your own worst enemy prone to self-sabotage. Learn to separate the facts, *through hard work you can become the best writer you can be,* from the feelings, *I'm not good enough! I don't deserve this!* Learn to deal with your emotions and let nothing hold you back."

—Kit Morgan, author of the Prairie Bride, Prairie Groom, and Mail-Order Bride Ink series.

PART 5
conquering fear

22

releasing perfectionism

Do not wish to be anything but what you are, and try to be that perfectly.

—ZEN SAYING

PARALYZING PERFECTIONISM

Perfectionism ties in with being too analytical. It's the fear of not doing a good enough job. We all want to write the perfect book to attract a publisher and a couple million readers. We want our stories to be the best we can make them. But when you're a perfectionist, you're never happy. Perfectionists are easily frustrated, angered, and discouraged. They need everything exactly so but can never achieve their idealistic expectations, so they become discouraged and give up.

Perfectionists are constantly disappointed—with themselves, others, and situations—and that's no way to live. Perfectionists are their own worst critics. It's not easy to change the habits of self-criticism and judgment, but if this is you, you already know you have to give yourself some slack, remove the pressure, and free yourself to write with abandon.

Perfectionism is yet another fear. It's a paralyzing fear, and it's made up of "what if" possibilities. *What if I write this book and no one likes it? What if it's rejected? What if I look like a fool? What if I'm no good? What if it's published and people think it's about me?* To combat this doubt and second-guessing, we must think more positively and change our thoughts. Instead of the debilitating "what ifs" listed above, you need to change that voice in your head, change those thoughts to, *What if an editor loves this book? What if readers love this book? What if I see my book at Walmart or the library one day? What if I feel good about myself once I've accomplished this achievement?*

It's tough being a perfectionist. I know. Perfectionists see the fault in everything. They have a difficult time letting anything go until it's perfect. But there is no *perfect* in writing. We can edit a book until the end of time, and it will never be satisfactorily perfect. The best we can do is enough. The best we can do at the time is all we're capable of. Sometimes you just have to let it go.

I was a perfectionist, usually a discouraged one. I've made my husband crazy with my obsessive need for alignment, even proportions and flawless paint jobs, to name a couple of things. I'm one of those place-for-everything-and-everything-in-its-place people, so I understand perfectionism. Now I call myself a recovering perfectionist.

Our finished manuscripts should be as perfect as we can make them, no doubt about it. This is a competitive market. But perfectionism has no place in the early drafts of our work. It has no place in our creative outbursts, brainstorming, or outlining. What is perfection in fiction anyway? What I enjoy, someone else won't. Two people will look at the same book and see it differently. I may write something I think is perfect, but the copyeditor thinks it needs improvement. What matters is the *doing*—putting one word after another until the book is finished.

Thinking we have to be perfect keeps us from attempting to write in the first place. Perfectionism kills creativity and puts a strain on your self-worth. It will suck the life out of your voice and make you crazy. If we can't be happy until we've done everything perfectly, until we've made everyone else happy, then we will never be happy. Those are unattainable expectations.

When you're feeling the pressure of perfectionism, remind yourself:

- Making mistakes doesn't mean I'm a failure.
- Being less than perfect doesn't mean I can't succeed.
- I'm human; I give myself permission to make mistakes.
- If I make a mistake, I get a do-over.
- I'll start, even if it won't be perfect the first time.
- I expect excellence from myself, but not perfection.
- I will learn to be patient with myself; I'll get there.
- I'll treat myself kindly, not critically.
- Obstacles happen and we all have bad days; I won't judge myself harshly.
- I'll share my fear of falling short with someone I trust and get a new perspective.

The thing that is really hard, and really amazing, is giving up on being perfect and beginning the work of becoming yourself.

—ANNA QUINDLEN, PULITZER PRIZE-WINNER

IN THEIR OWN WORDS

"What have I gotten myself into, trying to create an image I can't possibly live up to? That was me. When the image fell through due to negative book reviews, which I made the mistake of taking to heart instead of stepping back and looking at them objectively, so did my confidence. At that point, all I wanted to do was quit writing. Take the easy way out. That way, people wouldn't know I wasn't perfect. Or so I thought.

"My love for writing, however, had other ideas. It wouldn't let me quit. It took falling off my high horse to finally figure out that perfection was highly overrated and something I would never achieve because there is no such thing. *Perfect* is only a word in the dictionary. Pleasing everyone, including myself wasn't going to happen at the level I had set for myself. So what was I going to do about my dilemma?

"How was I going to get over the mind-set that insisted every word and story I wrote had to be perfect or it wasn't going to get written? Question after question raced through my mind like a racehorse on speed. What if I wrote as if I was the only one who was going to read it? Would I have the freedom to write without questioning every word I typed? All I could do was try. And you know what? It worked. As soon as I started writing for an audience of one, the stress of writing lifted. Now, when perfectionism tries to rear its ugly head and I start stressing over every little word and detail, I pause, take a deep breath, and remind myself that I am writing because I love it—and *perfection* really is just a word in the dictionary."

—Debra Ullrick, author of the Love Inspired Bowen Brides series

Recognize the differences in striving for excellence and being bound by perfectionism.

BOUND BY PERFECTIONISM	STRIVING FOR EXCELLENCE
Being motivated by your writing goals	Feeling anxious or fearful about your goals
Procrastinating because you're not ready	Excited to jump in and edit and learn as you go
Being dissatisfied and convinced your words aren't good enough	Celebrating and giving yourself credit
Getting bogged down in a word or small detail	Plunging forward planning to correct words later
Neglecting personal life and family	Balancing your writing and family life
Mistakes feel like failures	Laughing it off and learning from mistakes
Obsessing over mistakes you made before	Moving on with the intent of improving
Do it perfectly or don't do it at all	I'm proud of doing the best I can
Getting stuck in analysis paralysis	Preparing and knowing I can rewrite it later

Encourage yourself by going back and looking at your list of things you do well. If you didn't work on your list previously, do it now. Readers won't enjoy your stories because they're perfect. They'll enjoy them because of the characters you developed and emotions you portrayed in a realistic way. Readers would never know I wrote a depressing first draft of a novel (*Sequins and Spurs*, Harlequin Historical), and then tore it apart and rewrote it, unless they've read this book. Readers don't know and don't care that we don't get it perfect the first time or the second time. They simply want to be transported into your story world.

Are You Too Analytical?

If you over-analyze, over-think, or over-plan, you're too analytical. Do you worry over a thought to the point that you confuse yourself, not to mention others? Do you take something simple and complicate it? Those who overanalyze accept nothing at face value. They look for ulterior motives, back-up plans, and secondary issues. They pass up a perfectly good word in search of the elusive, all-encompassing "better" word. If this is you, you make other people crazy! Do you know that?

I have a good friend who is an excellent writer. A few years into writing, I recognized that she was editing and revising and thinking her stories to death. She would go back over the same paragraphs and pages so many times that they were unrecognizable the next time I saw them.

While it's always good to use the best word possible, obsessive perfectionism takes the spontaneity and freshness out of narrative and dialogue. I pointed this out to my friend, and she took it to heart. The chapters that followed were gems, containing great dialogue and her unique voice. By editing and tweaking and fixing until she reached what she thought was perfection, she had been draining the life out of her copy. In being too analytical, a writer can lose the fresh spontaneity of their voice

Raise your hand if this is you: A small detail will hold up the completion of a scene. A bit of elusive research puts a halt to your day's writing until the fact is found. You rewrite dialogue ten or twenty times to get it just right. You rewrite narrative and replace words with better words and use your synonym finder and reconstruct sentences until they are—yes—perfect.

The act of relinquishing perfectionism takes work. Try writing free-flow for ten or fifteen minutes without editing or looking back. Or try a writing session on an AlphaSmart (word processing keyboard)—the machine has only a small window, showing four lines of text, so you can't keep looking back and fixing things. My critique partner, *lizzie starr, changes her Word font to white and writes freeflow. I had never heard of that technique until she told me about it. These exercises can help you get out of the habit of crippling yourself by overthinking or editing a piece to certain death.

Behaviors are only things we do, they're not who we are. They are subject to change.

We can do things differently to arrive at different results.

Don't misunderstand me. Writers *are* rewriters. We edit. We adjust sentences. We reread and tweak. But if you're going back over the same thing countless times, it's possible you're stripping away every ounce of spontaneity and replacing your voice with what you *think* is a better voice.

A Writer Has to Grow Into Her Voice

I never knew I had a voice until my editor told me after I'd written about four books. "Really? I have a voice? Wow, who knew?" Voice is your personality on the page. It's your phrasing, word choices, and the way you string sentences together. It's your worldview. You don't have to *think* about it. When you're being real, it just happens.

A voice is developed: It takes work, effort, time and a lot of crappy throwaway pages. A writer can't actually edit their "voice" into their writing. When my editor mentioned I had a Hemingwayesque style, I wrote it down and then had to figure out what she meant. Put simply (no pun intended): I don't use flowery language or beat around the bush. It's kind of like me in person. If there's a straightforward way to say it or do it, that's what I do.

Write Smart, Write Happy

If you aren't improving, growing, or selling, consider this one crucial aspect of writing: If you keep writing new material and are mature enough to recognize that you didn't know it all three, five, or ten years ago, your writing actually improves.

In one form or another, fear is probably the number one culprit that keeps us from going after our dreams. Fear is often insidious, disguised as procrastination or poor time management, but it can be debilitating in any form. The first step to overcoming fear is to figure out exactly what it is that scares you.

Are you afraid of trying to write because you might find out you may not be as good as you thought? Are you concerned you might give it your all and never get published? Recognizing that something is holding you back is a huge step. Now take another step and figure out exactly what it is you're worried will happen.

Start by understanding this: The first thing you write won't be publishable. Neither will the first book, most likely. (Okay, it does happen.) And, most likely, neither will the second. But you will never learn, never grow, or never know that you can, until you put words on paper. It took me a long time to figure this out, but once I did, it was a revelation.

Read this until this reality sinks in for you: *They are only words. You can write more.* Realizing this was a breakthrough for me. Comprehending that words are replenishable is a sign of maturing in your craft.

Say it out loud: "They are only words. I can write more." If they're not great, you can toss them out and come up with different ones. There are plenty more words where those came from. Thousands, millions, in all sorts of combinations and patterns. And, you don't have to get them all right the first time.

Now, that's liberating.

Whenever a new member joins my RWA chapter or my critique group, I understand their nervousness. I was in their shoes once. I make it a point to tell them, "We all started out in the same place."

Action Steps

Find a couple of instrumental movie soundtracks. If you don't have any, you can check them out from the library, find them online, listen on Spotify or Pandora, or ask your Echo to play them for you. Instrumentals are best, something like *Cloud Atlas, Avatar, The Moon-Spinners, Last of the Mohicans, Titanic, Gladiator, Pirates of the Caribbean: At World's End, The Chronicles of Narnia, The Hunger Games,* or *Romeo and Juliet.*

Clear a half hour or forty-five minutes on your schedule, find a writing place that works for you, turn on the music, and let it show you shapes, people, and colors. Allow yourself to imagine what is happening as the music plays, and write it down. Now, as Drew Carey would say on *Whose Line Is It Anyway?*, "The points don't matter." No one is going to see what you put on the page. The points are like the talent portion of a beauty contest. The points are like pants to a tollbooth operator. Grammar, spelling, typos are out the window. Simply find a story in the music and write it without thinking, analyzing, or plotting. Just see a scene and get it on the page.

What I want you to take away from this exercise is that it's okay to do things haphazardly or, if you will, *imperfectly.* First drafts don't have to be finished products. They're only words. You can delete them. You can change and rearrange them. You can write more.

LISTEN TO MUSIC

Stephanie Ludwig, public relations manager of the Omaha Symphony Orchestra, local writer, and friend, compiled the following list of music she listens to while writing. "[The music I listen to] really depends on the scene I'm writing. [I choose something that will] get me in the right frame of mind and do the scene justice. I'm not a fan of songs with lyrics while I'm writing, because I find myself listening to their words instead of my own. I listen to most of my music on Spotify, so some of the music is on playlists as opposed to an album.

"Most of the movie soundtracks are either movies I've seen or that were recommended to me. I was exposed to much of this music through the symphony. In fact, I listen to most of our repertoire for upcoming concerts before I write a press release, so I know how to promote it properly. Subsequently, a lot of the music ends on my personal writing playlist."

Groups/Composers

- 2Cellos
- Dallas String Quartet
- Lindsey Stirling
- The Piano Guys
- Michael Giacchino
- Coldplay
- Norah Jones
- Emmy Rossum
- James Newton Howard
- James Horner
- John Williams
- Thomas Newman
- Alexandre Desplat
- John Ottman
- John Powell
- Howard Shore
- Enaid
- Oisin Mac Diarmada (Irish fiddle)
- Brian Bigley (Irish pipes)
- Vitamin String Quartet

Classical

- Tchaikovsky
- Rachmaninoff: Piano Concerto No. 2 and Rhapsody on a Theme of Paganini
- Aaron Copland: Appalachian Spring, Rodeo, Fanfare for the Common Man
- Beethoven: Symphony No. 2, Symphony No. 3 "Eroica," Symphony No. 6 "Pastoral," Moonlight Sonata, Fur Elise
- Respighi: The Pines of Rome
- Berlioz: Symphonie Fantastique
- Mendelssohn: A Midsummer Night's Dream
- Ravel: Mother Goose

- Rimsky-Korsakov: Scheherazade
- Gershwin: Rhapsody in Blue, An American in Paris
- Vivaldi: The Four Seasons
- Shostakovich: Festive Overture (referenced in my symphony mystery!)
- Joshua Bell: French Impressions (piano and violin album)

Soundtracks

- *Poldark*
- *Outlander* (each season/volume)
- *W.E.*
- *Far from the Madding Crowd*
- *The Piano*, Mark Nyman composer
- *Pride and Prejudice*, Dario Marianelli composer (the Keira Knightley version)
- *North and South*, Bill Conti composer
- *The Man from U.N.C.L.E.*
- *Anna Karenina*, Dario Marianelli composer
- *Jane Eyre*, Dario Marianelli composer
- *How to Train Your Dragon*
- *Robin Hood*, Marc Streitenfeld composer
- *In the Heart of the Sea*
- *Thor*, Patrick Doyle composer
- *Wonder Woman*
- *The Last of the Mohicans*
- *Cinderella*, Patrick Doyle composer
- *Miss Fisher's Murder Mysteries*
- *Robin Hood*, Prince of Thieves
- *The Incredibles*
- *Up*
- *The Lord of the Rings* trilogy (*The Fellowship of the Ring*, *The Two Towers*, *The Return of the King*)
- *Dragonheart*
- *Gladiator*
- *Pearl Harbor*
- *Strictly Ballroom*
- *Titanic*
- *The Tudors*
- *The 13th Warrior*
- *1491: The Conquest for Paradise*
- *Superman Returns*

proudly wearing your badges of honor

Success is not final, failure is not fatal: it is the courage to continue that counts.

—WINSTON CHURCHILL

Years ago, after my kids were all in school, my brother knew I was writing, and he brought me a newspaper article featuring a published author whose husband had been transferred to the Air Force base in my city. This woman was forming a Romance Writers of America chapter. I'd never heard of RWA. I was too inexperienced and uncertain—fearful and insecure, in truth—to even call the contact number. I was so afraid that I let another year pass before I saw that one of the chapter members was featured in the Sunday paper. My brother brought me that article, too, and said, "You're working in a vacuum. You need to get with these people."

It took me weeks to get the courage to call that phone number. When I did, I got an answering machine. Understand that back then only businesses had answering machines, and there was no such thing as voice mail. When I heard that recording, I promptly hung up. I was completely out of my league. I knew that I'd be stepping into a world of history and English majors—all professionals of course—and who was I? Just little old me, making up stories after my kids went to bed. Fear held me back. Fear of not measuring up, not being good enough.

Well, I was getting nowhere fast on my own, so eventually I did find the courage. I made the call and left a message. The woman called me back, and she was warm, welcoming, and delightful. I went to my first meeting with my knees knocking. It wasn't long before I discovered everyone there was someone like me—someone just making up stories for the pure love of it. There was a lawyer, a news reporter, a criminal justice teacher, an English teacher, a couple of Air Force wives, teachers, stay-at-home moms, and others from all walks of life.

Months later I finally showed a manuscript to that founding member—a published author. She took my manuscript home and returned it at the next meeting. She took me aside to a table and explained her critique in a kind and instructional manner. When I went home and looked at it, I discovered she'd crossed out page after page, repeatedly writing *nothing happening* in red in the margins. Eventually I understood she was right, but boy howdy, that hurt.

But she also showed me the things I did well, and showed me how to change and fix and rework the story. She was the first person who said to me, "You can do this."

To this day, I'm grateful that Diane Wicker Davis took the time to show a beginner what she was doing right and where she needed to improve. She was a warm Southern lady who mentored other writers and shared her knowledge. She passed away several years ago, and everyone who knew her remembers her laugh and her encouragement. Diane had a dramatic impact on my life. She's one of the reasons I pay it forward. Everyone starts this journey from the same place. I know exactly what it feels like to be uncertain, inexperienced, and out of place.

I pushed on after her critique, learning, studying, and rewriting, until a few years had slipped by and a stack of rejections piled up. I became so frustrated and so hungry for an agent or editor to assure me I could do this thing. Diane had assured me. My critique partners had as well. But I had to keep believing in myself. I had to remind myself why I wanted this and why I wouldn't be satisfied if I quit. Eventually, an agent told me she believed she could sell my story, and that validation was worth all the effort.

EMBARRASSMENT

It's time for some more honesty. Fear of embarrassment is actually your pride getting the best of you. We all had to start somewhere. We all wrote crap when we first started—most of us did, anyway. When babies first learn to feed themselves and walk, we don't make fun of them; they don't know any better. You didn't get on a bicycle the first time and smoothly take off. Training wheels aren't embarrassing to a four-year-old. Why do we think our first attempts at writing are humiliating? You have to be willing to make mistakes. You have to be willing to write poorly.

Fear held me back from attending that writers' group for the first time. I'd have found help and encouragement sooner if I hadn't held back for so long. Once I was there, I was timid about sharing my writing. I was self-taught, after all. I had learned what little I knew by reading outdated books in the library, by buying extra copies of my favorite books and highlighting sentence structure, viewpoint changes, and narrative. I subscribed to *Writer's Digest* magazine and checked out the annual edition of *Writer's Market* from the library. I never took a writing class or spoke with a published author. I was intimidated by the longer-standing members in our group.

Courage is not the absence of fear, but rather the judgment that something else is more important than fear.

—MEG CABOT

You Have to be Willing to be Bad

Trying something new or different can feel scary. When you're starting out, the odds of doing it wrong are pretty good. When I look back at the first manuscripts I actually submitted, I cringe. When I gave Diane

Wicker Davis that first manuscript, it was chock-full of mistakes. I had thoroughly researched a religious sect founded by a group called the Harmonists. My research was fascinating, and by learning all there was to know, I could put my characters right into the setting and describe it vividly.

But I went on and on about the dimensions of a bell tower. A fact no one needed to know, and worse, no one cared about. To add flavor to the story, the bell needed to ring at certain times of the day. That's all. I overdid it by immersing myself in research.

I had no idea how to get my story people from one place to another or move from one scene to the next, so I had them do mundane things like walk to another room or go to bed at night and wake up. No one needs to know that kind of thing. Everyone goes from room to room, everyone goes to bed, sleeps, and wakes up. I hadn't yet grasped the concept of moving from one scene to another with a hook and a drop down, then skipping over the rest. But that was okay, because I had written one hundred thousand words from beginning to end.

In the process of writing all those pages, I'd learned my best hours of productivity, how to delegate household tasks, and how to let go of perfection regarding those tasks. I'd learned that, as difficult as it was, I'd thoroughly enjoyed the process of writing that story. The most important lesson I learned was that I could accomplish something huge: I'd finished the book I'd set out to write. It wasn't great, it definitely wasn't salable, but I'd done it.

- Understand that when you undertake an unfamiliar task, you won't master it immediately. It's going to take some time to figure it out.
- Acknowledge that you're going to make mistakes.
- You don't have to do this alone. Others have gone before you, and while no one can tell you how to write your stories, other writers can give you tips and suggestions. What works for one person won't work for another, but we won't know until we try.
- Never compare your writing, your voice, or your pace to anyone else's.
- Compare what you've done today to what you did last week or last year.

In this book that I'd written, my mentor pointed out chapters that needed work. She also pointed out scenes she thought were good. I had included excessive amounts of research that had to go. I had a one hundred thousand–word manuscript to rewrite and make better.

Remember what I said in an earlier chapter: You can fix bad. You can't fix nothing.

My first book was rejected multiple times before I sold a different book and then contracted the first one. So as it turns out, I had something I could fix.

Rejection Is Not Failure

I have missed more than nine thousand shots in my career. I have lost almost three hundred games. On twenty-six occasions, I have been entrusted to take the game winning shot, and I missed. I have failed over and over and over again in my life. And that is why I succeed.

—MICHAEL JORDAN

According to CHMC Mental Health Center, a fixed mind-set leads to a desire to look smart, and therefore a tendency to avoid challenges and give up easily. This mind-set will ignore useful negative feedback. A growth mind-set leads to a desire to learn and a desire to embrace challenges and persevere in the face of setbacks. This person learns from criticism.

In the book *Mindset*, Stanford neuropsychologist Carol Dweck explains the differences between these two attitudes toward failure. Her research team gave children easy puzzles. After completing them, the children were given the choice of redoing the same puzzle or trying a more difficult one. Those with the fixed mind-set opted to redo the same puzzle, while children with the growth mind-set were excited to try a new one.

Is this mind-set changeable? Of course! By taking the steps to develop positive thinking, by rerouting your thought processes, by gaining confidence, by working on self-esteem, and by taking satisfaction in doing your best, you can do much to alter a fixed mind-set.

There's a funny meme made from two screenshots of *Pirates of the Caribbean: Curse of the Black Pearl*. Lieutenant James Norrington says: "You are without a doubt the worst writer I've ever heard of." Captain Jack Sparrow: "But you have heard of me."

Of course, in the film, Norrington says *pirate* in place of *writer*, but you get the point. This makes me laugh every time I see it. Jack is a the-cup-is-half-full kind of fellow.

FEAR OF SUCCESS

This might sound ridiculous to some, but fear of success can be crippling to motivation and progress. Why? The unknown. *If I sell a book, will I be able to do it again? What will people think?*

Make a list of the fears that are holding you back:

- *I am in an academic or male-dominated business. What if my employer or co-workers find out I am writing romance/science fiction/ you-name-it?* A pseudonym might be best for you. You can keep your two careers separate.
- *What if my mother/family is shocked or disappointed that I write graphic murder mysteries or sex scenes?* Most likely, people will not be shocked. If your mother or family is extremely conservative and doesn't know this is your genre, you can either talk to her about it first, deal with her disappointment, or don't tell her at all.
- *What if my spouse is unsupportive of my time commitment to writing groups and conferences?* I've seen spouses eventually come around and encourage the writer, and I've seen the writer who abandons her writing ambition to please her partner. I'm not a marriage counselor or a therapist, but I know enough to understand the perceived threat your writing is to that person. Anything that redirects your time and attention may be cause for feelings of jealousy. It's human

nature. Some writers have support from the beginning, but for others, it's a struggle.

My suggestion is to include your spouse and family in your excitement. Share your goals, the things you're learning; share where you see this taking you, where you'd like to be in a year or ten years. Let your spouse see that your goals aren't diminishing your primary relationship. Involve them at each step, and hopefully they'll want to be part of your journey. Balance family and work, and nurture the important relationships. If your spouse isn't onboard before you're successful, eventual support won't mean much afterward and may become a true point of conflict in your marriage.

- *What if my spouse is threatened by a potential increase in income?* Some spouses are indeed threatened by your passion for this activity that seems strange and unusual. It takes time and focus. It is an unfamiliar direction, and you'll form new relationships. Ask for help and support. Once that person sees you're serious about this, that you're not taking anything away from them, hopefully they will support and encourage you. So far I don't know any spouses who didn't eventually appreciate the income part of writing success. It is, after all, more to spend on your children's education, your vacations, and … it pays the bills.

When you write down these fears, they will probably seem far-fetched. Some are. Some aren't. But looking at them and admitting them gives you a place to start eradicating them with reason.

FEAR OF FAILURE

I'm not afraid of storms, for I'm learning how to sail my ship.

—LOUISA MAY ALCOTT

What if I do the very best I can, give it my all, and fail? Failure means to fall short; failure is a lack of success. But if we think falling short of perfection is failure, we're doing ourselves a disservice. This is where our thinking needs to change.

What is success? What is failure? Taking action reduces fear and stress, and increases your options. The more realistic your goals, the more determination you put into reaching them, the better your odds of succeeding. When we go back and look at the *realistic* goals we planned for ourselves, we can see where we didn't fall short in our commitment, resolve, or mission.

If you take the steps you planned to reach your goal, you succeed in doing the things that are within your power. Taking that action reduces fear and increases your options. Since failure is defined as an omission to perform an expected action, you haven't failed if you've *taken the steps* to reach your goal. In other words, failure isn't rejection; failure is not trying. You can succeed when you change your way of thinking and your self-defeating behaviors.

The only failure is in not trying.

Not every submission is a sale. That's just the way it is. But every submission is part of your journey, and you need to readjust your perspectives to see it in that light. A rejection is part of your journey, even if it doesn't feel that way. If I achieved my goal of submitting a project and my project was rejected, that act is part of my self-growth. I had the courage to take that step, and I learned one more thing that didn't work.

I have not failed. I've just found ten thousand ways that won't work.

—THOMAS A. EDISON

Step back from a sting of rejection and look at it from the editor or agent's perspective. To buy your book, that person has to feel 100 percent sure that your book will sell and earn out the advance. Did she give you good feedback explaining why she didn't feel sure? Vague rejections can be more difficult to accept, because you have no insight into the decision. However, if the person gave you feedback, try to understand her point of view.

Write Smart, Write Happy

I'm famous for asking a particular question when faced with a decision or facing something scary. I ask it of myself and then I ask it of others who hesitate: What is the worst thing that could happen?

Okay, people, we're talking about writing a book here, not jumping the Grand Canyon on a motorcycle. The worst thing that could happen? Your first three chapters could stink and need to be thrown out. Remember, there are more words where those came from. It could take you three years to sell a book once you know how. This is *my* story. It took me three years to sell a book once I learned how to write well—is that so bad?

You could write four books over twice as many years, not sell a one, and give up. So? You met wonderful people, you had a great time, you learned a lot, and you stayed out of the casino. What was the worst thing about that?

I'm giving you things to think about. I'm asking you to face your fears. I'm suggesting you take steps to put doubt and lack of confidence under your feet and stomp on them a few times—then don't pick them up and resuscitate them.

Fear is a lack of knowledge. Learn all you can about yourself, about how you work, and the things that get you motivated or the things that hold you back—and then take the menace out of the hindrances by taking positive action to put them behind you. Fear is always something that hasn't happened yet. You're projecting imagined failures on yourself.

If you want to kick up your productivity a notch and rid yourself of the burdens that are holding you back, face your fears and plan strategies to defeat them. One mistake or washout isn't a reason to throw in the towel. Neither are two—or three.

Learn from your mistakes. If rejections all point out the same problem, learn from those observations and improve. Learn from a book that didn't sell as well as you'd hoped it would. Or from a promotion that flopped. Look back at those numbers and say, "that sucked," but then move on. Go back to focusing on today. We can't be great at everything all the time. We have to be realistic.

Don't let yourself take the safest and easiest route, but challenge yourself to grow and learn, knowing it's okay to miss the mark.

FEAR OF REJECTION

Some writers aren't getting rejections at all. Yes, it's true. And do you know why? It's because they have never submitted anything. Fear of showing one's work to another person can hold a writer back from getting feedback, being critiqued, and submitting.

It's fair to say most people fear losing the acceptance and approval of others. Everyone wants to be liked, appreciated, and found pleasing. We seek approval from our parents, teachers, and community. We want to be accepted socially; we want to be good at our jobs to get promotions and raises. In school, good grades mean our learning is acceptable. Revealing something as personal as our writing risks disapproval.

Nobody Ever Said Rejection Was Fun

Most of us have dealt with a form of rejection all our lives, from childhood throughout our formative years, up until this moment. Every one of us can name a rejection we've suffered from a parent, spouse, or friend. Some of the rejection we've received has taken years of therapy or years of developing barriers to prevent it from happening again.

Rejection sucks. By definition, *reject* means "to refuse to accept, cast off, throw back, repulse; not wanted, unsatisfactory, not fulfilling standard requirements." It's not pretty, is it? It's hurtful.

We've become pretty good at developing techniques to protect ourselves from being hurt. When you think about it, what we do as writers is make ourselves vulnerable. We open ourselves up to be accepted or rejected. We know there aren't enough avenues of acceptance, not enough publishers or bookstores for every one of our manuscripts to find a home. Most of us will be receiving some rejections in the form of *No thanks, this story's not for us*. I actually received a rejection once with those words stamped (as in this person used a rubber stamp) on my returned manuscript.

We must learn to separate rejection of our work from personal, intimate rejection. A refusal of our manuscript doesn't mean we're not capable or worthy or valuable people. It just means the editor wasn't 100 percent convinced that the book would make him look good to his superiors. He wasn't convinced it would make enough money. That's the bottom line.

Yes, you must be sure that you've developed all the techniques and skills of a published writer. And then you must choose a story with wide-market appeal. And then you need to remember that the publishing houses have marketing strategies, special promotions, reader requests, and possibly even a cover and a title for which they're seeking a story to slip inside—this might not be a joke, folks. However, my point is that many aspects to this business are out of a writer's control. When the editorial staff gets together for a weekly meeting, or for their big staff seminar, they take various things into consideration. They make decisions on how they're going to buy and market books for the next year. And maybe yours just doesn't fit the criteria for whatever reason.

Of course, those things will not be reflected in your rejection letter. No, your rejection letter will say, "Although there was much merit in your story, I'm afraid that in the light of today's competitive market, I don't have the enthusiasm necessary for this project."

A publisher declining your manuscript is out of your control. But there are two things you can control:

1. the quality of your work
2. your attitude and strategy in selling

A rejection is not a step backward or a step down. Picture a side drawing of a stairway. Submission, rejection. Submission, rejection. Submission, rejection. Going up.

Now, I don't know how high that flight of stairs is! But I know it's going up. You don't have to turn around and go back down those steps unless you want to. It's a choice.

I always have more dreams. Bigger goals. Often my husband finds me the most irritating person in the world, because I will not let anything go. I will not quit, and I don't like to take no for an answer. When I start a project—whether it's painting a room, designing a flyer, refinishing a piece of furniture, getting a mailing ready, or just about anything—I cannot stop until it's finished. I'm impatient, and I want to see results. As I mentioned, I'm still working on the perfectionism thing. A job must be done perfectly and to my specifications. If I get hungry along the way, I grab a quick bite and get back to work; if my back hurts, I call the chiropractor and get a quick adjustment. If the phone rings, I talk and work. But I don't quit. I stick with my goal until I see it through.

Fear is a problem if we don't write or submit in order to avoid our feelings. If you don't take the risk, you allow fear to win. Acknowledge your feelings without letting them take charge. The key to becoming confident is to repeat the process until you can do it comfortably. Once you've stood in the face of fear and let yourself know you won't be stopped, fear will subside.

Focus on what you can control rather than the outcome; what you can control is today—the here and now—and the process of creating your story world. Focus on what you love about this story, not on all the distractions and tasks that drain your joy.

Rejection is a Badge of Honor to Be Celebrated

I've talked about rejection more than once, because rejection is a huge part of being a writer and can be a stumbling block to our progress. We must be able to look it in the eye without fear or cowering and be prepared to take it on. It's a fact of the writer's life.

Some years back I was asked to do a workshop on rejection. I looked for my rejection file. And do you know what? I couldn't find one. Surely, I have a rejection file. I keep every piece of paper that ever came into my house somewhere. I could put my finger on a receipt for something I bought fifteen years ago. I could find a specific e-mail message if you gave me a few minutes. After a serious search, I found a few rejection letters, but not many.

Why not? I just finished telling you that rejections are like badges of honor and courage, so why don't I know where all mine are? Because unconsciously, I focused on the positive. The heck with the negative. If you look at rejections differently, perhaps you can see them as achievements or at the very least, stepping-stones. Someday I'll run across that folder, and maybe I'll even open it for old times' sake.

Some screenplays are passed around for years before someone invests in them or the subject becomes a hot topic. And then the actual development of the movie can take years. But we watch it all flash by on the screen in a little under two hours. That project took years of effort—several people's effort. But it took someone to believe in that project enough to not let go, to not give up on it. That someone must be you, first and foremost.

One friend of mine had three books rejected after her previous book had made it to the *USA Today* best-seller list. What does that tell me? It tells me her stories weren't what marketing was looking for at that particular time. She's gone on to sell plenty more.

Remember to celebrate the goals you achieve. Don't dwell on what didn't work. Some writers are so fearful of rejection that they stay safely inside their comfort zones to avoid risk. You have to prove to yourself that you're brave enough to face rejection and not take it personally. Yes, our work is an extension of ourselves, and, yes, our stories are personal, but editors don't believe we're unworthy as people. Your story might need a little work. You've probably seen those lists of how many rejections famous authors received before they were published the first time. Louis L'Amour received 200 rejections before Bantam took a chance on him. Jack Canfield and Mark Victor Hansen heard that anthologies don't sell 140 times before their Chicken Soup for the Soul series sold and took off. After five rejections, L.M. Montgomery waited two years to submit her book again. When she did, L.C. Page & Company published the classic that was *Anne of Greene Gables*.

What if they'd given up? What if Stephenie Meyer had thrown in the towel after seven or eight rejections? You can read her story of submitting and selling *Twilight* on her website.

How many rejections is too many? Instead of asking, "How many rejections are enough?" ask, "What if the next one is the one?" That's the question that kept me going. What if I'd quit after three years of submitting and rewriting? I had a dream and I pictured myself achieving it. Even though I work toward and anticipate bigger and better achievements, many of my dreams still come to pass. Each book I see in print is a goal achieved. I appreciate the simple fact that I am an author. It's a job, a career I can mold around my life and family. When my young granddaughter called me—even though we already had plans to go to the salon together in the afternoon—she asked if I could come to her swimming lesson and watch her jump off the diving board for the first time.

I went, and I made up the work time that evening. Having more time for my family and the things I want to do was one of my dreams. When I have those hairy days when I ask myself if this is really what I want to be doing, it only takes me about a minute to answer myself. *Yes, this is what I want. This is what I dreamed of. But I still want better.*

Being able to quit my "real" job and write for a living was scary, but it was one of my dreams. I can schedule my own time and my own life—which is also scary, but it enables me to do the things I want to do.

Now I ask you: Can you dream too big? *Webster's* defines the kind of *dream* we're talking about as *a strongly desired goal or purpose; something that fully satisfies a wish; the ideal.*

And "dream of" means to *consider possible.* A dreamer is a visionary.

Look at your notes from chapter 8 now. Is your dream too big? Not if you consider it *possible.* Would having it come true satisfy your wish?

Or is your dream too small? You'll have to decide. As long as you're going to dream, you may as well dream big.

And while you're thinking about that, think about your number of submissions, and—if publication were based on the point system and each submission was a point—would you have enough points to accomplish your dream? A dream is only a state of mind until you make it a reality. It's a visionary creation of the imagination until you make it a possibility.

Dream big, and dream often. Dream with persistence and determination. How long you hang on to that dream depends on how badly you want to see it come to pass. Achieving a goal may depend on how willing you are to look at submissions and rejections as successful steps toward publication. I challenge you to dream the dream that's already in your heart.

Taking action reduces fear and increases options. How can you do things differently to get better results?

MAKE A PLAN

One of the imprints I've written for accepts about one out of every three proposals it receives from its authors. That's a lot of work produced, and a lot of stories declined. I always joke that the number of sales I make is a percentage of the proposals I've submitted; I just don't know what the percentage is, so I keep sending them. But it's true. Rejection is a common theme among writers.

Self-publishing isn't a means of avoiding rejection, though it may at first seem that way. A self-published book will eventually be reviewed by readers—and self-publishing doesn't guarantee any number of positive reviews. Most of the major online advertisers, like BookBub, require a certain number of 4.5 star or higher reviews to purchase an ad. If your book and its accolades don't meet their criteria, you can't even pay them to run an ad. That's harsh.

We're hardwired to protect ourselves against rejection, so stepping beyond that and believing rejection is part of the writing process takes some work. It takes discipline of thought.

As writers, we have to make progress without supervision or the constant oversight of a group. We look forward to the final payoff, but meanwhile, the task at hand requires us to chip away at the job on our own. It's so much easier to do that if we love what we're doing. If we can get excited about our story, that energy can make the solitary task of writing pleasurable. If we can find the joy in what was once a hobby or a dream, that pleasure can make the task more palatable.

Learn from your mistakes. Learn from the feedback you get from a reader, whether he's in your critique group or an agent you submitted to. Learn from a book that didn't sell as well as you'd hoped due to a promotional flop in your marketing plan. When you look back at your sales numbers, figure out to the best of your ability if low sales were due to distribution, the economy, the season, the cover, the genre, or the subject matter.

Make a plan to improve your chances and move on.

24

habitual success strategies

Good habits are worth being fanatical about.

—JOHN IRVING

There is another fear writers face, sometimes called Second Book Syndrome (or Third, Fourth, Fifth, etc.). This is comparable to Imposter Syndrome: *What am I doing here? I'm not as good as these other writers. I don't know what I'm doing.*

Many times, after a first book is accepted, a second book takes a while to find its publishing home. Often the publisher is waiting to see sales from the first book before offering another contract to that author. Other times, after three books, a period of panic follows with no sales. After selling multiple books, it's simply, *How long can I keep doing this? How long until they figure out I'm faking it, and they stop giving me contracts? How long until someone replaces me?*

Some of this fear is warranted. One publisher I'm aware of gives three-book contracts and then drops authors whose sales don't take off. I've known writers who have quit and faded away after that. I've also known writers in the same situation who rallied, pulled themselves together, reinvented themselves, and published elsewhere. Again, it comes back to how badly you want this. How much you're willing to sacrifice and dedicate to develop a career.

And there are real times when we simply get bored with a story, our genre, and the whole challenging process, throw our hands up, and ask, *Can I keep doing this?* To those who haven't published yet, it may sound impossible or be difficult to understand, but to those who've been branded into their cubbyhole and are expected to produce the same thing over and over—only different each time—it's a real dilemma. We reach a place where readers are buying our books for our names because they love the way we tell stories. *Awesome.* The publisher appreciates the sales numbers and wants more books. *Great news.*

We are branded, which is both good and bad. It means readers know and love our work, but it also means they expect us to write within our genres without veering off into anything unexpected. If we've been writing small-town feel-good stories, then we can't decide out-of-the-blue that the next book will be a dark paranormal; readers know what they want from us from now until infinity—at least that's how it feels. The publisher wants us to continue with a sure thing, i.e., the thing that's getting good results.

Writers often feel that a publisher wants homogenized stories, with little deviation from their themes and tropes, and that makes writing *hard.* Then there are the revisions to proposals or finished manuscripts that occur—revisions that have, on occasion, made the writer feel as though the story is no longer theirs. We might end up finishing a book that is nothing like the one we intended to write. And that makes writing *hard.*

We want to sell books and please readers, of course. But sometimes we want to write something different. We want to write about a road trip with clowns or a basketball player whose dog helps him find love at the museum.

But we have our niche. We have our readership. And that makes writing anything different *hard.* Editors expect a specific book because they want our partnership to be successful. Obviously we want to be successful. But we're bored. So bored we're playing spider solitaire and alphabetizing spices. And boredom makes writing *hard*. What's a writer to do? You must love what you're doing to keep at it. When you enjoy your work it doesn't feel like work. Being bored with your work makes it miserable. And, worse, that misery is reflected in the writing.

My critique group has one rule when brainstorming new stories: Hold onto the element about the story that excites you. I appreciate and need all the help my brilliant writer friends offer me. But I have one element in each story that I will never change; it's that one thing that excited me about the story in the first place. If I picture my hero as a futuristic renegade space cowboy in a brown coat who evades warring factions and the law, I will hold onto that one spark no matter how the plot, characters, conflict, or location transforms around him. That initial excitement will propel me through my story when the writing gets tough.

EDITS & THE EDITOR-AUTHOR RELATIONSHIP

I'm sure there are many different types of editor-author relationships. When you're independently publishing, you can choose your own editor based on the kind of help you want and the type of person with whom you work best. When you're at a publishing house, however, your editor is the person who acquired you or the person to whom you were assigned. This relationship can make or break your publishing experience.

Over the years, I've worked with plenty of editors. I was fortunate to have the same editor who acquired my first novel for eleven years. That's unusual in this business. I was beyond fortunate that she loved my work, writing style, ideas, and stories, and that she nurtured me as a new writer. I learned so much from her wise suggestions and gentle edits. I also worked with numerous other editors who were assistants at the time or who edited special projects I was involved in.

A book undergoes more than one type of edit—a line edit and copyedit are two different things. The line edit comes first. A line edit deals with creative content, style, and language. This editor checks sentences and paragraphs for clear communication and flow. This edit will catch clichés, overused words, unnatural dialogue, repetition of words or ideas, transitions from one scene to the next, pacing, and items that require clarification. Sometimes paragraphs or sentences are deleted, and sometimes sections are moved from one spot to another to make the introspection or narrative flow more smoothly.

A writer can learn a lot from the line edit. You can see why this is done first: It would be a waste of time to copyedit sections of a book that might be changed or deleted.

In a copyedit, an editor makes sure the text meets industry and house standards. These are spelling, grammar, punctuation, and syntax corrections. This fact-checking edit makes sure names and places are spelled the same way each time—and that capitalization and hyphens are consistent as well. Your copyeditor probably has *The Chicago Manual of Style* committed to memory.

A macro editor of this type will make corrections if your protagonist's eyes changed from blue to green, your find-and-replace missed when you changed a character's name, or you mistakenly placed the wrong president in the White House. Yes, I somehow did that once.

This editor will question your research. And that is why it's a good idea to have notes and records of where you found information, in case you need to prove you know what you're writing about. Both edits will make you look better and smarter.

These jobs are often outsourced, meaning the publisher knows and uses reliable copyeditors who aren't on the payroll regularly. Most often the author doesn't know the identity of this person.

Admittedly, overzealous editors have been known to make changes that are not pleasing to the author. If this happens, the wisest solution is to contact your editor and explain how you feel, and why. I've known situations where the offending edit was thrown out and a replacement offered. Your editor's job is to develop the best possible product while following the publisher's rules, reporting to her senior editor, and keeping her authors happy and productive. This is done while she edits books on a production schedule; writes cover blurbs, backmatter, and revision letters; attends staff meetings; reads manuscripts on the subway; travels to conferences; discusses cover art with the marketing department; and completes any number of other tasks. Yes, I'm saying she's quite busy.

Your editor wants your book to be the best it can be, *and* she wants it to be marketable. You want your book to be marketable, too. If a new title is assigned to the book, it's because the marketing department, who spends the big bucks on research, has figured out which titles sell. So don't panic. They haven't suggested the change in an effort to make you miserable. They always consider alternate suggestions for titles and cover art, and will do their best to make sure you approve. I'm always given the final approval on a title. If I don't love it, but I can live with it, I'm good because I know they have the reader in mind.

Choose Your Battles Wisely

Obviously, an edit that changes a character into someone I don't like is unacceptable. Completely changing sentences to sound like nothing I would ever say doesn't work for me, either. But changing words here and there, deleting a few paragraphs, asking me to rethink a section of dialogue or add a plot thread—these things are not a big deal in the overall scheme of a book.

What you have to remember is that together you and the editor are *product developers*. I understand this story is your brainchild, and you created these characters, so you know them better than anyone. Your editor knows this too. She also knows house style, what the marketing team is looking for, common complaints of readers, and what is discussed in editorial meetings. This is her job, and she likes her job. Writing is your job, and you like your job. With mutual respect, you and the editorial team develop your book into a marketable product.

Let's imagine for a moment a scenario in which the publisher has made a decision across their imprints that neither dogs nor cats may be named or described with food descriptions, because that may be offensive to a group of people. You are asked not to name your character's pet Mocha Latte because of this regulation. You really loved that name. You were married to it. Big mistake. Don't get your undies in a twist over something so inconsequential. Readers will never know how adorable you thought Mocha Latte was for this fictional animal. By abiding by the request, you appease your editor and prevent offending a group of animal rights activists.

Think this sounds like a ridiculous example? Not so much, I assure you. Some writers get bent out of shape over issues like this.

Don't nitpick if the editor changes a word here and there. Should you really waste your time and the editor's time writing a 500-word e-mail about one word in an 80,000-word book? As soon as you do, a flag goes up: *This author is difficult to work with.*

On the other hand, let's say you have a Ph.D. in pharmacology and you're writing a mystery novel. You use a drug in a murder case because of its specific properties, and an editor suggests a different one, since it's more familiar to readers. Um, no. You're the expert.

If you have a degree in aerospace engineering and the editor changes *hypersonic* to *supersonic*, highlight and correct it. You are the expert. You have every right to object to a change like that because it's *your* area of expertise and you chose the word for a reason. And here's the thing: Editors get it. They appreciate learning why one word is better than another, why a specific choice is correct, so everyone looks good in the end.

If you find something that was changed in editing, or you're asked to make a change and you can't get on board with it, explain the issue to your editor. Give strong suggestions for a way to change it that will make you both happy. I'm always thankful to the editors who find my mistakes and make me look better in the long run. It's my name on the cover of that book, and I want it to be the best it can be. Editors understand that, too, and have always worked with me to correct an edit I wasn't happy with. Good communication is the key.

Keep Perspective

Your editor is the mediator between you and the publisher. He has the education, skills, and trusted authority to acquire books and present them in a marketable way. You are partners on the journey of this book. He wants the best book possible, which means he wants the best from you and *for you.* A good working relationship is essential, and that type

Write Smart, Write Happy

of relationship comes in all shapes and sizes. Communication is probably the most important skill that should be developed between the two of you: The ability to communicate how each of you see the book, characters, and marketable package.

A friendly relationship is definitely important, and you may even share details about your families, pets, travels, etc. When you have the luxury of face time over lunch or drinks, it's good to exchange pleasantries and be on affable ground. The better you communicate, the better your working relationship will be.

Friendly is good. However, an editor is not your friend. The publisher signs your editor's paychecks, just like he signs yours. The editor likes her job. Her first loyalty is to the company she works for. When changes and instructions come from the top, she complies because it's her job. She will do everything in her power to keep you satisfied while writing for the publisher, but her power is limited to befitting administration rules.

I've been fortunate to work with editors who've coached me and with whom I've had excellent working relationships. When you click with an editor, the job is so much easier. I've also worked with a couple of editors with whom I was not on the same wavelength. I had to try harder to find a middle ground, but we still produced good books together. You're in this for the long haul. Working at these relationships is the key.

There's More to Focus on than One Story at a Time

Once your career gets rolling, and you have multiple books contracted, tasks begin to overlap. After a book is completed and delivered, I fill out art forms for the publisher's design team and begin plotting and writing another project. Often the next book is already contracted. I send out a synopsis and proposal for that book, and continue to write it while I wait for acceptance on this proposal. Somewhere in there the team might be running titles past me, because my title was too close to another one that's being published that month.

Several weeks after delivering book one, the copyedits arrive. I have to set aside book two and read through book one in search of errors, and adding text where the editor suggested something that strengthens the story. The turnaround time for this is a week or so, sometimes less. Sometimes I get a heads-up e-mail from the editor when it's coming, but more often I make an educated guess for when it will arrive and mark that guesstimate in my planner. It's almost guaranteed to arrive on a busy Friday with a return date of the following week. Murphy's Law.

If I have a book I wrote last year that's due to release soon, I may work on promotion for that book as well. By this time, I've forgotten what this new release is about (because I've written another book or two and a proposal since that one), and have to read it so I can guest blog and promote it.

I only write one book at a time. But I often pause in writing to edit, proofread, promote, and do whatever else needs to be done for other books. I know authors who schedule every step of their promotion on their calendar: when they will send advance copies for reviews, when they will buy ads, and when they will send newsletters, and on and on. I confess I am not that organized. I know when books, edits, proofs, and art forms are due, and I schedule those. I most often work on promotion in the evenings or late at night when my story-writing brain is drained for the day.

There are differing opinions on how profitable all the avenues of promotion are, and the best advice we always hear is "Write the next book." This is so true. We spend months writing a book, it's in production for months, and a reader devours it within hours. They enjoy it and move on to another book.

Once you've completed a book, you've shown the publisher and yourself that you can do it. Hopefully you learned some things about yourself in the process: about how you write, your pace, or what motivates you. Take notes every step of the way so you can remind yourself what works. Forget what didn't work. Move on.

Greek shipping magnate Aristotle Onassis said, "Always carry a notebook. Write everything down. ... That is a million-dollar lesson they don't teach you in business school!"

PART 6
time management

25

priorities

Until you value yourself, you won't value your time. Until you value your time, you will not do anything with it.

—M. SCOTT PECK

I don't like the expression time management. You can't manage time. It's there and it's unmoving. You can't schedule more hours into your day or switch morning with evening to suit your peak periods of productivity. Time is one of those things we can't change, so we have to change ourselves and the way we react to and use time.

If I asked you to tell me your top distractions when it comes to writing, your answers would likely be the things I've previously listed, like family obligations and scheduling conflicts. Some are life realities you have to work around, but others are poor decisions, like spending too much of the day checking e-mail and watching television.

Jobs and families are the reasons writers most often give for why there's not enough time to write. We're all busy people. We all have duties and obligations, and need time to relax and fill the well, too. Juggling all that is a challenge. There's a saying: "If you want something done, give the job to a busy person." Have you ever noticed it's the busiest people who get the most done?

Busy people are good at utilizing time and resources, and more likely than not, they're wise about when to delegate. Asking your family to share the load isn't expecting too much. It's teaching them to respect your time and needs. If you're carrying the load for meals and lawn care, plus working and writing, pretty soon you're going to become resentful—if you're not already. Your family will respect your writing only if you do. If you're willing to abandon your chapter each time Junior can't find his socks, Junior is going to get the message that your writing time isn't valuable.

Unpublished writers who don't pursue their dream have many reasons for not doing so. The expectations of people around them are every bit as restrictive as fear or insecurity. Your extended family may not understand your need to write. Your friends and neighbors can't comprehend what compels you. Only other writers get it. Only someone with the same drive can really appreciate your dream. Others will think it's not practical to spend so much time and effort on something that isn't paying the bills. You are the only one who can take control of your life and your time. If you don't find a solution that works for your family, you'll end up living a life that doesn't feel like your own.

Doing what society and others deem appropriate fails to fulfill your potential. Using your self-talk and surrounding yourself with positive people opens your eyes to the possibilities.

Many parents come up with a plan that allows them to pursue their dream; find one that works for you. If you're married, then of course your spouse and children are important, but so is your writing. Some parents guard their writing time with drastic measures: "If you're not bleeding, don't come into my office while the door is shut," they say. This is more difficult if you don't have a room to yourself, but you can still set limits within the space that you do have.

When my critique partner, a busy mom, started writing, she set up her work area in a large, open, upstairs hall, decorating and arranging the space to claim it as her own. With a used desk and new bookcases, she created a work space that delineates her commitment and points out the high regard she places on her writing. Because she values her area and her time, her family does as well.

I read about one mom who put on a specific smock-like shirt when she was writing. If her family members saw her wearing it, they were not to bother her. The smock is as effective as a closed door. The key is *whatever works*.

Maybe family isn't the problem for you. Maybe you're single, or married with a spouse who isn't making demands on your time, and you still don't get it all done. Here's an eye-opening exercise you can do: Record what you did each hour of the day for several days and make a pie chart using that information. In this way, you'll see how you spend your time. It might be a wakeup call. Maybe you don't realize how much time you spend on television shows, talking on the phone, or reading the news.

Prioritize the tasks you need to accomplish and try out a new schedule that creates blocks of time for each of these things. Fine-tune it until you get something that works for you.

Take note of successful people who are making sacrifices and being disciplined with themselves, and figure out how you can use similar wisdom in choosing how you spend your time.

TIME, CLUTTER, PRIORITIES

That which we persist in doing becomes easier, not that the task itself has become easier, but that our ability to perform it has improved.

—RALPH WALDO EMERSON

It's difficult to say no to well-meaning people and worthwhile activities. If you're getting called once a month to bake cookies for your kid's school, it's because they know you're easy. Buy the cookies next time. Or learn to say the magic word that hasn't killed anyone yet: No. Saying no isn't rude. It's healthy. It means you're setting your own agenda, rather than responding and reacting, which makes us feel out of control. Charles Dickens said, "Whoever is devoted to an art must be content to deliver himself wholly up to it, and to find his recompense in it."

If what you're doing isn't working for you, analyze your behavior and make some changes. If you're stressed out and resentful each time you have to present a program or workshop, accompany kids on a field trip, or show up for yet another dinner with the aunt you can't stand, draw some lines in the sand.

Set boundaries for yourself and make yourself clear. How you spend your time is your life.

Review your goals often and list your priorities to remind yourself what you're doing and why. If you haven't made a list of the reasons you want to achieve your goals, do it now. If your goal is to write one hour a day, define how that will benefit you. Add some emotion to your goal to make it part of you. "I will feel better about myself if I finish a chapter this week."

Voice your decisions in a kind manner and don't feel guilty for it. People who write on a regular schedule don't have any more time than you do.

AVOID PUBLISHING EXHAUSTION

This is a real thing. It comes after you've had a book released, and you're marketing; writing blogs for tours; doing book signings; hosting Facebook parties; accepting speaking engagements; handling copyedits, line edits, cover art, and title suggestions; and proposing new material so you're not out of contract.

Learn to say no. This is equally important after you're published as it is before. It always feels as though we should be doing something more, making an appearance on the publisher's community boards, participating in a holiday group promotion, joining a multiauthor anthology, attending a library event, speaking at a conference, donating a critique to a worthy cause, doing an interview. Plenty of things are worthy, but all of those activities demand our time and attention. It's easy to lose sight of the fact that writing the best book possible should be your focus. We do our best work when we're focused, so how can we be effective at doing twenty different things?

Fellow Nebraskan and billionaire Warren Buffett once said, "The difference between successful people and very successful people is that very successful people say no to almost everything."

Back off. Gain perspective. Schedule time to sharpen your saw between books. Schedule writing as your priority and learn to say no to things without the cost benefit. Focus is valuable. I need to remind myself of this constantly.

RETHINK MULTITASKING

I've been guilty of this one, but I'm making a conscious effort to single task and be more effective. I do laundry while I write, but I'm not actually performing those tasks at the same time. The washer and dryer are doing the work. I take a break from writing to fold, hang, reload, and think.

"People can't multitask very well, and when people say they can, they're deluding themselves," said Earl Miller, a professor of neuroscience. "The brain is very good at deluding itself." Miller, of Picower Institute for Learning and Memory at Massachusetts Institute of Technology, says that for the most part, we simply can't focus on more than one thing at a time.

What we can do, he said, is shift our focus from one thing to the next with astonishing speed. "Switching from task to task, you think you're actually paying attention to everything around you at the same time. But you're actually not," Miller said. "You're not paying attention to one or two things simultaneously, but switching between them very rapidly."

Miller said there are several reasons the brain must switch among tasks. One is that similar tasks compete to use the same part of the brain. So multitasking is actually "switch-tasking." It takes time for the brain to focus and remember what's needed to perform the next task; even seconds add up. Try giving your attention to one job at a time and see if you work more effectively that way.

Action Steps

Grab your notebook and make a list of the things you need to do this week. For example:

- Write 6,000 words.
- Prepare a workshop for next week.
- Answer reader mail.

- Post on the (author group) blog.
- Shop for groceries.

Now arrange these tasks in order of importance. When prioritizing, consider the consequences of not completing a task. The words have to be written, so word count is my number one priority. I have a few days to get a workshop ready—I'll do it in the evenings. Reader mail takes half an hour or so. I'll prepare the blog at night and schedule it ahead of time. We'll eat Chinese takeout.

Now make a list of the things you need to do tomorrow.

- Write 1,500 words.
- Pick up the kids from school.
- Prepare lunch.
- Schedule a dentist appointment.
- Take the dog to the groomer.
- Wash the towels.
- Return a package.

Now prioritize these tasks, considering the consequences of not completing each one. I have to write the words. I can't leave the kids at school, and they have to eat. A phone call takes only a minute. Ten minutes to drop off the dog. The towels can wash and dry while I'm writing. The package can wait.

Always attend to your number one priority first.

Do this each night in preparation for the day ahead. My page goals are in my planner—as well as other obligations—and the rest are in my head, like shopping and laundry. Keep track any way that works for you, as long as you set your writing goals and prioritize.

26

finding direction & overcoming stress

It took me a long time to not judge myself through someone else's eyes.

—SALLY FIELD

As creative people, "We're a breed of our own." Contrary to the stereotype, we are not flaky free spirits or unsocial beings. Writers are problem solvers and fact gatherers. We analyze plots, people, and motivations. We plan how to build stories, settings, and worlds. Even the most impulsive seat-of-the-pants writers need discipline to accomplish their goals. Creativity requires logical thinking, preparation, endurance, and a lot of self-control. It's a lot to handle, and there is so much more involved than mere imagination.

Someone looking in on us would be surprised to learn the enormity of knowledge, skill, and work involved in this career. Creativity itself is something rare. It's that mysterious quality that makes people ask, "Where do you get your ideas?" when that's something we don't stop to think about. But there is more to plotting and developing stories.

Just listening to new writers' questions tells us how much more is involved in the writing process. They ask about formatting manuscripts;

they ask about agents. They ask how to submit, where to submit, how to query. It's no small learning curve. A writer needs to learn craft. I don't know if anyone ever feels as though she has it all pulled together as far as writing skills are concerned. There will always be books to read, tips to discover, and processes to improve. We're always evolving, growing, and learning as writers. The fiction of today is not the fiction of twenty years ago.

Educating ourselves on the publishing process is a job all by itself. Every one of the components of being an author is a job in itself, really. There are editors who do nothing but edit. Book designers create covers and format the pages of the book. Website designers make websites. Marketing people handle promotion. But most writers have a hand in all these jobs.

We have to be experts at using a computer, knowing the intricacies of our word processing programs, and learning everything the actual physical part of writing entails—like fiddling with printers and surge protectors and updates, buying external hard drives and Jumpdrives, and using Dropbox for data storage. And simply because we learn something once doesn't mean we have the skill in the bag. That process will change. Newer versions of computers and software emerge. Technology evolves right before our eyes.

Some might not remember WordPerfect before Word became the common word processor. Word evolves with each new upgrade. Now Scrivener is a popular writing software, and it comes with its own hefty learning curve. Canva and Photoshop are only a couple of the programs an author might need to know how to use for graphics, social media headers, etc.

Add to this social media. Anyone remember MySpace? That sucked away more hours of my life than I care to acknowledge. Blogspot had its heyday. Blogs were once the hottest thing going. Now it's impossible to get a viewer to your blog unless you're The Pioneer Woman. WordPress is currently the most popular blogging and web host among authors, but that will eventually change, too.

Facebook dragged me kicking and screaming into its clutches. Just as you learn it, the platform changes. Only in 2015 did I get a grip on Twitter and learn to use it efficiently. In 2012, Pinterest reported more than 27 million unique visitors. In 2016, Pinterest reported 100 million active users, 67 percent of those millennials.

Think that's overwhelming? Consider the many others, including LinkedIn, Instagram, FourSquare, YouTube, Google+, and Snapchat. For readers and authors, you'll find Goodreads and Shelfari. Handling social media is another full-time job.

The arena in which a writer works requires a wealth of knowledge in many different areas. Social media is a huge part of being a writer. Who thought they had the Internet all figured out when they got the hang of *e-mail*? Many of you probably don't remember dial-up AOL. *Be glad. Be very glad.*

Research is another major part of your job as a writer. You can start a book without knowing about your setting or your subject, the time period or your character's vocation, but you won't get very far. Research is time-consuming and sometimes frustrating. Other times it's so engaging or fascinating that we have to remind ourselves to get back to writing the book.

Networking is another necessary task. The writer who works in a vacuum is rare. I don't know one, although sometimes I wish I were one. Some genres lend themselves to face-to-face contact and schmoozing more so than others, but if you want to know *anything* about the business, the editors, the rapidly changing face of publishing, the industry professionals, or even other authors, you have to be proactive. There are publisher sites, editor blogs, agent blogs, and market updates—all of which are important, but you must weed through them to determine which are beneficial. I follow a few, but I mostly lean on author listservs and my Twitter feed to send me links to the timeliest articles.

If you're independently publishing, you have to relearn everything you knew about formatting a manuscript. You have to learn about HTML conversion. And you'll need to find designers, freelance editors, and marketing pros, in addition to learning how to track sales so you can determine your taxes owed.

Promotion once involved buying ads, making flyers, and holding book signings. Now promotion involves social media campaigns, vlogs, Amazon bios, Facebook release parties, YouTube videos, and so forth. It can be overwhelming. And even though we're mired in an ocean of book promotion events—constantly in contact with other authors and readers—we can still feel very much alone.

Websites must be designed, and they sometimes crash. Editors move, publishers fold; we have trips to plan for, merchandise to order for signings, libraries to contact, blogs to write, posts to schedule, and that's only the career part of our lives. We might have a deadline and be humming along with our word counts when the washer quits—and now we have to call the repair person. Our bank account gets hacked, so we spend hours on the phone closing that account, going to the bank to open a new one, and then have to change all our auto payments. A toilet needs to be replaced. Water leaked and ruined a ceiling. We have elderly parents who need us, family emergencies, children or grandchildren who require care during school breaks. This is life. Life goes on. The clock doesn't stand still until we get our writing schedules back on track.

So much of our job relies on technology. And here's the scary thing: You can't plan for a computer crash, a storm that knocks out the power for a day, or the air-conditioning conking out. For this reason, you'll always experience setbacks and roadblocks. That's why sticking to your routine and staying on track is so important. If you're already behind and one of these things happens, you're doubly behind. If you stay on track and hit a snag, catching up isn't nearly as difficult or stressful.

Which brings me to the point of this chapter: Most of us experience stress at some time or another. Stress affects everything about us—jobs, relationships, sleep, health—and it affects everyone around us. Part of stress is caused by fear—fear of not finishing everything. Fear of not being efficient or missing a deadline, fear of letting someone down. We overestimate the time we have available and refuse to delegate.

I don't point these out to show you how challenging it is to be a writer. I bring it up to show you that you're not alone. That we all face the same overload of responsibilities. It helps to know you're not alone. It may appear that others don't have situations like this, but appearances can be deceiving. We rarely share the not-so-pretty side of our lives with the world. Everyone you know is walking their own path, dealing with their own set of complications.

So, what can you do about the stress? First, always plan for "life happens" in your writing goals. Inject some wiggle room. And always remember that the most important thing is how you react. I got angry when all of my bank accounts were hacked. That person stole money and time from me. I got the money back, but the time was lost. I couldn't change what happened. Instead, I could take every precaution to not have it happen again—which I did. And then I had to move past it. I don't plan to get sick or for one of the kids to get sick and need to stay home, but I work around it. I don't give up because I get behind. I work late nights until I'm back on track. Every writer I know deals with this stuff.

We like to think we're in control of situations, but life occasionally tosses us something unexpected. It's essential to plan for success, but we also must learn to roll with the punches. Accept that we can only do our best in every situation. I still remember how badly I want this. I take stock and discover again and again that the sacrifices are worth it.

Teach yourself to think and speak positively about yourself and your situation. Remember that saying I taped to my refrigerator? *If you say so.* My family takes words seriously. If one of us says, "This situation is impossible," another responds, "If you say so," which prompts a new confession. "I'm going to figure this out."

If you say so.

Learn to communicate well. Your family should know your schedule and when your most productive times are so they can work with you by giving you your space. Ask their needs and plans so you don't neglect them or the things that are important to them.

Action Steps

- Family is your priority.
- You will never have it all together; be okay with that.
- Show others you're serious and committed.
- Writing must be first on your to-do list, not an afterthought if you have time.
- Condition yourself to write around the ups and downs of everyday life.
- Have an outline, synopsis, or story board so you can pick back up after interruptions.
- Communicate your needs and be aware of the needs of others.
- Take notes and make lists in a notebook or an app.
- Never wait for the perfect time.
- Turn off your television until you meet the word count goal.
- Understand you will have to neglect something else in order to write.
- Set priorities.
- Make sacrifices.
- Surround yourself with people who support you.
- Schedule days for you; take vacations.

27

organizing material

For every minute spent organizing, an hour is earned.

—BENJAMIN FRANKLIN

No matter the genre, writers need a lot of information to write a book. Details must be accurate, and you must be able to back up research in the copyedit stage. You need some kind of organizational system so you're not wasting time searching for things. Binders, hanging files, Word files, whatever works for you. The website PBworks.com offers a great online storage space for saving and organizing research. I have friends who swear by it and have eliminated paper from their desks.

My longtime friend Pam Crooks, author of The Secret Six series, is a fan of Microsoft OneNote. OneNote is free and comes preloaded on Windows. Initially Pam bought an inexpensive e-book instruction manual, but once she learned the difference between Notebooks, Sections, and Pages, she didn't need it anymore. "I'm ready to start book four of my Secret Six series, which I envision to be six or seven books long. That's a lot of characters to keep track of. My time period is the 1920s, which requires research. I can create as many notebooks as I want and fill them with as many details as I need. No more clunky notebooks taking up valuable space on my bookshelves. No more flipping through notebooks to find that one kernel of research I knew I'd kept but couldn't remember where. OneNote makes information super easy to find. I can even copy images (the program documents the websites I get them from, which is really handy if I want to go back to that site again)."

Best of all, Pam says everything is saved automatically. OneNote syncs automatically to OneDrive cloud storage. If you're working with a team, OneNote can be set up so that everyone has access to the same information.

If you're a Scrivener user, you'll know that this program holds research, photos, notes, outlines, and everything you need to write your story.

I confess I am a paper person and work best with my research and character grids, etc., at my fingertips. I am, however, orderly and have each book's information in a binder organized with tabs and plastic sleeves.

My writer friends laughingly call my tried-and-true method The Binder of Wonder. I use a one-inch binder for each project. I use dividers to separate the categories of information. My desk gets cleaned only between projects, and I always have my current book binder open on my left. It holds the following:

- my GMC grids (goal, motivation, conflict)
- the story synopsis
- character grids that show inciting incident, long- and short-range goals, motivation, conflict, black moment, growth, and realization
- a list of character names and character analysis for each person in the story
- calendar of story events
- sketches of the house or town
- map of area, city, or town
- research details

Standing up behind that is my planner, where I have my page counts planned and recorded. I always have a cup of coffee or tea on the right. Add to all that my scribbled notes, Jumpdrives, and pens. My desk is a mess, but it's my method. I look at photos of clean desks and wonder how those writers do it.

PINTEREST AS A WRITING TOOL

I love Pinterest. It's easy to learn and easy to share. I had to dial myself back from being a Pinterest junkie—that's how much I love it. I don't even subscribe to decorating magazines anymore because Pinterest is my visual crack.

I create Pinterest boards for each book—a board each for characters, research, and clothing. Grab the Pinterest button for your browser toolbar, so you can pin from any site you visit. Create boards that will benefit your writing and your books. When you run across something you might want to use later, save it to an appropriately named board. Your board titles are important. Label them so you can easily find the information and photos you need. Keep boards for your current books at the top. When someone comes to look at your page, you want your books to catch their eye first.

You can also arrange your individual boards so the most interesting pins are at the top—I keep character photos up there. And you can select the cameo/featured photo. When you pin, add your own text to the space provided. Don't leave the previous pinner's text in that box. You want visitors to take interest in what you're doing. I invite you to visit my boards for ideas: www.pinterest.com/cheryl_stjohn/.

Pinterest is like any other form of social media. To create interest and encourage followers, here are my tips for using it:

- Pin often, at least a couple of times a week.
- Rearrange your boards occasionally.
- Delete boards that you lose interest in.
- Like other people's pins often. It encourages them to visit your page.
- Don't pin another person's entire board. That's considered rude (and lazy).
- Add your website address to your original photos. This is easily done in PowerPoint.

If you are working on a series with other writers, create a shared board so all of your information can be found in one easily accessible spot.

One of the most convenient features of Pinterest is that you have all your photos in one place. When it's time to fill out the art fact sheets for your cover and send cover art ideas to your editor, you don't have to scan or hunt or search.

Pinterest is good for collecting anything in one place: recipes, room décor, paint ideas, crafts, clothing, hair, and beauty, but its main value for a writer is in the collection and organization of research. You can also keep boards private for works-in-progress or miscellaneous information.

GETTING ORGANIZED

I mentioned before that you need a place to work. If you don't have a room to yourself, create a corner in a bedroom, the basement, or the dining room. You need a spot where you can keep the materials you need handy. My first attempts at writing happened while lying on my bed composing longhand. I wouldn't recommend it, but I know writers who still create longhand. My first office was a tiny cubicle in our house, which was built in 1913. The room, located behind the fireplace, barely fit my secondhand desk. But it had terrific leaded glass windows and a solid oak pocket door that closed me in and shut out the world. In that tiny room I wrote several books that were later published—the first few on an Apple IIC with no hard drive, printed on a dot matrix printer. Both came from the hockshop. My editor was ever so thankful after I'd published a few books and could afford a real printer.

It's not an expensive computer or a beautiful desk or all the bells and whistles that make you a writer. It's the determination to get into the zone no matter the place. There isn't a writer who doesn't understand and crave the zone. Arriving there should be your daily goal.

If you work well in clutter or don't even notice it, then obviously disorganization is not a problem for you. But most people don't thrive in such an atmosphere. Many of us find that disorganization impedes our ability to keep our thoughts organized.

Organzational Tools

Ask for help if you feel overwhelmed. A friend or family member would most likely love to lend a hand in cleaning or designing your work space. When we moved quite a few years ago, one of my daughters did a clean sweep for me, and she's ruthless. I begged for trades to keep the things I wanted. But it was great. I need to schedule her again. I did my own clean sweep again a few years ago and tossed out years' worth of old magazines and slimmed my books from ten tall bookcases down to four. My husband built shelves in a closet for me, and I purchased all new streamlined office furniture. Organizing my space and reorganizing my work space was one of the best things I ever did for my productivity.

If uncluttering makes you more productive, do it. You need a writing space that works for you.

If clutter makes you crazy and you know it makes you crazy, then get a handle on it. My desk is always cluttered, but I call it organized chaos. I know exactly where everything is. I clear it off about once a week and then it piles back up again. If I'm on deadline, it can be a long while before the desktop is unearthed. But I have a pattern: When I'm ready to start a new project or hunker down for a deadline, I straighten it all up.

Eliminating or Ignoring Distractions

My friend Cyndy Salzmann is known as America's clutter coach. If clutter is a big problem for you, check out her website and read her advice and tips. She has many helpful suggestions for writers at her website, http://cyndysalzmann.wordpress.com/. The important thing is to take action so that your writing space is effective. Clutter wastes time.

I know a lot of writers who grab their laptops and sit in a recliner with the television on or music playing, and that's where they write. If an easy chair or recliner is a comfortable place that works for you, then that's your spot. Other writers have huge elaborate rooms with enormous desks and mountain views.

Your ideal work space is the space and position that works for you. Honestly, once I'm at my desk, with my head in the story, I could be anywhere. But getting to that place is why I need my chair in my room at my desk. I get in the zone at my desk and nowhere else. I've learned that writing weekends with my writer's group are a waste of time. Perhaps I'm easily distracted. But right now there are cartoons on in a nearby room and I only noticed because I happen to be writing on this subject. The dog is snoring downstairs (the dog is *loud*), but I was oblivious. The washer probably played its tune half an hour ago, and I didn't hear it. I've been in the zone.

E.B. White was an American essayist and contributing editor to *The New Yorker* best known for his beloved children's novels *Charlotte's Web* and *Stuart Little*. White said, "The members of my household never pay the slightest attention to my being a writing man—they make all the noise and fuss they want to. If I get sick of it, I have places I can go. A writer who waits for ideal conditions under which to work will die without putting a word on paper."

Not everyone can write in chaos like that. We're all different. If you require solitude and you don't have a dedicated place to be alone, that lack of space is a symptom of the lack of respect you have for your writing and the time and commitment it deserves. According to Stephen King, the main thing a writer needs is a "door that closes."

I dream of renting an office, where I will go to work alone in an ideal environment with no interruptions, but I know myself well enough to know that the perfect dream office is not the answer to productivity. The key to productivity is a secret weapon I like to call "Butt in Chair." Add "Fingers On Keyboard" to "Butt in Chair" and words appear.

Reader Mail

I believe responding to reader mail (whether letter or e-mail) in a timely manner is extremely important. While the letter might be from a single reader, it represents a lot more than that. I read once that a single copy of a book is often read seven times. That means the average reader buys your book and loans it to friends or gives it away to a thrift store or to a group like the Friends of the Library. Many writers probably cringe at the letter that says something like, "I borrowed your book from the library," or worse yet, "I found your book at a garage sale."

Okay, so you didn't make any royalties off that particular copy, but this person enjoyed the book enough to write to you. She will possibly write a review, and maybe pass the book to a friend. We can't discount how many books are purchased or read thanks to personal recommendations. When we read great books, we want to share them with our friends. "You have to read this!" we insist. Whether a reader bought or borrowed your book, he may write a review and rate the book on Goodreads or Amazon. Readers pass the word. Plenty of them discover a writer by reading a used or borrowed book and subsequently buy every book the author has written.

A reader who enjoys your book to the point of sharing and communicating oftentimes feels he knows you. He loved your style, your intimacy, the way you made him feel; and that's personal. He's in awe, and he feels a connection.

You can either reply to each communication as you receive it or schedule a slot once a week or month to respond to reader replies. To save time, you can create a couple of templates and customize one for each new release. If you haven't already, you might want to create a letter template for how to get started writing, with advice and perhaps a list of books for beginners. You'll hear from a good many readers who also want to be writers and hope you have all the answers. Suggest they find a group, recommend a few online sources, create a short list of books, and wish them well. If they imply they'd like you to read their material, suggest your agent doesn't allow you to do that, but be kind and encouraging.

Sadly, physical mail is a dying art. Years ago I received mail every week, but now I rarely do. When I receive a handwritten note, I always write a handwritten response and use a stamp—those little square or rectangular things you don't even have to lick anymore. And from reader mail, I've collected a database of mailing addresses. I send the people on this list Christmas cards or Valentines to keep in touch—not to promote.

E-mail readers receive a reply thanking them for taking time to let me know they enjoyed the book. I ask them to join my newsletter mailing list and to follow my Facebook page. Once prompted, many do.

TAMING THE E-MAIL VORTEX

Gayle Lantz, author of *Take the Bull by the Horns*, has a tried-and-true trick to handling e-mail. "E-mail becomes overwhelming when you're not clear about your priorities," she says. "The more clear you are about what's most important, the easier it becomes to manage e-mail."

You love to hear from your readers, but do you want to be bogged down by an overwhelming amount of mail in your inbox? Of course not. Reader mail is yet another area of our writing lives that needs organization. Writing books is our main priority, and e-

Write Smart, Write Happy

mail sucks time away from that. There's really only one way to handle the e-mail vortex and that is ruthlessly. An inbox with thousands (or even hundreds) of messages is due to a lack of effective handling.

- Read your e-mail client's documentation to understand settings and time-saving tricks.
- Google tips for Gmail or Outlook or whichever e-mail program you use.
- Use the filter feature if you have one.
- Unsubscribe from advertisements, retail stores, and newsletters.
- Change your settings on Yahoo! Groups to digest, so all the day's posts come in one e-mail.
- Turn off Facebook and Twitter notifications.
- Use spam filters; block words and addresses.

Some people advise not checking e-mail first thing in the morning, so you don't get sucked in. However, I check it first thing, delete everything that's not relevant, and reply to important matters. I don't check again until later in the day. This works for me.

Either way, you should process your e-mail only once or twice a day. Switch off your phone's notifications, or if you don't, refrain from looking every time you have a new mail alert.

I have a one-time handling policy for snail mail—either toss it into the trash or file it. I don't leave it lying on the counter for later or next week. Whenever possible, I apply my one-time handling policy to e-mail as well, but sometimes it's impossible, so I leave it until evening when I'm finished writing, or until my once-a-week time slot during which I gather info and make replies.

Some writers I know use a triage method to divide their mail into three or more folders labeled "Follow Up," "Archive," or "Hold." You can use any labels that make sense to you. Commit to moving every read message in your inbox. This is not easy, but with some practice and discipline you can do it.

When my e-mail has grown to a ridiculous number, one of the ways I get it under control is to divide all the mail into senders and delete huge blocks of mail I haven't read and won't miss if I don't. Let's say I subscribe to a listserv of cat lovers, but I haven't read the digests for weeks. I want to get back into it after this busy season is over, however, so I can either unsubscribe for now, or I can search my inbox for the listserv name and delete them all in one chunk. I can knock out hundreds at a time with that method. I've deleted my entire in-box accidentally in the past and haven't missed out on anything.

Another tactic you can use is to select every e-mail that's older than thirty days and click delete. If there was anything important in that group, you would have taken action or the sender would have been in touch. If you're terrified to do this, here's a fix: Create a folder or box labeled "Old Inbox" and move it all there. In a few weeks or a month, when you realize you haven't missed anything, delete it. The feeling of relief that comes when 3,000-plus e-mails disappear clears your mind.

One last tip for the road (literally): If you're waiting in a dentist's office or a parking lot outside the café where you're meeting a friend, don't check your Facebook; clear out your inbox.

Now apply the one-touch/one-read method and either handle each missive immediately or put it in another folder. Keep templates of information you need often, like lists of ISBNs, bios, where to purchase your books, etc. Make certain your outgoing e-mails are clear and precise and cut down on recipients responding with requests for clarification. Most important, develop your system and stick with it

28

eat the frog

If it's your job to eat a frog, it's best to do it first thing in the morning. And If it's your job to eat two frogs, it's best to eat the biggest one first.

—MARK TWAIN

Behavioral scientists have discovered that we retain a more pleasant memory of something if the difficult part comes first and the pleasing or rewarding part comes next.

For example, let's say you have a doctor's appointment: You sit in the waiting room for fifteen minutes and in the exam room for fifteen more minutes before the doctor appears. When you leave, you feel as though you waited forever. Or, you sit in the waiting room for thirty minutes and as soon as you get into the exam room, the doctor arrives and performs his exam. Which of these scenarios leaves you feeling as though the experience wasn't so bad? The second one, of course, because the impatient part of waiting was over and done in one shot.

So researchers know that stacking the painful part of a process early and the best part of a process last leaves us with a more enjoyable experience. We enjoy our vacations and trips more if we pay for plane tickets, day passes, etc., in advance. We've done the painful part first—forking over the money—and then enjoyed the fun activities last.

If the house is a mess, and it all needs to be cleaned, I know I should do the things I don't like doing first. I like doing laundry, but I hate doing dishes. If I don't do the dishes first, I will dread that task the rest of the day. But if I clean those dishes first and get that job behind me, my experience improves and the rest of the day goes better.

How does this relate to our writing? If we stack the hard part up front, our experience will improve because we'll get the difficulty out of the way. The hard part for many is getting started. Putting it off makes it worse. So if we discipline ourselves to get started, thereby removing this obstacle, we should be able to get into the zone and have a better experience overall.

Tom Ziglar, CEO of Ziglar, Inc., shared the following: "Invest the first part of your day working on your number one priority that will help build your business." As a writer, what task will have the biggest impact on reaching your goal? Writing the words, of course.

STRATEGIES FOR EATING THE FROG

I couldn't find solid evidence that the quote at the beginning of this chapter attributed to Mark Twain truly came from him, and it's been paraphrased in many forms over the years. The gist is that if the first thing you do each morning is to eat a live frog, you can go through the day with the satisfaction of knowing that is the worst thing that will happen to you all day. Eating the frog is the ugliest, most difficult task of the day.

Staring at that frog is why we procrastinate and sort our pens. My husband and his brother love oyster stew because their mother and sister made it, so it's a family tradition. The first time I mentioned that oysters are disgusting, they admitted they don't chew them—they swallow them whole so they can enjoy the broth. I believe that's an object lesson.

Why chew the oyster if you only like the broth? Why stare at the frog until it becomes more revolting? Get it over quickly, so you can get to the good parts. What's the good part of writing, you ask? Reaching the zone of course. That place where the story flows, where you love your good guys, hate your villains, and think a section of dialogue is complete genius. That place where a scene makes you laugh to yourself. You can't get there if you don't eat the frog.

Getting started is the challenge. I'm not talking about the beginning of the book—that's a piece of cake. Everything is fun and exciting in the beginning of the book. I'm talking about your daily writing session, about actually sitting down and getting to work. (I know some writers stand, so when I say sit in your chair, I mean get into your writing position.) Tackling the most difficult action first must become a habit. Procrastinating is emotionally uncomfortable, because it causes guilt and stress. You have the power to change all that here and now. Be aware that a habit can take three months to establish. As your productivity increases, making excuses for not writing will decrease.

To keep the momentum going, at the end of today's session make a plan for where you'll start writing tomorrow. Make yourself a note or write it in your planner. Whenever possible, I like to stop my scene at a spot where I know what will happen next. I can make notes about what's to follow, and the next day it's easier to pick up where I left off. Think about it before bed. Visualize the scene you're going to write the next day.

Don't beat yourself up or feel bad if you've been dreading a section of the book. If you blew it off yesterday and went to the mall, that was yesterday. Remember you don't have to get anything perfect today. All you have to do is get words on paper.

It might be painful to write badly at first. It might be painful to struggle with those first words, pages, chapters. But as you flex your writing muscles, you're getting closer to mastering your craft. Writing will never be easy, but your confidence will imbue you with stamina and determination.

If you need more help getting started, set a timer for fifteen to thirty minutes. Assure yourself you only have to write for this amount of time. Start small if you want. Work into it. You will sit down and write for fifteen minutes. When the timer goes off, you can stop. Most likely, once you've been writing for fifteen minutes you'll know where you're going and want to continue until the scene is finished.

- Start with small segments; write for fifteen to thirty minutes.
- Give yourself rewards.
- Count your blessings—what else would you rather be doing?
- Review your goals.
- Remind yourself you're empowered and in control of reaching for your dream.
- You're the god of your story world—anything is possible.
- Take time to recognize how good it feels to have accomplished your daily quota.
- Plan exercise, take time with family, meet with friends as part of your routine.

The first months or years of your writing journey might be painful as you learn, stretch, make mistakes, and get feedback or rejections. You're backloading your writing career with the hard stuff. You're eating the frog. It will never be easy, but you will develop skills, learn your abilities and pace, and discover the enjoyable part of being a writer.

PART 7
celebrate success

29

resiliency

> I was set free, because my greatest fear had already been realized, and I was still alive, and I still had a daughter whom I adored, and I had an old typewriter and a big idea. And so rock bottom became the solid foundation on which I rebuilt my life.
>
> **—J.K. ROWLING**

Burnout is not a mental block. Nor is procrastination or a lack of ideas. Burnout is being sick and tired of the frustrations and being ready to give up on writing. Burnout is being over the whole writing thing. On Facebook, your friends are in hashtag heaven with their #amwriting. They're in their writing caves and posting their sprints, and you just want to run, hide, go off the map.

Negative thoughts try to worm their way into your head. *Something's wrong with me. I'm not a real writer. Others can do it all. I don't have what they have.* This is the moment you've prepared for. Take those negative thoughts captive and put a lid on them. There is nothing wrong with you. You're normal. You're a real writer. No one can do it all; you're tired. And that's okay.

Burnout is a common topic for authors to talk about when they get together. We must develop tools to strengthen our stamina, but we also have to learn techniques of self-care to avoid the pitfalls of stress and mental exhaustion. I believe the stories and suggestions I've made throughout these chapters will encourage you and give you options. You're not alone in your endeavor. You are unique and special because of who you are. Your contribution to the world is important.

I asked two of the most prolific and enduring writers I know for their tips and advice on being resilient in this business.

IN THEIR OWN WORDS

JULIE MILLER is the *USA Today* best-selling author of *Military Grade Mistletoe* and more than sixty other books. She has a National Readers Choice Award and two Daphne du Maurier Awards to her credit. She was honored with a career achievement award in Series Romantic Suspense from *Romantic Times* Book Reviews and has been a finalist for Romance Writers of America's prestigious RITA Award.

"One of the key things that helps is to mix up the process every now and then, to keep things fresh, not only in the content of my writing, but in the way I approach it.

"Probably my number one piece of advice is to write the book as quickly as you can. No stops and starts with breaks in between. The longer it takes me to write a book, the more likely it is for my enthusiasm to wane. I'm not a draft writer, so it doesn't work for me to sit down and spew out an eighty-page version of my story, then go back several times and layer in all the elements. By the time I reach 'The End' my brain is pretty much done with the story, and at that time I'm just going back through it to check for typos and continuity. So it's important for me to stay in the zone for as long as I can. Nothing slows down productivity like losing the joy of telling that story, and it becomes a catch-22: Taking too long kills the excitement about a project, and then it can be painful to make myself sit down and write, so it takes even longer.

"That means being really strict with my real-life commitments. If it takes me two months to write a book, then I can't go on vacation or to a conference or remodel a room in my house in the middle of those two months. I need to commit to those two months of writing every day, and increase my word count as the book goes on. (The first third of a book is always the slowest for me, getting everything set up just right. I naturally write faster as I near the end of the book.)

"I say no to big projects that aren't writing related, no matter how fun or interesting. It involves more planning and less spontaneity to schedule my fun time—or time to work on other things—but that's what I have to do. In addition to freeing up more time to write quickly, those plans act as my reward for time well spent. If I have a good writing day/week/month, if I finish a book on time or early, I feel like celebrating. And at that time, I make the most of it. I refill the well with reading, activities with friends and family, time away from writing. I've also discovered that by the time my scheduled reward is finished, I'm eager to get back to my writing, and that, in turn, is motivating, too.

"I give myself daily rewards, too, such as an hour away from my computer at lunchtime to read a book. I try to schedule the daily things that need to be done around my prime writing time—running errands in the evening, scheduling appointments for later in the afternoon, etc. And I make a point to train my friends and family to respect my needs. So, write fast, guard my time, meet my goals, reward myself for a job well-done—then get back at it."

CHARLENE SANDS, author of *Redeeming the Texas Rancher*, has more than forty-five novels published. She's a recipient of the National Readers' Choice Award and The Cataromance Reviewer's Choice Award, as well as a double recipient of the Booksellers' Best Award and has won *Romantic Times* magazine's Best Harlequin Desire Award. She's a member of and contributor to the Los Angeles Chapter of RWA.

"I try to surround myself with upbeat writers who love the work as much as I do. Enthusiasm and joy feed off one another.

"I never follow trends unless I adore the subject matter. And more important, I never start a book I don't love from the get-go. I need to feel excited about the project before I start. The outside world offers us so many distractions and it's tempting to fall into the trap of meandering and not staying focused. The best way for me to keep the happy juices flowing is to invent, discover, or create a story I am dying to write.

"When I stall, I sit down with a good book from a favorite author and as the inspiration flows, I refocus and get back into my story. Another thing I think is imperative is to live life. You need to experience life in order to write about it, is my motto. Do something out of your comfort zone; say yes, more than you say no. I learn something new with every experience, and I think it makes me a more rounded writer."

If you're experiencing symptoms of burnout, don't worry. It's normal and others go through it. It's not here to stay. This too shall pass. Remember as always—be kind to yourself.

Action Steps

- Give yourself permission to be sick of writing for a while.
- Unplug.
- Get six or more hours of sleep a night.
- Don't isolate yourself—talk it over with someone who understands.
- Give your head a vacation—don't think about writing.
- Give your body a vacation—visit museums, see movies.
- Redirect your creative energy and do something that excites you.
- Read—replenish the word well.
- Enjoy your friends and family.
- Don't feel guilty.
- Reevaluate priorities and change goals or directions if need be.
- When you're ready, write something that isn't what you normally write.
- Write something no one will ever see.

GETTING BACK INTO A ROUTINE

Whether procrastination, circumstances, or burnout was the cause of your hiatus, the longer you've been away from writing, the longer it's going to take you to transition back into the routine. Your current routine doesn't allow for writing time or getting into the zone. If you've been away for a month or more, you're going to need to create a new routine. You have to relearn how to reach the zone.

Take a deep breath. You'll get your focus back. You will build a new habit of concentration. Refamiliarize yourself with your desk and clean your work area. Prioritize what needs to be done. Concentrate on the first task and put the rest out of sight, in your planner for the future. If you've missed a deadline or it's a sure thing you will, contact the necessary people and reschedule those deadlines. It happens. I've never had an editor or project manager who didn't understand and who didn't want to help me get back on track.

In the 1950s, after observing how long it took his patients to get used to their new faces, plastic surgeon Maxwell Maltz published his thoughts in *Psycho-Cybernetics*, a book that sold more than thirty million copies. In the decades that followed, every self-help guru from Zig Ziglar to Tony Robbins used Maltz's story, until it morphed into, "It takes twenty-one days to form a new habit." More recent research studies have discovered that it actually takes more than two months—more like sixty-six days—for a new behavior to become automatic. Of course, results vary depending on the person, the behavior, and the circumstances, but the point is that developing new routines is a process. Changing our behavior takes commitment.

This realization makes me think of Chris and Heidi Powell's *Extreme Weight Loss* television show. If you've ever watched it, you've seen how the couple guides people to learn new routines and habits for a healthier life. Everyone does well when they're being observed and given daily reminders and encouragement, but as soon as they're on their own, back in their own home, faced with cooking their own meals in addition to working and taking care of families, they have trouble following through. If the subjects are going to backslide, that's when it happens. Motivation is imperative, but commitment is key. Chris and Heidi have been living the healthy lifestyle for years; the couple they're trying to help is working to develop a new habit. It's a process. They can expect to make mistakes, and they need strategies for getting back on track.

A good piece of advice is to change one habit at a time. Know why you want to change. Write it down. Make a step-by-step plan. Tell someone what you're doing and make him your support system for accountability. Keeping it to yourself means you can back out and no one's the wiser.

We do the same thing the same way automatically (without thinking about it), using psychological patterns we've developed. Call them triggers if you like. Have you ever gotten in the car and later arrived at a destination without remembering how you got there? It's pretty scary, actually. Neuroscientists attribute habit-making behaviors to one part of the brain and decision-making to another part. We put on our socks and shoes the same way every day. Our morning routine is a habit. If someone interrupts our habit, we're likely to forget a step.

When I get to the kitchen, I make myself a protein shake and take my vitamins with it. If my granddaughter asks me to help her find her shoes or to fix her hair while the blender's running, I'm likely to forget to take my vitamins. Why? The automatic routine has been interrupted.

Changing a habit while on vacation is one of the most successful ways to change. All of the cues from your daily life are missing, so it's easier to develop a new pattern. It's never too late to form a new habit, and it's easier to do if you create a new environment around that habit. For instance, rearranging your office or sitting in a new chair interrupts your previous triggers and makes you think about the new habit you want to perform.

We are what we repeatedly do. Excellence then, is not an act, but a habit.

—ARISTOTLE

be a professional

> Professionalism in art has this difficulty: To be professional is to be dependable, to be dependable is to be predictable, and predictability is esthetically boring—an anti-virtue in a field where we hope to be astonished and startled and at some deep level refreshed.
>
> **—JOHN UPDIKE**

What does being a professional mean? This might sound obvious, but be prepared to work. You're solely responsible for your business—including the product, marketing, taxes, and accounting. You'll find that you do everything yourself, or you'll hire professional help. Anything worth having is worth the work. Anything worth doing is worth doing right.

CHECK YOUR EGO

Regardless of your publishing status, you are a reflection of your entity, company, and body of work. A professional attitude and conduct will serve you well in all aspects of your writing life.

For most of us, writing is a self-motivated job. If we don't write, we don't get paid. Acquiring more degrees, taking more classes, or publishing more books does not make you the king of the writing world. Be humble and gracious. If you're asked for advice, offer it kindly.

Professionals are good listeners. Listen carefully to what others are saying. Don't think about what you're going to say next while they're talking—that behavior is easy to spot. Be responsive, even if you don't have anything to say or add. Nod and smile. Never let your body language show that you're bored; never let your gaze wander to something that seems more interesting.

Be present and don't text or look at your phone during meetings, sessions, luncheons, or critique groups. You can look at your Facebook feed when other people are not around. If you get a call you think is important, excuse yourself and answer it somewhere in private.

As a professional, you'll also want to ask leading questions. Share experiences if you're comfortable doing so. Be a good listener, but don't feel like you have to solve issues for other people or take on the weight of the world.

KNOW YOUR BUSINESS

Industry knowledge is one of the most important areas where a writer can educate himself. Learn everything you can about the publishing business and the avenues available. Good writing is good writing, so while writing is your number one priority for education, there are other things you need to know.

Traditional and independent publishing are two different things. There are a multitude of traditional publishers and small presses in North America. Each publishing house has unique guidelines and requirements. Traditional publishers are investors who pay you an advance and royalties. They can afford to take the financial risk on your book because they have best-selling authors who offset their losses. Most often they lease the rights to your story for a certain amount of time. They do the marketing and advertising. Some accept only agented submissions. Learn whether or not you want or need an agent.

Self-publishing, or independent publishing, is another way to publish but requires a different skill set and, to produce a quality product, requires the hiring of professional editors and designers. Independent publishing means you hire the work you can't do yourself.

You are responsible for the marketing and advertising. You own 100 percent of the rights to your book, and the ISBN belongs to you. Usually 70 percent of the profits are yours.

There are websites and online writer groups for both kinds of publishing, as well as for hybrid authors—those who do both.

A subsidy, or vanity, publisher is one who asks you to pay up-front for the cost of the production of the book. Writers beware: Even though you've paid them to produce the book, they own the ISBN, cover, and typesetting. You're required (often contractually) to buy your own copies, to market and advertise, and to sell the books yourself. You take all the risks, including the risk of ending up with a garage full of books.

If there's something you don't know, find out. Learn about contracts, advances, agent fees, copyrights, author earnings, tax deductions—as much as you can to make informed decisions.

BE PREPARED

When you're asked to speak to groups or sign books, always show up on time—or better yet show up early enough to work out any wrinkles like microphone trouble or other set-up issues.

I once planned a book signing at a local store. I checked with the PR person ahead of time and made sure she'd ordered enough books. Whenever I do a book signing, I send postcards to local readers. So when I arrived, there was a line of people already waiting and only six books on the table. Six. I checked with store personnel—sometimes the person you work with ahead of time isn't even there—and yes, they had checked in plenty of books and put them out on a rack. Where they had already sold.

Readers left the store, went to Target, and brought back books to have signed. Of course, Target ran out. I always bring a box of books with me to signings and leave it in my car. Thankfully my husband had come with me to this event, so he went for the books and checked them in with the booksellers, who afterward ordered more books and replaced mine. This isn't a common occurrence. Sometimes I only sell a handful of books. But I've used my own personal copies more times than I can count, so I always arrive prepared.

BE GRACIOUS

Authors get all kinds of letters and e-mail from readers. And some of that mail is about mistakes they've come across in your book. It's true that mistakes sometimes get through the editing and publishing process. They're usually simple things, like using the wrong name in one place or forgetting an eye color. Sometimes it's something more important, like an incorrect attribution for a quote or a mistaken detail from research. These things can happen during production. And sometimes they're just an oversight. Of course, authors are mortified by errors. By the time this book is in print and on the shelves, it's too late to make changes. The book, with its mistake, is out there for the world to see. I believe most readers who write us about these mistakes are well meaning. *I loved your book, but did you notice you said Susan on page 114 when it should have been Cindy?*

As much as you're dying to reply, "I didn't know until the first fifteen people e-mailed me, and had I known, I would have fixed it," resist the urge. Always be courteous. These readers love our genre, they have paid for our books, they want to love them and us, and most often they do. Reply with something like, "I only became aware of that error after the book was released. I hope it didn't lessen your enjoyment of the story. Thank you for picking up my book. I always enjoy hearing from readers. Follow me on Facebook at ..."

Remember this charitable response even when you can tell by the tone of the letter or e-mail that this person is gloating and feeling superior over finding a mistake in your book. Even when he mentions he's been an English teacher for thirty-five years and this kind of mistake sets his teeth on edge. Even if he complains about the poor quality of books these days. Even when he tells you he went through your book with a red pen and found all the places you could have done something better. Even when he tells you he borrowed your book from the library or bought all your books at a garage sale. Resist.

All readers are a win-win.

RELATIONSHIPS WITH AGENTS AND EDITORS

Never ever, ever, under any circumstances, write a letter to an editor who rejected you and tell him why he's wrong. A thank-you is professional. Anything else confirms their decision to turn you down. Lynn Price, editorial director at Behler Publications, wrote the following on her blog at http://behlerblog.com: "Authors who write out of anger diminish themselves in a way they don't even understand. This industry is filled with rejection and tough love. If authors don't learn that one lesson of grace under fire, then their career will be decidedly short and filled with angst."

Don't be a Tattletale

Don't ever gossip to your editor about other authors because you think it will magnify you and your performance in their opinion. It does not. If you're having trouble working with another author on a group project, work it out with that author like an adult. Find a middle ground or find a way to do it their way. Do not go behind the other person's back and rectify the problem without their permission.

Do not tell your editor things you heard in private author loops. That behavior always comes back and bites you in the rear, and your peers will have a difficult time trusting you.

- Do not share personal drama online.
- Do not, by any means, engage the social media trolls. Ignore or block them. Delete their posts if they're on your page.
- Do not post your promotional post on another person's wall. Ever.
- Use social media to interact with readers and authors, not to bombard your followers with "buy my book" advertisements.
- Genuinely show interest in others; comment on and like their posts. The percentage of posts promoting your books should be small.
- Share your friends' books; share books you've read and recommend. You are a reader, not only a writer.
- Do not use direct message for advertising. Personal messages are for conversations with people you know.
- Do not add people to groups without their permission. Invite them and give them the choice.

PROTECT YOUR CAREER

On listservs, privacy is not guaranteed. Do not say anything on a group listserv that you wouldn't say in public. I've been online since the days of dial-up AOL and mailing lists (the precursors to Web forums and newsgroups), and I've seen a lot of people get burned sharing something personal that got back to the wrong person—usually an editor. Technology has changed, but sadly the nature of people has not. Venting could be detrimental to your career. A sixty-second rant is not worth losing face or risking your career.

Don't burn bridges. You will run into authors you knew years ago. Maintaining good relationships may benefit you in the future. Editors change houses and show up again. Editors talk to each other. Even if you've ended a working relationship because it wasn't in your best interests, don't tell anyone off. Always leave the doors of communication open. Badmouthing another person never ends well. End relationships with mutual respect, not anger.

Your dress, language, and conduct are all part of your professional image. When you behave like a professional, you become a professional.

HAVE A PROFESSIONAL PHOTO

Your author photo identifies you as someone who is a professional. It shows you went out of your way to have a photo taken just for this purpose. It's fine to use a photo in which you've cropped out another person on your personal Facebook page, but don't use it for professional purposes (i.e., your author page, professional publications, or websites). Please file away your Glamour Shots portrait from the nineties. Save it for #FlashbackFriday on social media and share a good laugh with your friends.

Don't try to incorporate your genre into your photo. Wearing a cowboy hat (western), a low-cut dress (erotica), or a feather boa (romance); holding a magnifying glass (mystery); or looking menacing (horror/suspense) is nothing but cheesy. Let the person with the camera suggest ideas. Good photographers are geniuses at making people look good.

Be consistent by using your author photo on all your sites and in advertising. If you want, purchase more than one pose at a time so you have a few different angles to choose from, but keep them similar.

moving forward

> No steam or gas drives anything until it is confined. No Niagara is ever turned into light and power until it is tunneled. No life ever grows great until it is focused, dedicated, and disciplined.
>
> **—HARRY E. FOSDICK**

We've gone over a lot of problem areas. I can't tell you specifically how to fix each one. The solutions are as different as we are as people. My purpose is to help you look at behaviors that are holding you back and encourage you to honestly recognize some of them in yourself. Facing a problem is a huge part of overcoming it. Once you own up to it, you can plan steps to correct it. These behaviors are just things you do, they're not who you are. They are subject to change.

WHAT JUNK CAN YOU GET RID OF?

Take time to reflect over the chapters in this book; look at the notes you've taken, the behaviors you're going to change, and choose to get rid of them now.

In chapter 1, I mentioned how I gave a similar class in person and asked the members to write down the behaviors they wanted to be free from. We then placed the notes in a trash bag and threw them away—symbolic of the step required to permanently remove the behavior. Hopefully you've been taking notes as you read through these chapters; if you think a symbolic gesture will work for you, toss your bad behaviors in the fireplace or the trash can. Throw old spaghetti on top, if you have to. It's garbage now!

George Bernard Shaw said, "People are always blaming their circumstances for what they are. I don't believe in circumstances. The people who get on in this world are the people who get up and look for the circumstances they want, and if they can't find them, they make them."

This might sound a little harsh, but when you think about it, it's true. So much of the population today has a victim mentality: *Poor me. I can't make anything of myself because I grew up in a dysfunctional home and my parents didn't have any money and all my relationships have ended badly.* We become what we think about, what we focus on, and what we think of ourselves. If you think of yourself as a victim, or as down and out, you probably are. But if you have the mind-set that you are an achiever who can overcome any adversity and make something of yourself, you will.

More than once I've heard the mind compared to land or soil. Land is lying there, available. If you have a yard or a garden, you know this. A farmer knows it, up close and personal. Land doesn't have an opinion about what becomes of it; it's ready for anything. If no one ever plows or plants seeds or fertilizes, the land will produce only weeds. Maybe a stray wildflower or tree seed will happen by, and if the weather permits and there is adequate rain and sun, those seeds will grow into plants. Anything that grows is by happenstance.

But a farmer can plow and prepare the soil and plant any crop he wishes—anything from corn to deadly nightshade. Land doesn't care. It will produce whatever is planted. *But land always returns what is planted.*

The same is true for our minds. We can let our minds fall idle to whatever happens to fall in and take root. Or we can create goals, prepare our thoughts, and plant success. Our minds don't care what we plant, but whatever we plant is what will grow and be returned to us.

Perseverance isn't simply doing the same thing over and over. We've all heard that Einstein's definition of insanity is repeating the same behavior over and over while expecting different results. Set new goals every year. Evaluate them a few months into the year and again at least halfway through the year. There's nothing wrong with revamping your goals or trying a different method of reaching them.

Make this your year of change. You're worth it.

Evaluation Checklist

- Are your goals realistic and have you broken them down into achievable bites?
- What do you expect from yourself?
- I can change my thinking about _____.
- I will not allow _____ to affect me negatively.
- If you knew that you could not fail, what would you do this year?
- If you were to take complete charge of your life, what is the first thing you would change?
- What have you been tolerating or putting up with that you're going to change this year?
- List the things you want more of in your life.
- List the things you want less of in your life.
- How do you most often sabotage your own goals?
- Who will you ask to hold you accountable if they see you behaving like that?
- Are you willing to make a commitment to your goals?
- Make a list of things that have to change to see those goals accomplished.
- When I picture success for myself, I see _____.
- I am going to speak with confidence about _____.
- I want to prioritize my time so that _____ _____.
- Is your writing space working for you?
- This year I'm going to sharpen my writing skills by _____ _____.

- What one thing can you change that will bring you peace and relieve stress?
- My next step is _____

  _____ .
- Who will you tell about this commitment so they can hold you accountable?
- What are three steps you can take every week to keep a positive attitude?
- Who should you be spending time with so that setting goals becomes a habit?
- On a scale of one to ten, how excited are you about taking these actions?
- What will the cost be if you don't take any action?
- What have you been doing well?
- What can you do better?
- What would you most like to be acknowledged for so far in your life?
- What would you most like to be recognized for five years from now?
- Is there anyone you'd like to acknowledge for something? Tell them today.

It's not what you've got, it's what you use that makes a difference.

—ZIG ZIGLAR

ENCOURAGE YOURSELF

Don't let anything hold you back from being the best you can be.

- Make a list of things you want to change.
- Make another list of why you want to change.
- Make a third list of how an improved attitude will advance your writing, energy, and ambition. Writing down goals and referring back to them helps you check progress and hold yourself accountable. It also helps you remember.

- Take time to meditate on how you're going to think differently.
- Make yourself note cards as reminders to think positively and place them on your mirror or above the sink or at your desk.
- Use your self-talk to encourage yourself.

IT'S A WRAP

The greater danger for most of us lies not in setting our aim too high and falling short, but in setting our aim too low and achieving our mark.

—MICHELANGELO

In the previous chapters, I have asked you to take an honest look at yourself. I have pointed out areas in your writing life where you may be able to change and improve. If you've been keeping a journal or notebook, look back over your notes now to remind yourself.

Grab Your Notebook

Answer these questions now:

- How many manuscripts have you sent out this year?
- How about last year?
- Have the rejections gotten "better"?
- Do you target the right houses and agents?
- Have you entered contests? If so, have your scores/placements improved?
- Are you entering contests rather than writing?
- Are you revising previously written material rather than writing new material?
- Are you in a critique group or do you have a critique partner?
- Do you take constructive criticism well?
- Have you said negative things about your writing?
- Are you willing to learn, change, and become a better writer?

- Do you attend workshops to improve your writing?
- Are you analyzing your work?
- Did you set a writing improvement goal this year?
- Are you still flogging the same manuscript you started six years ago? (Someone had to ask.)

Each time I sit down at my computer, I read something inspirational to get started. And I tell myself something positive. *I'm writing a best-selling book. I'm writing an award-winning book. Readers are going to love this story.* Do I feel silly saying things like that out loud? Not at all. Too many positive things have come to pass thanks to this kind of inspirational talk.

Do I still have doubts? Of course I do. Every time I receive a particularly ugly line edit. Every time I stand up to speak in front of people. Every time I get to the middle of my current book. Every time I stretch my writing a step further. Every time I have a proposal rejected.

But every accomplishment is a confidence builder, and those outweigh the negatives by far.

Deal with feelings. Get your thoughts and emotions under control. I heard somewhere that if a computer were built to have the capacity of the human mind, it would take the space of the Empire State Building to house it. And yet we use only a portion of our brains. We live in a society that believes we're all victims; nobody's responsible for their actions, feelings, or thoughts. Well, I don't know about you, but I'm responsible for me. I may not be able to change my past or change other people, but I can change how I feel and how I react to situations. I can change my behavior. You can too.

Do I still have bad habits? Yes. I just ate my supper while seated at my desk finishing this book. But I'm always working on improving my writing and self-care habits. There is no one rule or schedule or writing goal that works for everyone. Unfortunately, we have to figure out this stuff by trial and error. My hope is that it reassures and encourages you to know there are other writers who understand what you're dealing with as a busy spouse, parent, employee, writer, breadwinner. A lot of us have been there and not only survived but written books that many readers have enjoyed. You can do this too.

Remember to celebrate the goals you achieve; don't dwell on what didn't work. Never compare yourself to anyone, because you're special just the way you are. You have the ability to dream a dream no one else can. You're going to write the books only you can write.

Continue to learn. Be aware, curious, and open-minded. Be a reader. Most of us came to be writers because of our love of reading. When we get busy with deadlines, it's easy to let that first love slip away. Renew that love. Fill the well. Remind yourself why you love stories, why you want to write.

And above everything else: Believe in yourself. Draw on and draw out the writer inside. You're the only writer like you—the only person who can write your unique individual stories. You're the only person who can make your dream come true. You have the tools and the desire. Hold onto the unshakable truth that you can do this and you will move forward.

FINAL REMINDERS

- Write down one thing you are thankful for every day.
- Give yourself deadlines.
- Minimize distractions.
- Use your planner to stay organized. You'll thank yourself.
- If you don't have one, claim your own work space. If you do, clean your desk.
- De-clutter your e-mail and list subscriptions.
- Surround yourself with those who inspire and encourage you.
- Be kind to yourself. You are unique and amazing.
- Learn to say no. Say no to toxic people.
- Figure out what your priorities are. Spend more time on priorities and less on unimportant matters.
- Read a devotion, a verse, a poem, an affirmation—something uplifting—every day.
- Plan a day or weekend trip with friends.
- Plan to meet a friend for lunch regularly.

- Find an accountability partner who is not a best friend.
- Spend a day or weekend completely unplugged from social media.
- Meet new people. Carry on a conversation with someone very different from you.
- Celebrate milestones and successes. You are awesome.
- Take a step out of your comfort zone.
- Make a list of your strengths.
- Take a class.
- Create a dream board or post visual affirmations.
- Read books by authors you've never before read.
- Enjoy a hands-on hobby that isn't electronic.
- Send a note of encouragement or appreciation through the U.S. mail.
- Perform random acts of kindness.
- Tell people you love them.
- Buy someone an unexpected gift.
- Visualize success.
- Reward yourself.
- What positive thing can you say about yourself and your writing dream right now?

Success is not final. Failure is not final. It's the courage to continue that counts.

—WINSTON CHURCHILL

index

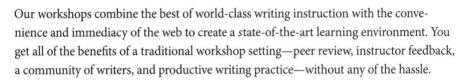
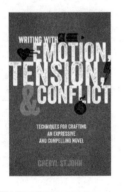